# PAGAN VIRTUE

# PAGAN VIRTUE

*An Essay in Ethics*

John Casey

CLARENDON PRESS · OXFORD
1990

Oxford University Press, Walton Street, Oxford OX2 6DP

Oxford New York Toronto
Delhi Bombay Calcutta Madras Karachi
Petaling Jaya Singapore Hong Kong Tokyo
Nairobi Dar es Salaam Cape Town
Melbourne Auckland
and associated companies in
Berlin Ibadan

Oxford is a trade mark of Oxford University Press

Published in the United States
by Oxford University Press, New York

British Library Cataloguing in Publication Data
Casey, John
Pagan virtue: an essay in ethics.
1. Ethics
I. Title
170
ISBN 0-19-824958-6

Library of Congress Cataloging in Publication Data
Pagan virtue: an essay in ethics/John Casey.
Includes bibliographical references.
1. Cardinal virtues. 2. Ethics. I. Title.
BJ1531.C29 1990 170-dc20 89-39296
ISBN 0-19-824958-6

Typeset by Cambrian Typesetters, Frimley, Surrey
Printed in Great Britain by
Bookcraft (Bath) Ltd, Midsomer Norton, Avon

# PREFACE

THE study of the virtues was for centuries the central tradition in moral philosophy. The virtues were those dispositions of character that enabled men to live good and happy lives. Courage, temperance, prudence (or practical wisdom), and justice in particular were taken to be central, or 'cardinal': a good and happy man had to have all of these virtues. At the same time, many other dispositions—wisdom in the use of money, wit, pride, magnificence, friendship, truthfulness, shame—were also thought to be useful or necessary. Some writers, of whom Aristotle is the most important, thought that the virtues were not simply means to an end—such as happiness—but were also to be valued in themselves. In addition, other qualities and gifts of fortune were often thought to be relevant, not only to happiness, but also to goodness: cleverness, wealth, good birth, beauty, fame, children and descendants who would keep alive the memory of their ancestors. Aristotle himself held that although a man could not be considered truly happy unless he were also virtuous, his virtues would not in themselves guarantee happiness without the assistance of material prosperity. An element of contingency, the limits of which cannot easily be defined, enters into the good life for man.

This book is not a historical study of the cardinal virtues, but a contribution, by means of reflection upon them, to modern moral thought. For some this will seem an impossible enterprise. How can a study of the 'pagan' virtues be other than merely archaeological in a world, the moral sensibilities of which bear the ineradicable imprint of Christianity? For Christianity rejects the worldliness implicit in the ethic of the virtues, and abhors the values that go with such worldliness. Pride, the desire for honour, and still more wealth and beauty, have nothing to do with Christian goodness. Even those active virtues (so admired by Hume and Gibbon) which make a man formidable, great, a valuable member of a city state, have always met with an equivocal response from the Christian tradition. Meekness, humility, a conviction that human corruption cannot be overcome by human effort, a rejection of the world and its pomps, are at the centre of the Christian moral consciousness. And Christianity, like Stoicism, has always held that the true good for man—including what we would now call 'moral goodness'—cannot possibly depend upon the vagaries of fortune.

Self-abnegation lies at the heart of the Christian vision. St Augustine connects this with happiness. Unhappiness springs from our desiring what it is essentially not within the power of our own will to enjoy. This includes all that can pass away—'fine reputation, great wealth, or various goods of the body.' We are contented only if we possess the 'good will', which is the only good fully within our power, and of which we cannot be deprived by worldly circumstances (Augustine, *De libero arbitrio*, bk. i. ch. 12). The good will consists in our directing our desires ultimately at God alone.

The most memorable philosophical attempt to derive moral principles purely from reason—that of Kant—issued in a view of the moral life quite compatible with Christian tradition. For Kant the good man is not someone endowed with intellectual gifts, or even good feelings. He certainly owes nothing to fortune: a slave is as capable of moral goodness as an emperor. Indeed, the 'moral' is a category hermetically sealed from all natural human desires and satisfactions. The good man is he who possesses the Good Will—which is the determination to do the right for the sake of the right. Unlike the traditional virtues, the Good Will does not depend at all on worldly circumstance. We respect people morally simply as possessing a Good Will, and not for any other gifts or attractive qualities they might have. One way of understanding this is that we should ultimately value ourselves and others simply as *persons*. We approach the idea of a person partly by discounting those accidents of fortune and endowment that divide people—intelligence, sex, race, culture; and also a greater or lesser capacity to be brave, wise, calmly deliberate, generous, witty, or good-tempered. The concept of a person ideally coincides with that of a rational agent who expresses his rationality, and hence his universal humanity, in the principles of action he adopts and obeys.

The hold of Christian values on our moral imagination is so strong, so incapable of being disowned, that a vigorous advocacy of some sort of 'paganism' might be thought to amount to nothing more than an exercise in irony. Yet we can explore areas of life and value which do not appear to belong to the Kantian category of 'the moral'. As well as being agents who can succeed or fail in willing the right, human beings have emotions and attitudes, such as love, hate, anger, admiration, and contempt. They are capable of friendship, civic pride, political loyalty. They may be practically wise, mastering many arts and skills. We may love and admire people for their simple goodness of heart, their integrity and unselfish devotion to principle; but also for their genius, imagination, wit, physical courage, the refinement of their pleasures, their vitality, taste, individuality, ambition, scepticism, grace, and self-possession. We can also admire and praise people for the culture which they inherit, and for their breeding and beauty. What we may value most deeply in people need not be—perhaps usually is not—limited by what is clearly within the control of their will. We may *praise* people for qualities the absence of which would not prompt us to *blame* them.

This points to the continuing vitality of a 'pagan' ethical tradition. Furthermore, I believe that this ethic is founded on virtues which constitute personhood, and that an ethic of the virtues significantly, although not entirely, overlaps with an ethic of persons. In valuing others for possessing the traditional virtues, one implicitly recognizes and values their personhood. Indeed it may be that as modern men we are constrained to approach the virtues through an ethic of persons, and even to test it by such an ethic. Yet at the same time one's idea of what it is to be a person and recognize others as persons will have neither the clarity nor the simplicity that the Kantian tradition claims for it. Our problem as moderns in taking an ethic of the virtues seriously—of accepting that it makes sense of our experience and can have a claim to guide our lives—arises at the point where we may think that there is no overlap. Any advocacy of the 'pagan' position must therefore acknowledge that we are of necessity in two minds in our thought about ethics. My stress in what follows on an assertive, proud ethical tradition, on a certain worldliness, and on the relation of personal morality to politics is a deliberate attempt to remind us that we *are* in two minds, and that it is desirable to be aware of this. But being in two minds should also mean that we will not easily conclude that worldly, or proud, or self-regarding virtues, and various gifts of nature and fortune, cannot possibly form part of an *ethic* at all.

Aristotle was in the enviable position of believing that his account of the virtues was based upon a metaphysical biology. My own suggestion is much more modest—that an ethic of the virtues makes sense of our experience. This does not mean that we have an independent picture of 'our experience' which we can hold up against the Aristotelian tradition in order to see whether it fits. It is only by entering sympathetically into the tradition and *ipso facto* modifying our understanding of 'our experience' that we can be persuaded that it does make sense. We may come to see that a 'pagan' ethic is more persuasive than our prejudices (if we may so call them) allow. My assumption is that in practice we do take these virtues more seriously than we are usually prepared to recognize. Therefore the enterprise of this book is less an antiquarian reconstruction than an appeal to what we already know but may for all sorts of reasons be unready, or unwilling, to acknowledge. Our unreadiness to confront the 'pagan' in our ethical tradition may reflect mere inconsistency, or (on the contrary) an unhappiness at the inconsistency which we may discern in the tradition itself. It may arise also from egalitarian convictions, democratic sentiments, and liberal sensibilities. None of these motives is to be disowned or despised. Nevertheless, to become more aware of them is implicitly to acknowledge the spirit of Nietzsche's great enterprise: the reduction of bad faith.

The cardinal virtues are undeniably worldly. By that I mean that they include an element of self-regard, and that they rely upon material conditions for their fulfilment. Courage (for instance) can be understood—is perhaps best understood—as a public virtue, which finds its fullest expression in the political realm, rather than in the quiet heroism of private life. Friendship is best understood in relation to justice, which in turn presupposes a certain sort of polity. Pride and honour are part of the moral life.

It would be wrong, of course, to think of such an ethic as having existed only in the ancient world. It was revived in the Italian republican writers of the Renaissance as the concept of civic virtue; it is found in Hume; it is central to the understanding of virtue as above all political—expressed in a readiness to fight for the fatherland—of the French Revolutionaries. And this means that it is an element in the most important movements in modern radical politics, and also (whether or not acknowledged) in our modern understanding of patriotism.

We are not in Aristotle's happy position of believing that we can base an ethic upon a metaphysical biology. What I offer instead is 'tradition'. This book therefore engages in a modest rediscovery and (hence) criticism of a tradition which we inherit. My enquiry into moral philosophy in some ways resembles an exercise in literary criticism. The literary critic rearranges and criticizes a literary tradition, and may even propose new and unexpected perspectives on the literary past, but he does not usually presume to invent a tradition *de novo*. In much the same way the moral philosopher cannot fruitfully assume that what he does stands outside history. Indeed it will become apparent that I think that 'the tradition', with its inconsistencies—and surprising connections—is often best approached through art and literature. I shall therefore resort to literary and artistic examples with a frequency that may seem excessive in an essay on ethics.

Of course, tradition allows a good deal of latitude. In the twentieth century the term has been used by literary critics—in particular, by T. S. Eliot—to allow the most radical reinterpretation of the past. Indeed, what counts as a tradition has often been taken to be simply what we can be persuaded to see as one. In this spirit, I have taken considerable freedom in my discussion of the virtues. While I always begin with an Aristotelian description of each particular virtue, this is invariably the starting-point for reflections which sit very loosely with Aristotle, or (as in the discussion of temperance) radically diverge from him.

I do not aim to present a systematic, historical account. Any attempt to delineate different ways of thinking about the good for man, and to describe these as 'traditions', is inevitably somewhat artificial. Aquinas—whose exploration of moral psychology in the *Summa theologiae* is one of my chief sources of inspiration—made an heroic effort to reconcile the ethics of Aristotle with those of the New Testament. Some writers—of whom Shakespeare in his comedies is the supreme example—have so blended 'pagan' and Christian values as to make it seem that there is no conflict. Indeed, this is true of the Renaissance as a whole. Whether a modern writer can attempt anything similar without being *merely* eclectic must be doubtful. It is for the reader to decide whether my recourse to writers as diverse as Homer, Aristotle, Augustine, Aquinas, Shakespeare, Hume, Kant, Hegel, Jane Austen, Nietzsche, and Sartre expresses a coherent point of view, or only a confused response to a complicated inheritance.

J.C.

*Cambridge*
*September 1989*

# ACKNOWLEDGEMENTS

An early version of the work was read by Roger Scruton, S. L. Goldberg, Christopher Cordner, and Noel Malcolm, and I am extremely grateful for their criticisms. Parts of the book were also read by Mark Archer, James Tregear, and Joachim Whaley, all of whom made helpful suggestions. For the final version I am especially indebted to John Vallance, who extensively corrected my amateur classical scholarship, whilst remaining perturbed that I should so often approach Aristotle through Aquinas, and Colin Burrow, whose acute and relentless criticism brought about numerous improvements in structure and style. Perhaps it would not be amiss to mention two books which greatly stimulated my thoughts on the subject: Alasdair MacIntyre's *After Virtue*, and Martha Nussbaum's *The Fragility of Goodness*.

The book was first conceived during my tenure of visiting fellowships at the Humanities Research Centre and the History of Ideas Unit at the Australian National University, and I have happy memories of both institutions. The last two chapters were written, and the book finally revised, during five months at the University of Doshisha, Kyoto, in 1988, for the delightful hospitality of which I am most grateful.

Portions of this book, in earlier versions, have been previously published as follows: pp. 67–78 and 91–9 were published as 'The Noble', in A. Phillips Griffiths (ed.), *Philosophy and Literature*, Royal Institute of Philosophy Lectures (Cambridge, 1984), pp. 135–55; pp. 85–9, originally the text for a sermon for The Commemoration of Benefactors, in Caius College, were published as 'How Can we Have a Duty to the Dead?' in *The Salisbury Review* (Spring 1983), pp. 4–6; pp. 118–28 were published as 'Emotion and Imagination', in *The Philosophical Quarterly* (January 1984), pp. 1–14.

Finally I record my gratitude to Gonville and Caius College for providing an environment in which research can be carried out, and life lived.

# CONTENTS

# I

# PERSONS

## I RESPECT FOR PERSONS

THE world contains persons. We cannot doubt that we encounter other people; and no man can doubt that he is a person himself. An account of human nature must recognize a necessary connection between being human and being a person. Any attempt to describe the good for man which has nothing to say about what it is to be a person, if it gives rise to an ethical theory at all, is likely to issue only in a supremely crude utilitarianism.

Some philosophers—including Kant and Hegel—have sought to base an ethical doctrine upon what it is to be a person. This book is greatly influenced by them. Yet it is difficult to move surely from the concept of a person to ethics. It is not certain that we all agree about what we mean by 'person'; and it is certain that we do not all agree about what flows from the concept of a person—for instance, what it is to 'treat others as persons'.

Perhaps everyone will allow that a person is at least a self-conscious, rational being. This would presumably allow us to regard God as a person. Self-consciousness and rationality mutually imply each other, since a rational being is one to whom reasons can be offered, and who can accept reasons: and all and only self-conscious beings can accept reasons. It may also seem obvious that self-consciousness and rationality imply language, so that persons must also be language users. Yet disagreement is possible even here. Some theologians, for instance, have held that God is a person, but seem to have thought that His knowledge of Himself is somehow not mediated through language.[1] So it would be absurd to speculate

[1] This seems to be the doctrine of Aquinas, even though he does not raise explicitly the question of God's language; for he says that in God to be and to know are the same (*Summa theologiae*, Gen. Ed. T. Gilly (London, 1972) 1a, 14, 4), and that God's knowledge is not discursive, since he sees everything at once and not successively (1a, 14, 8). It is difficult to see how knowledge of that sort could depend upon, or even be expressed through, language. Richard Rorty, whilst including 'ability to use language' amongst those features which philosophers have, at one time or other, taken as marks of the mental, does not include it as an 'item bearing on personhood'. See *Philosophy and the Mirror of Nature* (Oxford, 1980), pp. 35–7.

(as does the young Stephen Dedalus in *Portrait of the Artist*) on whether God's language could be English or French.[2]

Philosophers have also included, among the conditions of personhood, the ability to act freely, and the ability to be included within a society or polity, even to be 'one of us'.[3] We can characterize as 'persons' those beings who can make claims, who can incur and acknowledge obligations, can be wronged, can be the objects of and can reciprocate love, respect, hatred, and contempt. This understanding of persons assumes that part of what it is to be a person is to make and recognize claims. The existence of persons introduces the normative into the world. A natural corollary will be that our knowledge of other people, and even our sense of ourselves as persons—our recognition of what is self-conscious and rational— will entail our having certain attitudes towards ourselves and others. If we include all these ideas in the concept of a person, then we will not think that the world 'contains' persons in quite the way in which it contains bodies. We would not think that, even if we were to add another element to our idea of a person—that persons are mind / body unities. Although it has often been held that being a person must include having a body, most people would not identify a person with any particular thing in the world. A person is a 'for himself' and not simply an 'in itself'.

If morality is essentially concerned with persons and the relations between persons, then the moral law can plausibly be thought to derive from what constitutes their essential personhood, rather than from features that may characterize all whom we know who actually are persons—for instance, human beings. This could lead to the conclusion that all that does not express self-conscious rationality, all that is simply 'empirical' in man, and does not characterize his universal, rational essence, is irrelevant to morality. It is possible to regard as 'empirical' man's life as a sentient, desiring, and passionate being, and to hold that men are truly persons only when they are fully free and rational; and that is when they are least under the dominance of 'nature'. On this view, our understanding of man in his freedom is quite different from our understanding of him as an object in the world determined by the

---

[2] James Joyce, *A Portrait of the Artist as a Young Man* (London, 1956), p. 16.
[3] Cf. Rorty, *Philosophy*, pp. 35–7. See also Daniel Dennett's 'Conditions of Personhood', in Amelie Rorty (ed.), *The Identities of Persons*, where six conditions are mentioned.

laws of nature. Man as person is absolutely free to choose his destiny, his values, even his nature. His existence as a person, and hence as a moral being, is not determined by something called 'human nature'. Morality must be concerned with man in his freedom, and the moral law is the law of freedom. Ideas such as these we can associate with Spinoza, Kant, and Sartre. Kant argued that since the moral law must apply to all rational beings generally, then it must apply to man simply as a rational being. No truly moral command could be based on man's 'empirical' nature—upon particular desires, strengths, or skills.

If we think like this, we are likely to conclude—as Kant in effect did—that an ethic of the virtues would fall into the error of 'heteronomy' since it must be concerned with man's empirical nature, and not purely with his nature as a rational being. The virtue of temperance, for instance, controls sensual pleasures; the virtue of courage regulates fear of pain and death. No scheme of the virtues could be evolved which did not assume, as well as the conditions of personhood which have already been mentioned, the human condition itself. This will include the fact that man is a sentient, desiring, passionate animal. The classical virtues could not be the virtues of all rational beings without exception: the Schoolmen, pondering on which virtues could survive into the next, heavenly life, found that almost none could, except perhaps justice, and the theological virtue of charity.[4]

In fact, the concept of a person, and its consequences for values, is a focus of ideological disagreement. 'There is neither Jew nor Greek, there is neither bond nor free, there is neither male nor female: for ye are all . . .'[5] *persons*. To insist that someone is above all a person is to insist that all these other characters he may have are irrelevant to that distinct pattern of response that is appropriate to rational beings. To say that someone's colour, or sex, or caste is irrelevant to his personhood is usually to say that it is inappropriate or wrong to withdraw certain sorts of consideration from him because of these features or accidents of birth, or to accord certain sorts of consideration to him because of them.

Few, however, would deny that some 'accidental' characteristics are grounds for serious consideration, for respect, or for reverence. These might include someone's being one's parent; one's benefactor;

---

4 Cf. Aquinas, *Summa*, 1a2ae, 67, 1–6.
5 Gal. 3: 28.

one's Creator. Many cultures would go much further than this and include as proper objects of such consideration that someone is one's lawful king, one's commanding officer, or one's employer, one's teacher, one's elder, one's master. The Greeks seem to have thought that beauty (*to kalon*) was a proper grounds for reverence. And among characters which, while not simply 'accidental', are none the less not obviously and simply 'conditions of personhood', and which have often been thought the supremely appropriate objects of praise and esteem, are the virtues, especially courage, wisdom, temperance, and justice.

Kant isolates a peculiarly pure form of respect, the object of which is righteousness embodied in another person. And it can be understood finally as respect for another simply *as* a person. He writes:

A man can . . . be an object of love, fear, or admiration even to astonishment, and yet not be an object of respect. His jocular humour, his courage and strength, and his power of rank may inspire me with such feelings, though inner respect for him is still lacking. Fontanelle says, 'I bow to a great man, but my mind does not bow.' I can add: to a humble plain man, in whom I perceive righteousness in a higher degree than I am conscious of in myself, *my mind bows* whether I choose or not, however high I carry my head that he may not forget my superior position. Why? His example holds a law before me which strikes down my self-conceit . . .[6]

We may be puzzled in the face of such austere requirements. We can, for instance, love someone for all sorts of reasons—for beauty of character, genius, beauty of person. (The Rhinemaidens to Siegfried: 'So schön! So stark! So gehrenswert!'—'So fair! So strong! So worthy of love!'[7]) The love of friendship, of parenthood, and (less uncontroversially) erotic love bring with them a profound appreciation of another person. If a philosopher believes that he can draw a sharp distinction between such attitudes and a respect for persons that is uncontaminated by the mire of human veins, then we *may* acknowledge that he has evolved a conception of what it is to be a person and to treat others as persons that is different from ours. Yet we may equally say that he is actually expressing not a metaphysical theory about personhood, but a particular morality. (This is essentially Nietzsche's riposte to Kant.)

---

[6] *Critique of Practical Reason*, trans. Beck (Indianapolis and New York, 1956), pt. II, bk. i, ch. 3.       [7] Wagner, *Götterdämmerung*, Act III.

It is scarcely possible to doubt what is at the core of our idea of a person. We cannot regard as persons those whom we think incapable of being offered reasons for action. We almost certainly could not regard as persons those whom we thought incapable by nature of being the objects of and reciprocating love, respect, anger, and contempt. And our having such attitudes to others may actually constitute our practical belief that they are indeed beings to whom reasons for action can be offered. Such interpersonal attitudes[8] may also amount to the practical belief that other persons are free agents.

It may also follow that we are rationally obliged to treat a person as 'one of us'. As a person he is 'one of us' in a deeper way than that in which, because of his race, his caste, or his fortune, he may be 'not one of us'. We cannot, therefore, accept Aristotle's account of slaves as by nature not their own men, but another's, 'animate articles of property' and animate 'instruments'.[9] A person must indeed be 'one of us' in the sense that he is by nature potentially capable of forming part of a society and a polity. He is always capable of entering into the society of marriage, family, and tribe. In this sense man is (as Aristotle elsewhere says)[10] a political animal. To treat people as though they were not capable of these social relations (as American slave-owners in the South seem often to have done) would be to treat them as though they were not fully persons. Yet it is still possible to withhold certain forms of political participation from those whom one may regard as too primitive to take part in the life of a highly sophisticated polity, without as a result failing to treat them as persons. Australian Aborigines were treated, politically speaking, as children, and it is likely that most Australians thought that this would be their permanent condition. Whether this was right or wrong, it cannot be conclusively argued that the denial of certain political and civic rights must necessarily amount to treating others as less than persons. To do so might be to incorporate a political requirement into our concept of a person which will be persuasive only with those who already share our ideology.

All persons whom we in fact encounter are human beings, and

[8] See P. F. Strawson, 'Freedom and Resentment', *Freedom and Resentment and Other Essays* (London, 1974), pp. 1–29.
[9] *Politics*, trans. Ernest Barker (Oxford, 1948), 1253$^b$25–1254$^a$20.
[10] *Politics*, 1253$^a$.

almost all human beings we encounter are persons. We may doubt that some of the insane are persons, or fully persons; and a very young baby, or a child in the womb, is a person only potentially. Some people express their sense that some of the insane, and infants in the womb, are not fully persons by asserting that they are not human. In doing this they acknowledge that it is the normal destiny of a human being to be a person.

In our experience, then, the world of persons is the human world. In describing that world we describe the activities of persons. Yet this does not certainly entitle us to assume that the world of persons is necessarily the world of human beings, or that in characterizing persons we are *ipso facto* characterizing the human world which we inherit, its particular history and culture. There remain powerful reasons for suggesting that in characterizing the concept 'person' we are not thereby characterizing a particular species. Indeed, it is possible to go further and argue, as Kant did, that there are two quite distinct ways of looking at man. We may see him as essentially a rational being, a being to whom reasons for action can be offered, and whose essence is therefore to act from reasons, and hence to be *free*. Or we can see him as part of nature, subject to natural laws, and as such not free but determined. As a person and a rational being man is conscious of himself as free and as subject to the moral law, which is the law of freedom. We can, however, also see men from the outside, look upon them 'objectively',[11] as caused to act by forces which exert power over them whether they will or no. This view—which we can call the 'two worlds views'—can indeed lead (as it led Kant) to the conclusion that everything which expresses man's 'empirical' nature, rather than his nature as a free, rational agent, must stand in opposition to his being as a person, and hence as a moral agent.

If our ideal of rational self-consciousness is simply that of a being who can be moved to act simply as a result of accepting motivating reasons, then we will be driven towards the 'two worlds view'. The most complete statement of this view—that of Kant—sunders all connection between man as a moral agent and as a human being, between man as free and as immersed in nature. It has the consequence that obedience to the moral law, which is of supreme importance for all men, must be detached from any natural

---

[11] See Strawson, 'Freedom and Resentment', p. 9.

disposition to do what the law commands. Our motive for action must be not kindness, gratitude, sympathy, or good nature, but respect for the moral law simply *as* the moral law. Only thus can moral merit, in its supreme importance for all, be possible for all men simply as persons, and not only to those fortunate enough to have been born with lively sympathies, kind hearts, and good natures. Such a morality, detached as it is from all natural human satisfactions, becomes profoundly mysterious. It becomes difficult, perhaps impossible, to see what its point might be, or why it should occupy a position of supreme importance in human life.

If we reject the 'two worlds view' as implausible, and as leading to obscurity, we might try to replace it with the possibility of there being two ways of looking at a single world. We might agree that there are two broadly different ways of understanding people, which, although they may overlap, nevertheless produce very different pictures of them. In understanding other human beings, we may aim to predict their behaviour in various ways, to understand the forces, the unacknowledged desires and fears, the 'economic laws' that seem to govern their behaviour. Alternatively we may pay most attention to developing our understanding of interpersonal relations and feelings. This does not imply either that there are two worlds or that people can be seen in two radically different ways, but rather that there are two ideal poles in our understanding of people, and that the nearer we approach one pole rather than the other, so our understanding of them as persons will be lessened and increased. These ideal poles might also correspond to certain moral polarities: understanding and recognizing others as persons may be connected with treating them as existing in the same moral realm as ourselves.

We may develop this third possibility by reflecting on those emotions and attitudes which in fact seem to contribute to our sense of ourselves and others as persons, and upon others which do not. It may be that this will lead us to accept that there is a very strong connection between the notion of a person, defined as a self-conscious rational being, and that of a human being, with all his desires, culture, and social institutions.

Reflection along these lines would be very helpful in finding a rationale for an ethic of the virtues. The reason why an ethic of the virtues seems to war against an ethic of persons is that the possession of at least some of the virtues seems to depend upon contingency. Not everyone is born with the potential of becoming brave, wise, and self-controlled. However, it may be that some emotions and attitudes both increase our sense of ourselves and others as persons, and are at the same time the basis of certain virtues. Contingency is not thereby ruled out: some people may find it impossibly difficult to cultivate the feelings necessary to their fullest development as persons. Being fully a person and respecting others as fully persons[12] may be an achievement that is not simply guaranteed for all of us. In reflecting on the attitudes and emotions that go with a full sense of being a person, we may be led naturally to reflect upon man's social life, his institutions and culture. To try to think about 'inter-personal attitudes'[13] without these larger reflections may be to set arbitrary limitations on our understanding.

The consequence of this line of thought will be that we will have supplemented our provisional (and formal) definition of persons ('self-conscious rational beings') with an understanding of rationality that we can associate with Aristotle and Hegel. We will look for rational self-consciousness primarily, and perhaps only, in a certain sort of *nature*. In reflecting on man's emotional nature, for instance, we will *ipso facto* be reflecting upon him as a rational being. We might be attracted by an understanding of the virtues which assumes that passions and appetites can be well or ill-ordered; that appetites can be brought under the control of the rational principle. This would at the same time be an exploration of our rational nature. The fullest development of such a line of thought was Hegel's. For Hegel the only adequate account of man's rationality was one which was also an account of human institutions and history. In other words, all human phenomena are expressions of rationality and, in turn, rationality is only to be understood through its expression in human phenomena. All of human nature, from the body to the emotions, to our ability to have a history and to express ourselves in institutions and practices—the realm of 'objective spirit'—expresses our nature as rational beings. As Sartre writes: 'Every human fact is of its nature significant, and to deprive it of its significance is to deprive it of its status as a human fact.'[14]

---

[12] Cf. Hegel: ' . . . the imperative of right is: "Be a person and respect others as persons." ' *The Philosophy of Right*, trans. Knox (Oxford, 1967), sect. 36.

[13] See Strawson, 'Freedom and Resentment', p. 9.

[14] *Sketch for a Theory of the Emotions*, trans. Mairet (London, 1962), p. 27.

This may lead us to be unclear about what sort of boundary there might be between what belongs to human beings purely as persons, and what is simply the result of contingency. We may find that there is an easy transition from what clearly counts as 'being a person and respecting others as persons' to those very qualities which call forth admiration, but which Kant thought not worthy of *respect*—to qualities of grace and style; perhaps even to such gifts of fortune as wordly power and physical beauty.

This points to a great contention in human values. If there is no adamantine distinction between what characterizes someone purely as a person, what sorts of response constitute respect for him purely as a person, and all other advantages and attractive qualities a human being may have, then the way is clearly open for a 'worldly' scheme of values. Christianity has disposed all of us, whether believing Christians or not, to assume that ultimate values must be internal, and to feel more or less scandalized by any ethic which elevates special strengths, rare gifts, and luck. We all inherit from Christianity, and from Kant, the assumption that there must be some set of principles of conduct which apply to all men simply as men. We further assume that if there is such a set of principles of conduct, they will have authority superior to other, more particular principles. Paganism does not seem for most of us a real option. To be interested in how far an ethic influenced by 'paganism' can be taken seriously is to be interested in an ethic that does not rigorously exclude contingency.

## II EMOTIONS

We can treat other people in ways which diminish our sense of them as persons like ourselves. Some of the things we do can amount to a withdrawal of recognition of others as persons. Rulers who authorize saturation bombing of enemy civilians have to be thought of as doing this. We also talk (whether wisely or not) of 'psychopaths'—people who can exploit, and to that extent recognize, persons, but who seem to be intervening in sublunary affairs in which they are not deeply interested. 'Psychopaths' treat others purely as means, and they seem capable of committing crimes coldly and for extraordinarily trivial reasons. They may have a cunning understanding of their victims; yet we feel that their complete lack of emotional response is also a failure to understand. The 'psychopath' does not really see himself as a person amongst persons, and the egoism he manifests in his coldnesses and cruelties may be apparent rather than real; for he does not treat himself as a person any more than he does others.

The 'psychopath' is an extreme case of emotional failure. How far do our normal emotions and attitudes contribute to and detract from our understanding of others as persons?

### i *Anger*

Aristotle and Aquinas make some interesting remarks about anger. Distinguishing anger from hatred, Aristotle says that whereas it is possible to hate a universal class, or under a universal description, we can be angry only with individuals. So 'we all hate any thief and any informer' he says, meaning that we hate them simply as a class, whether or not we have any particular examples of theft and informing in mind.[15] I can, indeed, hate all thieves and informers past, present, and to come. But I cannot be angry with the whole class of thieves and informers, only with particular ones on particular occasions. Aristotle also says that we are angry with those who laugh, jeer, or mock at us, for such conduct is insolent; and with those who inflict injuries upon us that are marks of insolence; and those who show contempt for us in connection with the things that we most care about. So those who are eager to win fame as philosophers are angry with those who show contempt for their philosophy.[16] Aquinas, following Aristotle,[17] says that 'all the motives of anger are reducible to slight.'[18] Aquinas argues that anger and justice have the same object; and that anger pursues its object under the aspect of a good—punishment and revenge, and hence justice. Hatred, by contrast, pursues its object under the aspect of an evil. It simply wishes harm.[19]

Aristotle's interest in anger may seem strange to the modern mind. The Christian suspicion of the deadly sin of wrath makes it difficult for us to entertain the idea of a virtuous anger. The decline in subtlety with which anger has been understood by later

[15] *Rhetoric*, trans. W. D. Ross (Oxford, 1924), 1382ᵃ4–6.
[16] *Rhetoric*, 1379ᵃ.          [17] *Rhetoric*, 1378ᵃ.
[18] *Summa*, 1a2ae, 47, 2.          [19] *Summa*, 1a2ae, 46, 6–7.

philosophers is revealed in Spinoza's definition of it as 'the desire by which we are impelled, through hatred, to injure those whom we hate.'[20] The distinction between hatred and anger is, as we shall see, important.

The ancients could regard anger as a noble emotion. One doctrine of the soul which went with this belief saw anger as a 'spirited' rather than an 'appetitive' emotion. It might help us approach this belief sympathetically if we notice how important anger is to personal expression. Anger can be peevish and petulant; it can be the impotent irascibility of the old, or the wilful rage of infants. An anger that does not command respect is well described by Johnson:

Nothing is more despicable or more miserable than the old age of a passionate man. When the vigour of youth fails him, and his amusements pall with frequent repetition, his occasional rage sinks by decay of strength into peevishness, that peevishness, from want of novelty and variety, becomes habitual: the world falls off from around him, and he is left, as Homer expresses it, φθινύθων φίλον κῆρ, to devour his own heart in solitude and contempt.[21]

Johnson is describing a passionate anger that goes with weakness. What is repulsive is not the anger itself but its failure (as it were) to be impressive. Johnson sees this anger as proceeding from pride. Yet one would think that his irascible old man was as little capable of true pride as of serious anger.

Successful anger frequently makes a man impressive, and commands fear and respect. This was noted by Keats: 'May there not be superior beings amused with any graceful, though instinctive attitude my mind may fall into, as I am entertained with the alertness of a stoat or the anxiety of a deer? Though a quarrel in the streets is a thing to be hated, the energies displayed in it are fine; the commonest man shows a grace in his quarrel.'[22] Anger compels our respect, even against our will, unless it is so impotent, spiteful, or deformed that our natural respect is overcome by contempt, dislike or embarrassment. Ian Donaldson quotes the speech of Kastril in *The Alchemist*, where Lovewit, 'needing to win Kastril's consent so that he may marry Kastril's sister, Dame Pliant, turns upon Kastril

---

[20] *Ethics*, trans. Gutman (New York, 1949), pt. III, 'Definitions of the Emotions', prop. 36; see also prop. 40.　　　　　　　[21] *The Rambler*, No. 11.
[22] Letter to the George Keatses, 19 Mar. 1819, *Letters*, ed. Rollins (Cambridge, 1958), No. 159, pp. 58–109.

with a sudden display of dazzling anger. Kastril is at once delighted and converted . . .':

God's light!

This is a fine old boy, as e'er I saw!

. . . . . . .

'Slight, thou art not hide-bound! thou art a *Jovy* boy![23]

It is essential to anger that it be active. It is at the active quality that Aristotle is pointing when he says that anger 'must always be attended by a certain pleasure—that which arises from the expectation of revenge. For since no one aims at what he cannot attain, the angry man is aiming at what he can attain, and the belief that you will attain your aim is pleasant.'[24] I suggest that it is an outcome of what Aristotle says—and, more importantly, that it is true—that if you try to be angry with someone whom you know to be very much more powerful than yourself, then your emotion will be not anger, but a sort of melancholy sadness. For he says that anger is accompanied by pain,[25] and that the pleasure which also always attends it arises from the expectation of revenge. So if there is no hope of revenge, all that would be left would be a despairing pain of mind—which is the definition of melancholy. I could not be angry with the Pope unless I thought that I was in a position to rebuke him, to have my resentment taken seriously. To be angry with someone is to be disposed to rebuke him, to remonstrate with him, demand that he apologize, have him punished. One could not satisfy one's anger simply by causing another person to be harmed. One cares about his attitudes as well as his acts. If one's anger cannot be appeased by apology or restitution, and if it concentrates not upon someone's attitudes and intentions, but purely on what he has done, or even on what he is, then it has ceased to be anger and has become hatred. (Hence Aristotle suggests that hatred is more incurable than anger.[26]) So the natural accompaniment of anger, as well as the desire to rebuke and punish, is forgiveness. This is perhaps why Aquinas says[27] that anger seeks to harm its object under the aspect of a good, since it is concerned with punishment and revenge, and hence with justice.[28] Hatred, by contrast, seeks to

[23] v. v. 132–3, 144; Donaldson, 'Jonson and Anger', *Yearbook of English Studies*, 14 (1984), 56–71.     [24] *Rhetoric*, 1378ᵇ1–10.
[25] *Rhetoric*, 1378ᵃ30–5, 1382ᵃ10–15; *Ethics*, 1149ᵇ20–5.
[26] *Rhetoric*, 1382ᵃ5–10; see also Aquinas, *Summa*, 1a2ae, 46, 6.
[27] *Summa*, 1a2ae, 46, 6.     [28] *Summa*, 1a2ae, 46, 7.

harm its object under the aspect of an evil. One may simply wish that the person one hates cease to exist.[29] Anger cannot be a lingering, passive state that can exist in a subterraneous form all one's life, breaking out occasionally, as can hatred and envy.[30] So it is part of the nature of anger that one make certain demands, that one seek a certain response. The angry man claims that his feelings and attitudes be taken seriously. He makes certain claims, and considers himself justified. Anger and apology are concerned with claims, justification, recompense.[31]

## ii *Anger and Respect*

One way we can treat an angry man is simply to be interested in his anger as a display, as we might be interested in the aggressive display of an animal. For instance, it is possible maliciously to provoke anger in order to enjoy the spectacle: schoolboys do this to vulnerable masters. Yet we can also respond with respect, awe, and fear; and this can actually be part of what it is to understand anger.

It is often said that fear must necessarily have as its object something that is thought to be harmful. But if we fear someone's anger simply because we think that it will lead to some harm— physical assault, for instance—then we are treating it as grounds for a prediction—as the hiss of a snake is a sign that it is going to strike. Yet we may respond fearfully to anger without expecting any harm. For fear may be an expression of respect. 'Fear of the Lord' may well include fear of the consequences of offending Him; but it also includes respect and awe, which go with love and a desire to obey. Even our respect for other people includes an element of fear. A man in the presence of another, whom he greatly respects and reverences, fears to be judged ill by him, and may be embarrassed, tongue-tied, or ashamed. And the natural reaction to anger is something like respect, something like awe, and something like fear. These reactions are a way of recognizing and understanding anger, rather than of fearing the consequences of it. They are also a

[29] Cf. Aristotle, *Rhetoric*, 1382ª15–20.

[30] In this respect anger is rather like jealousy, which is itself characteristically a more active—one might even say 'healthier'—emotion than envy.

[31] We might note the Stoic distinction between *ira* and *excandescentia*—the latter, a sudden violent blaze, was taken to be noble by Renaissance theorists (e.g. Politian); whereas the former, identified with *kotos* (rancorous anger) is uniformly condemned.

way of respecting the angry person, and of taking his demands seriously. Yet it is only where anger is successful that this response is more appropriate than, say, embarrassment or amusement. It is not easy to determine exactly the conditions for successful anger, but Aristotle seems to have come as close as anyone to doing so: 'The man who is angry at the right things and with the right people, and, further, as he ought, when he ought, and as long as he ought, is praised. This will be the good-tempered man, then, since good temper is praised.'[32] But when are these conditions satisfied? I have already suggested that they are not satisfied when one tries to be angry with someone whom one knows to be remote, or far more powerful than oneself. When Gulliver in Brobdingnag is indignant with the giantesses for taking no account of his presence as they dress and undress (he salves his pride by saying that they were 'far from being a tempting sight')[33] he makes himself ridiculous. The senile anger which has become peevishness, which Johnson describes, or the wilful anger of a child, will also not exemplify 'good temper'. Equally, one cannot be angry with someone who acts contrary to one's wishes, but without consciously rejecting one's wishes. In *Coriolanus* the tribunes use their knowledge of Coriolanus to provoke him to rage and reckless speech, so that he loses the consulship. Had he acted out of character, and retained his self-possession, the tribunes would no doubt have been chagrined or disappointed at the failure of their plot, but they could not have been angry with Coriolanus. If you try to influence someone's behaviour by a stratagem, and not by offering him reasons for action or for taking up a certain attitude, which he might accept or reject, then you cannot be angry with him for not behaving in the

---

[32] *Ethics*, trans. W. D. Ross (Oxford, 1915), 1124$^b$5–10 (all quotations from the *Ethics* use this edition unless otherwise stated). It is perhaps doubtful whether 'good temper' properly conveys Aristotle's meaning here. The Greek is *praotes*, which means mildness, meekness, or gentleness. It seems paradoxical to say that the meek man is the one who knows how to be properly angry. Presumably sensing this difficulty, a German translator of the *Ethics*, Franz Dirlmeier, coins the term *Vornehm-ruhig*—'noble calmness' (*Aristoteles' Werke in deutscher Übersetzung*, ed. E. Grumach, vol. vi: *Nikomactische Ethike*, Berlin, 1956). I am grateful to Christian Wildberg for drawing this to my attention. It would seem that Aristotle is envisaging a man who is gentle in that he is strong and capable of anger, and a virtue which includes qualities of self-restraint and justice. Perhaps we lack a word for it in English just because we lack the concept of it. The coinage 'noble calmness' seems as good a gloss as any, and reminds us of an ideal of Nietzsche's.

[33] Swift, *A Voyage to Brobdingnag*, in *Works*, ed. J. Nichols (London, 1801), ch. 5.

way you want. Anger entails reacting to someone personally, setting a value on his attitudes and intentions. It implies treating him as an agent capable of accepting or rejecting reasons for action. And that means treating him as free.

## iii *Sympathy*

Hume uses the term 'sympathy' to explain our recognition and understanding of the passions of others.[34] He has a particular theory of how sympathy comes about: we form an 'idea' of the passion of another—which is just like the perception of an ordinary fact. Then, since we are similarly constituted, we convert this idea into an 'impression', and hence sympathetically enter into the feeling of another. We need not accept Hume's peculiar (and peculiarly implausible) doctrine about ideas and impressions in order to find useful his essential contention—that we grasp the passions of others through imaginatively entering into them. We certainly have the impression that we directly hear the passion in someone's voice. This seems still more obvious when we are listening to music. We also seem to see his emotions directly in his physical gestures and facial expressions.

Sympathy implies the power of imagination. Indeed, an unimaginative man may often fail to notice someone else's feelings. Sartre says some things about mimicry that have a bearing upon this.[35] He is discussing the actress Franconay mimicking Maurice Chevalier. We *could* conclude that she is mimicking Chevalier simply because we in fact know that that is what she is trying to do. And we could see how certain of her gestures, the way she holds herself, what she does with her lips, the angle at which she wears a boater, resemble Chevalier. Yet that would not be recognizing the mimicry. To notice her intention, even to discover literal resemblances to Chevalier, is not to recognize a successful mimic. Indeed, Sartre points out that the literal resemblances between the actress and Chevalier are almost non-existent: 'How is Maurice Chevalier to be found in these fat painted cheeks, that black hair, that feminine body, those female clothes?'[36] Franconay is short, stout, brunette, and female; Chevalier is tall, slim, blond, and male. According to

---

[34] *A Treatise of Human Nature* (Oxford, 1888), bk. II, pt. i, sect. ii.
[35] *The Psychology of Imagination*, trans. Frechtman (London, 1972), pp. 30–1.
[36] *Psychology*, p. 29.

Sartre what Franconay projects is 'the expressive nature' of
Chevalier, his essence as 'delivered to intuition'. His conclusion is:
'When I see Maurice Chevalier (i.e. in the mimicry) the perception
involves a certain affective reaction.'[37]
Our grasp of the emotions of others is not dissimilar. Confronted
with an angry gesture, for instance, I do not have to recall to mind
how I usually behave when I am angry, and then make a correlation
between my anger, my usual angry behaviour, and the angry
behaviour of the other person, whom I then conclude to be angry. I
may be unable to recall the particular angry gesture or the
particular anger that goes with it. Yet I have no difficulty in
recognizing the gesture as an angry one. Merleau-Ponty (from
whom this idea is taken) writes: 'I do not see anger or a threatening
attitude as a psychic fact hidden behind the gesture, I read anger
into it. The gesture *does not make me think of* anger, it is anger
itself.'[38] However, there are other bodily gestures which I may be
precluded from understanding in this way. Merleau-Ponty suggests
that the sexual expressiveness of the body is a perception barred to
the child 'unless the child has reached the stage of sexual maturity
at which this behaviour becomes compatible for it.'[39] My recognition of bodily gestures is a recognition of intention; but it is a
recognition of intention the condition of which is that I enter into,
imaginatively grasp, the intentional act. 'It is as if the other person's
intention inhabited my body, and mine his.'[40] Merleau-Ponty is
surely right in suggesting that my ability to grasp the expressiveness
of a bodily gesture depends upon its seeming to be in some sense a
possibility for me. Sex is particularly interesting because children
do not seem to grasp the expressiveness of sexual behaviour or, if
they do so, they show this by uneasiness or fear. A child's
understanding, and also his failure to understand, is related to
his sense of possible intentions and hence to his sense of the
meaning of his own bodily gestures. It is precisely here that we want
to say that knowledge depends upon experience—although the
experience may simply be that of coming to see one's own body as
the vehicle of a new set of possible intentions. My understanding of
the bodily gestures of others is a matter of their answering to my
own 'inner possibilities'.[41]

---

[37] *Psychology*, pp. 30–1.
[38] *The Phenomenology of Perception*, trans. Smith (London, 1962), p. 184.
[39] Ibid.          [40] Merleau-Ponty, *Perception*, p. 185.          [41] Ibid.

Even our understanding of the behaviour of animals seems to require an imaginative sympathy. We are very strongly inclined to see animals as acting intentionally. Indeed to see an animal as conscious is to see it as acting intentionally. For this it is not enough that we see the movements it makes. We also see these movements as expressing desire, fear, appetite. We have some sense of how the world presents itself to the animal as fearful, edible, capable of being occupied as his territory. Towards insects we may be more ambivalent. We may remind ourselves that bees are much more like automata than genuinely purposeful beings, and that their behaviour can entirely be explained by traces of sugar, the position of the sun, the direction and concentration of food.[42] Their apparently intentional behaviour is really a response to a stimulus, which can be expressed in causal laws establishing regular correlations between states of affairs in the world and the state of the organism of the bee. At the same time, despite what we know, when we actually watch them at work it is natural to see them as purposeful creatures.

Our comparative willingness to see the behaviour of bees as intentional is curiously like 'sympathizing' with them. At the same time, our readiness practically to accept that they are really quite like automata goes with a real difficulty we have in entering imaginatively into the consciousness (if that is what it is) of a bee. Certainly—as a matter of phenomenology—we do project ourselves into the creatures: it is something more solid than sheer sentimentality that may give us a revulsion from needlessly crushing a bee. As Wittgenstein says of the struggles of a fly: pain seems to get a foothold here.[43] In observing the movements even of an insect one is immediately in a different world from that of stones and plants. (And yet we are tempted to use intention-like language to describe even the flourishing of plants: 'It likes this soil'.) It would be true to the phenomenology of how we regard animals to say that we both do and do not attribute true intentionality to them, and analogously that we both do and do not sympathize with them. To sympathize

[42] Cf. Jonathan Bennett, *Rationality* (London, 1964), discussing Karl von Frisch.

[43] 'Look at a stone and imagine it having sensations.—One says to oneself: How could one so much as get the idea of ascribing a *sensation* to a *thing*? One might as well ascribe it to a number!—And now look at a wriggling fly and at once these difficulties vanish and pain seems able to get a foothold here, where before everything was, so to speak, too smooth for it.' *Philosophical Investigations*, trans. Anscombe (Oxford, 1958), p. 284.

with an animal is not quite like having certain beliefs about it. We may feel revulsion at killing some insects without any particular belief about what they feel. Rather the modest possibility of revulsion is also the modest possibility of sympathy, and the equally modest possibility of attributing consciousness to them. Our comparative readiness to think of bees as automata goes with the relative difficulty there is in entering imaginatively into their consciousness. We can read an angry gesture as anger; but it is very difficult to 'read' the behaviour of insects at all, or even to see it as expressing pain or fear. And if we feel a much greater revulsion at mistreating some of the higher mammals, this need not be because we believe—falsely—that they have a consciousness just like ours (as children who read Beatrix Potter may believe that animals think and talk like men), but rather that there is a greater possibility of imaginative sympathy. Some remarks of Thomas Nagel are relevant: '. . . the fact that an organism has conscious experience *at all* means, basically, that there is something it is like to *be* that organism. . . . the essence of the belief that bats have experience is that there is something that it is like to be a bat.'[44] But our grasp of what it is like to be a bat (as Nagel says, not what it would be like for me to be a bat, but what it is like for a bat to be a bat) is conditioned by some similarity between the creature's body and my own. The further I am from being able to interpret the movements of the animal's body on the analogy of movements of a human body, then the further I am from having any idea of what it is like to be that creature.

We might set ourselves to believe that all sorts of things besides animals are conscious. Magnetism and the adaptation of plants to their environment can be seen as analogies of desire and will: 'Yea plants, yea stones detest | And love'.[45] Yet such a belief would remain fanciful, as the language of will and desire, applied to plants and stones, would remain metaphorical. We certainly have no temptation to see plants and stones as conscious: on the contrary, to do so requires exceptional imagination—and even that is not enough.

By contrast, it is virtually impossible not to see animals—and especially the higher mammals—as conscious beings which engage in intentional behaviour. We see animals in a profoundly different

---

[44] 'What is it Like to be a Bat?', *Mortal Questions* (Cambridge, 1979), pp. 166, 168.          [45] Donne, 'A Nocturnall upon St Lucy's Day'.

relation to the material things around them from the relation these things bear to one another. Perhaps I approach a large pile of twigs and branches and suddenly realize that there is a swan on a nest. The presence of the animal makes me see the scene as arranged around it—though not arranged around it as the moons of Jupiter are arranged around the planet: rather I am impelled to see the scene from the creature's point of view; or, in observing the scene, I inevitably make allowance for a new factor in it—the creature's point of view. But to make allowance for the swan's point of view is not merely to add another feature to the scene. It is to participate in the scene imaginatively. This imaginative participation is not something we can simply decide to engage in or not to engage in, but rather something that we naturally do, unless we make an effort to do something different. Among the things that make it possible for us to sympathize with an animal will be its having a sensory intake that orientates it towards the world in ways analogous to that in which our own senses orientate us towards the world; a sense of the ways in which its body can be hurt, and consequent behaviour by the animal that reveals it can feel pain.

Coming back to anger, we can draw some analogies. There are ways of recognizing anger that are external or 'objective'.[46] We may treat the behaviour of the angry man simply as providing evidence about his probable future behaviour. It can also provide evidence about his present state of mind, in that we may discount the description under which he sees his own feeling. I may think of my anger as a response to injustice: you may take it as a sign of envy. One might even take someone's righteous anger as proof that he is absorbed in infantile wishes and fears—*that* is the state of mind it reveals.

To take up such an objective attitude will from time to time be necessary and, given that self-deception is common, may be correct. This does not make it less chilling. In *King Lear*, for instance, the response of Goneril and Regan to their father's anger is a sort of venomous irritation. It is not simply blank. Regan dismisses Lear's denunciation of Goneril with 'So will you wish on me when the rash mood is on.'[47] She is right of course, in that he curses her almost immediately. However, Goneril and Regan do not simply refuse to respond to Lear's anger: they are quite unable

---

[46] See Strawson, 'Freedom and Resentment', p. 9.
[47] II. iv. 166–7.

to. This inability is conditioned by their language, which is stripped of all emotional content—except cold irritation and (later) lust—as it is stripped of almost all metaphor. A metaphorical language suggests a heightened ability to sympathize, to enter imaginatively into the world of man and nature. (For metaphor, when used by Donne, for instance, involves extending the limits of the human realm, appropriating alien objects by language.) The poverty of the language of Goneril and Regan certainly dissociates them from 'nature' in several senses—natural feeling, natural loyalty, womanliness. Lacking imagination and the language in which it would be revealed, they can express only the most primitive emotions— above all a childish (but not the less dangerous for that) irritation and spite. Their coldness to the demands of Lear's rage extends also to a coldness towards the body itself—so that Gloucester's sense of what should be a natural, and womanly, kindness to an old man meets with no response. And Kent's high-spirited (and high-born) banter is met with a spite that is notable for its humourlessness and priggishness. His assertion that 'anger hath a privilege'[48] could scarcely have found a less receptive audience. In failing to respond to Lear's anger, his two daughters treat him as an object who provides specimens of his 'rashness' ('he hath ever but slenderly known himself', 'The best and soundest of his times have been but rash . . .')[49] and can hence reject his demand.

In rejecting or being insensible to someone's anger I am withdrawing sympathy. Keats's remark that 'the commonest man shows a grace in his quarrel' is rather ambivalent, for he adds 'the energies displayed in it are fine'. He seems to be suggesting that the possibility of seeing anger from the outside—rather than of entering into it—means that we can look on anger aesthetically, as something 'fine'.[50] In the same letter he imagines what it would be like to observe human beings from the outside, but with a certain imaginative sympathy, as we ourselves observe animals:

I go among the fields and catch a glimpse of a stoat or fieldmouse peering out of the withered grass—the creature hath a purpose and its eyes are bright with it—I go amongst the buildings of a city and I see a man hurrying along—to what? The creature has a purpose and his eyes are bright with it. But then as Wordworth says, 'we have all one human heart'—there is an ellectric fire in human nature tending to purify—so that

---

[48] II. ii. 65.     [49] I. i. 293–4.     [50] See n. 22 above.

among these human creatures there is continually some birth of new heroism.

We can connect anger (if we can understand 'a quarrel in the streets' as an expression of anger—which is perhaps not quite what Keats means) with 'the birth of . . . heroism', for anger involves a flaring forth of the whole personality. We experience the anger of another as a claim being made upon us, a claim that we treat the other as a person, take his attitudes seriously, enter into a world of reciprocal relations where rebuke, apology, forgiveness, are intelligible. And that must be the world of beings who can make claims, can incur and acknowledge obligations, can be wronged, can be the objects of and can reciprocate love, respect, hatred, and contempt.

I may aim to be capable of proper anger. A failure to feel anger may amount to a defeat: if instead of anger all I feel is a dumb, subterraneous resentment, then I may be failing to regard myself as on terms of equality with the person at whom my feeling is directed. Achilles has not the slightest difficulty in expressing anger towards Agamemnon, even though Agamemnon is the 'king of men'. To learn to articulate my anger—and hence to feel it *as* anger rather than as dumb resentment—may be to introduce an active quality into what I would otherwise simply suffer. In entertaining the active emotion of anger towards someone I imply that we are both part of the same moral universe, that an exchange between us is possible, that rage may be assuaged by apology and restitution. Anger can, therefore, be regarded as a moral emotion. And failure in anger can plausibly be described as 'pusillanimous'. Later I shall pursue this line of thought and see what reason there may therefore be for connecting the Aristotelian virtue of 'proper temper' with another virtue: courage.

## iv *Hatred*

Unlike anger, hatred can be passive. Certainly one who hates can be expected to harm the person he hates if he has the opportunity. Yet it is possible to hate without wishing to confront the object of one's hatred with any justifying reasons. In hating you need not make any claim against the person you hate, and you need not look for any recognition of a claim. Apology is therefore not necessarily relevant to hatred. Anger must necessarily tend to be appeased by an apology—otherwise it is hatred, not anger. When we are angry with someone we do not simply wish him to be harmed, and we certainly do not wish that he cease to exist. Anger desires that the person with whom one is angry acknowledge his wrongdoing. Hence, as Aquinas says, anger and justice have the same object.[51] In hating one need not claim any justification. A man may simply be an obstacle to my plans and I am determined to remove him. And Aquinas writes: 'But anger seeks evil only by way of just revenge. When the evil inflicted exceeds the measure of justice, according to his estimation, the angry man will relent. Hence Aristotle says that the angry man is appeased if many evils befall whereas the hater is never appeased.'[52] And Aquinas also says that in anger 'one wants the man whom one is punishing to be aware of it, and to suffer and realise that his suffering is in retribution for the wrong he has done. One who hates cares nothing about this because he simply wills evil as such to the other person.'[53] I wish to see him harmed, but it is not essential to me that he realize that his suffering is in retribution for a wrong he has done.[54] So the fact that Odysseus was determined that Polyphemus should know that he had been blinded in punishment for his cruelty shows that Odysseus was angry with him.[55]

A further difference between anger and hatred is that one treats the person one is angry with as responsible, and therefore free. In being angry with someone one believes that he ought to have acted differently, and that he can be offered reasons for regretting what he did, or for having different attitudes and feelings. By contrast I can hate someone simply for what he is, whether he can help it or no.[56] In *Middlemarch* Dorothea comes to ask herself of Casaubon 'Is he worth living for?' and in coming to suspect that he is not, realizes that she is beginning to 'shut her best soul in prison, paying it only hidden visits, that she might be petty enough to please him. In such a crisis as this, some women begin to hate.'[57]

Yet it is easy to exaggerate the sharpness of the distinction between anger and hatred. It is doubtful that in hating someone I simply treat him as an object—say, as an obstacle. That hatred can reveal an intense fascination with the hated person is one reason

---

[51] *Summa*, 1a2ae, 46, 7. See also p. 12 above.
[52] *Summa*, 1a2ae, 46, 6, referring to *Rhetoric*, 1382ª14. See also p. 12 above.
[53] *Summa*, 1a2ae, 46, 6.                                        [54] Ibid.
[55] Homer, *Odyssey*, ix. 475–9.
[56] Aristotle says that we may hate someone simply because of what we take to be his character (*Rhetoric*, 1382ª5–10).                [57] Ch. 42.

why it has often been thought to resemble love. Although in hating you are characteristically uninterested in apology, and are unwilling to be appeased by it, this does not show that you think of the hated person simply as an object. For another way of describing hatred is to say that in hating you close your eyes to the claims of the other person, you refuse his demand to be treated as a person. In so far as we hate someone we do not treat him as responsible and free. This does not necessarily mean that we have ceased to believe that he is free, but that practically we set our knowledge aside. Yet can we hate something which is not a person? Can we truly hate animals, or plants, or humid weather? Although we talk of hating these things, it must be doubtful that we really mean it. My 'hatred' here does not go with a desire to harm. Perhaps we cannot really hate what is of its nature beyond someone's control—the colour of a man's hair, or of his skin. Hatred is always directed at a person, even if it is based on features which it is beyond his power to change.

So can we really hate someone for a trait of character which we know is entirely outside his control? There can perhaps be no conclusive answer to this question. Some might say that it is precisely the disgusting or irritating features of someone's personality which we know he can never change that we hate most: we hate him all the more for being unable to change. Another line of thought might lead us to say that since hatred must be directed at a person, then the more clearly we see that the people whom we hate are genuinely not responsible for their actions, so we cease to feel hatred for them—even though we might still feel a sort of resigned contempt. Most of the time we are incapable of such clearness of seeing, because we are in the grip of passion. Hatred, it could be argued, is an intrinsically confused emotion, for in hating we treat a man objectively: yet if we really regarded him as an object, and his hateful qualities as purely natural features, then our hatred could not find its target. So it could be argued that hatred, if pursued, involves a contradiction, for it involves a refusal either to become angry, and hence to admit the possibility of forgiveness, or to see the person whom one hates as determined by causes beyond his control, and therefore to transform one's passion into under- standing. Something like this line of thought is found in Spinoza.[58]

---

[58] *Ethics, passim,* but esp. pt. v.

Dorothea does not, in fact, 'begin to hate' Casaubon. The scene ends with her waiting to express her resentment to him as he comes up the stairs to bed. But she has a perception of him not as a man in command of his character and behaviour, but as 'creature' who should not be harmed. Thus does she exclude him from the possibility of hatred:

'Dorothea!' he said, with a gentle surprise in his tone. 'Were you waiting for me?'

'Yes, I did not like to disturb you.'

'Come, my dear, come. You are young, and need not to extend your life by watching.'

When the kind quiet melancholy of that speech fell on Dorothea's ears, she felt something like the thankfulness that might well up in us if we had narrowly escaped hurting a lamed creature. She put her hand into her husband's, and they went down the broad corridor together.

## v *Envy and Jealousy*

Envy more resembles hatred than it does anger. If one is jealous, then one claims for oneself something that another possesses, and claims some sort of justification. Jealousy resembles anger in that it is particular. I could envy under a universal description. I could envy all rich men without enumerating them or knowing who they all are, whereas I am jealous (or disposed to be jealous) of particular people on particular occasions. Jealousy is not entirely analogous to anger in this respect. We might say of a wife that she is jealous of all women whom her husband talks to. We mean that she has a disposition to be jealous on every occasion on which her husband talks to another woman. Yet we probably mean that she also has a certain attitude to all other women, and that she has this attitude all the time. Here 'jealous' is like 'irascible'. Jealousy is active and, like anger, implies personal recognition. We could see jealousy as a 'healthier' emotion than envy just in that it is active. A jealous man typically believes that his feeling is justified, and is ready to confront the person of whom he is jealous with his grievance.

Furthermore, although someone may be very strongly disposed to jealousy—may be a jealous sort of person—this does not mean that he can be jealous of just anything and everything. When we describe someone as jealous we have to have some idea of the sorts of thing that excite his jealousy. We can call someone envious without having any definite idea of the likely objects of his envy. Jealousy involves a claim or at least pretence of justification—a claim to prior or proper possession, to superior merit, to equal treatment. This applies even to sexual jealousy. The jealous lover has some claim to possession. The rejected suitor, jealous of a successful rival, has some belief—however deluded—of unjust displacement.

Envy, by contrast, can be largely passive. We need have no desire to justify our envy to those who are the victims of it. Furthermore we can be envious of someone for possessing what we cannot and do not hope to possess ourselves. (One can doubt how far it is possible to be jealous without hope. That would have something of the melancholy of impotent anger.) There are no limits to envy, and it can come close to simply disliking the good fortune of others just in that it is not one's own, or even just because it is good fortune. And that goes with taking pleasure in the misfortune of others just in that it is not one's own misfortune, a human trait described in some famous lines of Lucretius:

> 'Tis pleasant, safely to behold from shore
> The rowling ship; and hear the tempest roar:
> Not that another's pain is our delight;
> But pains unfelt produce the pleasing sight.[59]

So envy is more like hatred than anger: it is passive, as hatred is, and it does not claim something as its own. Like hatred, and unlike anger, envy can be directed at someone so far above one in power, talent, or fortune that there is no possibility of action or even significant expression. By contrast, jealousy, like anger, involves some disposition to confront the person of whom one is jealous with one's claims or reasons. Jealousy can, therefore, issue in a self-assertion which can have a certain grandeur, and a confrontation with another person in which malice may be overcome. Envy, by contrast, cannot have any greatness of spirit. Envy wishes to pull down the envied person rather than to confront him. In their passivity envy and hatred are comparable to vanity; in their activity, readiness to make claims, and to engage directly with others, jealousy and anger are comparable to pride.

[59] *De rerum natura*, bk. ii (Dryden's trans. in Dryden, *Poems*, ed J. Kinsley (Oxford, 1958), vol. i, p. 403).

Yet although for all these reasons I have described jealousy as a 'healthier' emotion than envy, it must also be allowed that it is more dangerous. For as well as envy which is expressed in malicious action (a poor man lets down the tyres of a rich man's car) there can also be a sort of innocent, harmless envy. If I say 'I envy you your fine sons' there need be no malice in my feelings. There must presumably be some slight pang, or sadness in my attitude, in my comparing my own fortune with yours. But I need have no wish to pull you down; nor need I take pleasure in any harm which befalls your sons. If I am jealous of your having such a fine family, then there is something malevolent in my feelings. The 'healthiness' of jealousy, arising from its being active, can make it more dangerous.

### vi *Fear*

I have already suggested that the fear one may feel towards someone whom one respects and loves need not be inspired by the thought of some harm other than the danger of losing his affection and approval. A child's love of its parents is at the same time a sense of dependence and an intense fear of loss. It would be difficult to imagine human relations which excluded fear and which yet included respect, consideration, and civility. Human relations without fear would also be without shame and pride. I shall later discuss the role that shame and pride play in the moral life.

### vii *Admiration and Contempt*

I have mentioned the tradition going back to Kant that there is a sharp distinction between all that we may admire in someone and what we respect ethically. We can admire a man because he is brave, generous, clever, witty, good-looking, talented, fortunate with women. Admiration can take in the gifts of fortune and of nature, as well as those qualities of character which perhaps everyone has a reason for cultivating, and which perhaps everyone is capable of cultivating. By contrast the respect that we owe to the morally good man cannot be directed at qualities he has purely contingently—skills, endowments of nature, the gifts of fortune— but only at his moral character. His moral character might be understood as his possession of the virtues, or as his being the man of 'Good Will'.

I shall throughout be concerned to suggest that no such sharp distinction between those moral qualities which are the proper object of our *respect*, and all other qualities which we may admire, is decisive in our understanding of the ethical life. It is clearly a distinction which does not consort easily with an ethic of the virtues. More importantly, if pressed it leaves the notion of purely 'moral' goodness mysterious. It may be that certain virtues—for instance, courage—properly inspire admiration. I shall leave the question of whether such admiration expresses a moral judgement until the discussion of courage. However, my discussion of anger has already suggested that the respect which is inspired by successful anger includes the possibility of an admiration that can be directed at something other than 'purely moral' qualities. It can, for instance, be called forth by force and greatness of mind.

We can think of contempt as an important part of the moral life only if we do not assume that there is an absolute distinction between moral and non-moral qualities. A man might turn aside with contempt from certain courses of action because of his pride. He may contemn the lack of spirit or strength of purpose in another. Contempt may be expressed in my failing to be angry with another person, since one can be angry only with someone whom one respects.

The successes and failures in action and character that may call forth our admiration and contempt will include both what someone is clearly responsible for, and much that we might regard as contingent. It may be that the virtue of courage, for instance, includes in its highest form qualities and opportunities that are denied to most men. Nevertheless in praising courage we are making an ethical judgement.

## viii *A Natural Kind*

This suggests that certain emotions are incompatible with treating another person purely 'objectively'. Anger is one of these and so, to a considerable extent, is jealousy. By contrast, when one hates or envies another, one's sense of him as a person may very well be lessened. Anger especially is directed at the attitudes of others. For instance, one is angry with another because of his contemptuous attitude. His apology shows a withdrawl of contempt, and therefore one's anger is appeased. Hatred need not take account of another's attitudes and is hence, as Aristotle says, more incurable than anger.

Yet it is wise not to aim at too much neatness. Hatred can be actively directed at what is wicked. We can hate cruelty and injustice, and as a result we can actively oppose them. Hatred and envy are in their own way directed at persons, even if they may often cloud our fullest sense of their personhood.

A person must *at least* be someone who can make and acknowledge claims, and can be the object of and can reciprocate love, respect, hatred, and contempt. Some emotions—and certainly anger—express one's sense of oneself as a person amongst persons, and help to illuminate what it is to regard oneself and others as beings to whom reasons for action can be offered. So emotion, far from derogating from the idea of rational agency, reinforces it. At the same time, this sketch of some emotions presupposes man's life as a social being. We could not understand anger without knowing about what counts as respectful and contemptuous behaviour, what people value, what grounds people have for self-esteem, what is regarded as admirable and disgraceful. In so far as reflection on the emotions gives us an insight into what it is to be a person, it also gives us insight into what it is to be a human being. Indeed I shall be assuming throughout that the only idea we have of a self-conscious rational being is of a human being. Our notion of a person, therefore, will be less like that of a 'nominal essence' functionally defined,[60] and more like that of a member of a natural kind. If the idea of a person is the foundation of ethics, then moral philosophy will concern itself with 'human nature'.


### III SELF-CONSCIOUSNESS: THE GLANCE

Persons are self-conscious, rational agents who make and recognize claims upon each other. Persons are therefore essentially social beings. If we are to go further in finding a necessary connection between the notion of a person and the notion of a human being,

---

[60] See David Wiggins, 'Locke, Butler and the Stream of Consciousness: And Men as Natural Kind', in Amelie Rorty (ed.), *The Identities of Persons* (Berkeley, 1976), pp. 139–74.

then we must presumably take seriously the fact that none of the persons whom we encounter are disembodied minds. They all have human bodies. Our experience of the human body is necessary to our sense of ourselves and others as persons; and our sense of ourselves and others as persons is necessary to our perception and understanding of the human body.

We can sometimes, but not always or usually, regard human bodies simply as objects in the world. It is possible to do so when we are engaged in certain specialized activities. A cobbler fitting a pair of shoes is mostly concerned with how the shoes fit the feet. To an extent he does regard the feet simply as physical objects— although part of what he understands as the shoes fitting properly is that they be comfortable. An eye-surgeon specializes in one part of the body, and does not always think about the body as a whole. Yet it is very difficult to imagine how we could set about systematically treating human bodies simply as 'objects'.

Following Sartre's brilliant discussion in *Being and Nothingness*,[61] we might begin with an activity which essentially involves the body, but which at the same time entails self-consciousness and consciousness of others: looking and being looked at. In meeting someone's glance it is difficult simply to look him in the eye. At any rate, it is difficult simply to look *at* his eye, for his eye seems to vanish into his glance, to be absorbed in his intentional activity of regarding me. As Sartre puts it: 'If I apprehend the look, I cease to perceive the eyes . . . The Other's look hides his eyes; he seems to go *in front of them*.'[62] If I am asked to say what I see, then I can naturally and correctly reply that I see him looking at me. If I am asked whether I see his eyes, I obviously have to reply that I do. Yet it would be equally true for me to say that what I see is his glance, his gaze. His eye as a physical object seems to have vanished into the activity of looking: it seems to me that what I see is the glance itself—rather than an eye which I interpret as looking at me. But in seeing the glance I am aware of an intention: I see him intending me in his gaze. Again I naturally say that what I see is him looking at me, as though I see his intention directly. To see the eye looking at me is to see someone regarding me and being conscious of me.

I can set myself to look through a glance at the eye itself. This can be a way of avoiding a certain consciousness of myself—the

[61] Trans. Barnes (London, 1957), pt. III, ch. 1, sect. 4.
[62] *Being and Nothingness*, p. 258.

consciousness of being gazed at. To look through the glance may be to take up an attitude to the intention of the other person: I refuse to become an object to him, and insist that I am a subject, and he the object. An eye-surgeon examining an eye is not doing this. He examines it from close to, and separates it from the complex expression of the face. He does not see the gaze, but only the eye. The eye as he examines it does not gaze, since to see the expression requires his seeing it in the context of the expression of the face. For him the eye of a living man is different from the eye of the dead only in its physical features, in the fact that the pupil contracts and that the eye is clear. To observe the eye simply as physical object is profoundly different from apprehending the glance. Following Husserl, Sartre writes: 'It is never when eyes are looking at you that you can find them beautiful or ugly, that you can remark on their colour. . . . to apprehend a look . . . is to be conscious of being looked at'.[63]

To return or meet a gaze therefore implies a recognition. In returning the gaze, or failing to meet it through shame, I am acknowledging him, his consciousness of me, his subjectivity. I acknowledge myself as an object in the world, and at the same time as a subjectivity that can be objectified through being observed by another.

Sartre argues that my consciousness of myself as an object for another is not a simply a matter of my attending to something. Suppose, for instance, that moved by curiosity or jealousy I eavesdrop through a keyhole. I am not at first conscious of myself as 'eavesdropping' or 'curious' or 'jealous'. Rather, behind the door a spectacle is presented as 'to be seen', a conversation as 'to be heard'. If I am jealous, 'I *am* this jealousy; I do not *know* it'.[64] My jealousy just is the overwhelming urgency with which I strain to hear the conversation, to see what there is to be seen. But 'all of a sudden I hear footsteps in the hall. Someone is looking at me.'[65] I suddenly become for myself what I appear to the person who observes me. I am ashamed, and in my shame I recognize the image that he has of me: 'It is shame or pride which reveals to me the Other's look and myself at the end of that look. It is shame or pride which makes me *live*, not merely know, the situation of being looked at. . . . Now shame . . . is shame of *self*. It is *recognition* of

[63] *Being and Nothingness.*   [64] Ibid., p. 259.
[65] Ibid., p. 260.

the fact that I *am* indeed that object which the Other is looking at and judging.'[66]

Sartre is arguing that when I apprehend the glance of another, what is essential is that I am the object for another subject. All that would reveal the Other as an object—his physical qualities, for instance—is irrelevant: 'If this gross and ugly passerby shuffling along toward me suddenly looks at me, then there is nothing left of his ugliness, his obesity and his shuffling. During the time that I feel myself looked-at he is a pure mediating freedom between myself and me.'[67]

It would follow from this that I could not be made self-conscious—embarrassed, ashamed, proud—through the look of an Other who was not a free subject. I could not, for instance, be embarrassed by the gaze of an animal. This point is made by Merleau-Ponty:

In fact the other's gaze transforms me into an object, and mine him, only if both of us withdraw into the core of our thinking nature, if we both make ourselves into an inhuman gaze, if each of us feels his actions to be not taken up and understood, but observed as if they were an insect's. This is what happens, for instance, when I fall under the gaze of a stranger. But even then, the objectification of each by the other's gaze is felt as unbearable only because it takes the place of possible communication. A dog's gaze directed towards me causes me no embarrassment. The refusal to communicate, however, is still a form of communication.[68]

Merleau-Ponty is saying that the gaze is intrinsically part of human communication, and hence naturally treats the other person as a subject. The Sartrean account of it as transforming the person looked at into an object describes, on this view, a gaze which retains the intention of being conscious of the other whilst withdrawing from that context of communication in which the gaze has its natural place. What Merleau-Ponty says seems true to experience. We feel uneasy when someone stares at us unflinchingly—in the manner, perhaps, of a child, but not with the unselfconsciousness of a child. There is a difference between an awareness of the other that acknowledges his subjectivity and one which denies it. And the two contrary attitudes may occur at almost the same time; or one may pass into the other. For instance, I stare at someone absent-mindedly and suddenly become aware that he is

---

[66] Ibid., p. 261.     [67] Ibid., p. 276.
[68] *Perception*, pp. 360–1.

returning the stare. He has transformed himself from being an object, and I become embarrassed in becoming aware that I am staring at him.

The self-consciousness that is enacted in the giving and returning of glances is not a matter simply of knowing something, but of an interchange amongst persons. My knowledge of myself depends upon my communication with others. When I recognize someone as looking at me, I do not infer his intention from his glance, rather (as in the case of anger) I 'read' his intention in the glance. In recognizing the eye as looking at me I see myself as an object, I am self-conscious.

This line of thought clearly has its roots in Hegel's account of awareness of the Other as necessarily a struggle, a striving against something, and in his corresponding doctrine that 'self-consciousness exists in and for itself when, and by the fact that, it so exists for another; that is, it exists only in being acknowledged.'[69] My earlier discussion of anger and of those emotions which dispose us to knowledge of ourselves and others fits with this line of thought.

We can nevertheless ask whether we could imagine a self-consciousness that had no connection with looking and being looked at. It could be urged that when I blush at the gaze of someone, what I am reacting to is his *thought* of me—which is why I could not be embarrassed at the glance of a dog. It is my knowing that the Other thinks of my action as vulgar, or as showing curiosity or jealousy, that is the cause of my shame—not the mere fact that he looks at me. Suppose there could be a race of beings who never looked at each other, but thought about each other and communicated their thoughts by telepathy. Could one of them be ashamed because of what others were thinking about him? After all, people can feel ashamed of their sins 'in the sight of God'.

It is difficult to see how this would in fact be possible. In apprehending the look of another I recognize an intention. Yet I recognize this intention because what he does is a possibility for me also. That is to say, my recognition of this intention implies the possibility of action, and not simply of directed thought. The possibility of a community of beings who recognize each other as intending each other by thought must in the end presuppose a community of beings who can recognize each other as intending to

---

[69] *The Phenomenology of Spirit*, trans. Miller (Oxford, 1977), sect. 178.

act. Only in such a context could I distinguish between a thought that I believe that another has about me from a thought that is merely in my own mind. In a community of beings who communicated purely telepathically this distinction would not exist.

Self-consciousness depends upon the possibility of my actually being looked at (or its auditory or tactile equivalent). It presupposes my being in the world, possessing a body, and being in relation to others in the world who also possess bodies.

We have therefore moved from an abstract notion of self-consciousness to a slightly more concrete picture of how emotions contribute to our consciousness of ourselves and others, and to our nature as embodied beings. The glance is a symbol of all this. The eye vanishes into the glance, and we see the person looking rather than the eye itself. Analogously, the body as sheer physical fact is swallowed up by the sign: we concentrate on the sign rather than upon the signifier. The expressiveness of the body too plays a role in our understanding of ourselves and others.

## IV BODIES: MYSELF AND OTHERS

According to Schopenhauer the body is given to us in two different ways, first as 'an idea in intelligent perception'—that is, as an object amongst objects and subject to the laws of objects; but secondly 'as that which is immediately known to everyone, and is signified by the word *will*.'[70] For Schopenhauer the body as 'object' is a Kantian phenomenal object; whereas the body as will is real in a way in which no object is real, since it is the 'thing in itself'—a noumenon. Therefore the body has a special metaphysical status: it is the expression of will, an object of direct knowledge, and that through which the individual knows the world. According to Schopenhauer the body 'is nothing but objectified will'. At the same time it is 'the immediate object'. Thus the will is 'the knowledge *a priori* of the body, and the body is the knowledge *a posteriori* of the will'.[71]

To talk of the body as the expression of will through which the individual knows the world is to say more than that the body is the necessary vehicle for an individual's encounter with the world. It is

[70] *The World as Will and Representation*, trans. Payne (New York, 1958), bk. ii, pp. 18–20.      [71] Ibid., p. 130.

also to say that there is an intimate connection between our
awareness of our bodies and our awareness of the world. Our
disposition to act upon the world is realized through our bodies;
but at the same time our sense of our bodies is a sense of our
disposition to act upon the world.

How do I know that this body is *my* body? Stuart Hampshire has
argued[72] that for this body to be my body it is necessary that I be
able to move it at will. When I move my body I do not perform a
mental act which is then followed by a physical event. I do not, for
instance, wish that my body move, and then find that it does so.
And if I 'willed' that a matchbox jump up off the table, and it
miraculously did so, I would not have moved the matchbox in the
way I move my arm. It is not part of my body.

Sartre develops this line of thought with considerable subtlety.
He suggests in effect that my sense of my body is first given to me
by my sense of the world—the world as to be acted upon,
manipulated, traversed—from my particular point of view.[73] If I
am writing, I do not focus upon my hand which holds the pen. I do
not use my hand in order to hold the pen. What I apprehend is the
pen which is writing. For Sartre this means: 'I am not in relation to
my hand in the same utilizing attitude as I am in relation to the pen;
I *am* my hand.'[74] What Sartre seems to mean is that my various
projects towards the world presuppose my body, its form and
capacities, but my intentions are directed towards the world, not
towards my body which realizes my intentions. In a sense what I
*know* is the world to be acted upon—to be grasped, loved, hated,
resisted—rather than my body. For at first I am simply immersed in
my activities, aware of what I pursue and avoid (for instance) rather
than aware of myself as doing these things. It is only when I have a
sense of how I appear as a body to another that I become fully
aware of my own body. This is another instance—a more general
one—of that passage to self-consciousness from mere consciousness
that Sartre illustrated with the anecdote of the man looking through
the keyhole who becomes ashamed—and hence conscious of the
character of his actions—only when he is seen by another.

If we say, with Hampshire (and in effect with Schopenhauer),
that my body is that which I move at will, then it will be natural to

---

[72] *Thought and Action* (London, 1959), ch. 1.
[73] *Being and Nothingness*, p. 318.
[74] Ibid., p. 323.

say that someone who sees my body and understands what it is sees my intentions, and sees my body as the vehicle of my intentions. And I see the body of another person as what he is because I see what he plans and intends.[75] Sartre expresses this by saying that 'consciousness of the body is comparable to the consciousness of a sign'.[76]

Let us revert to looking and being looked at. When Adam and Eve realized that they were naked, what did they know that they had not known before? We are told that 'the eyes of them both were opened, and they knew that they were naked.'[77] They see themselves naked in the sight of each other and later—or so Adam claims—in the sight of God. If we know our own and others' bodies simply as we know physical objects, it is difficult to make sense of the change in Adam and Eve. Yet we know that modesty and shame are connected with seeing and being seen, and that after an early age they are a normal part of our feelings about our bodies. We may regard the self-awareness of sexuality as a special case—but it does point to the general question of how our self-consciousness is related to our awareness of our body as an object for others.

People are self-conscious about their bodies. To show one's body is a significant gesture. ('Nudists' who make a point of showing their bodies do not remove significance from nakedness; rather they try to give it a different meaning.) Between the sexes the showing of the body has a complex range of meanings: it may aim at exerting fascination and influence, or it may express a wish to be an object for the other. Then there is curiosity, and the sense of the other's body as something to be explored ('Oh my America! My new found land!').[78] Sexual curiosity is perhaps as strange as knowing that one is naked since there is little that one does not already know about the body as object. But it is not like one's curiosity towards (say) an unusual shell: it is, rather, a fascination with the other person through the body.

In an adult, who is capable of shame, there is no mere unconsciousness of one's body that does not amount to shameless-ness; there is no mere instinctive embarrassment at showing the body that does not amount to shame. Shame and modesty are ways of acknowledging the role played by one's body in one's relation to

[75] Cf. Mary Warnock, *The Philosophy of Sartre* (London, 1965), p. 83.
[76] *Being and Nothingness*, p. 330.  [77] Gen. 3: 7.
[78] Donne, Elegie XIX: 'Going to Bed'.

another—for instance in being the object for another, or in seeking to be a subject exerting influence over the other. Therefore, as Merleau-Ponty says, '. . . we must recognise in modesty, desire and love in general a metaphysical significance.'[79]

Milton (imitating a passage in the *Iliad*)[80] captures this in his account of the Fall. Adam and Eve first begin to cast looks of lust upon each other; Adam quite explicitly makes Eve an object for his newly discovered sexual connoisseurship:

> Eve, now I see thou art exact of taste,
> And elegant
>
> .    .    .    .    .
>
> For never did thy Beautie since the day
> I saw thee first and wedded thee, adornd
> With all perfections, so enflame my sense
> With ardour to enjoy thee, fairer now
> Then ever, bountie of this vertuous tree.[81]

It is only after each has used the other lustfully that they both awake (literally) to the fact that they are naked. Their sense of their nakedness is connected with their new-found readiness to see each other as sexual objects.

To understand the body of another person as *him* is to see what his projects are, what he plans and intends. However, in reading the physical as the intentional we do not take the body as disclosing something that quite transcends it. Rather we read the signs of the body. This idea used to be taken for granted as (despite Hegel) it no longer is. For instance, poets and philosophers of the past have been able to describe the human form itself as 'noble'.[82] Milton so describes Adam and Eve (with a certain self-conscious insistence on what was then possible) in Paradise before the Fall:

> Two of far nobler shape erect and tall,
> Godlike erect, with native Honour clad
> In naked Majestie seemed Lords of all,
>
> .    .    .    .    .
>
> His fair large Front and Eye sublime declar'd
> Absolute rule . . .[83]

---

[79]  *Perception*, pp. 360–1.
[80]  xiv. 315–28.
[81]  *Paradise Lost*, ix. 1017–34.
[82]  The idea of the noble will be discussed more fully in ch. 2.
[83]  *Paradise Lost*, iv. 288–301.

Later Adam says to Raphael that not only does he know that Eve is inferior to him in mind, but he knows also that this inferiority finds a physical expression:

> For well I understand in the prime end
> Of Nature her th'inferior, in the mind
> And inward faculties, which most excell,
> In outward also her resembling less
> His image who made both, and less expressing
> The character of that dominion giv'n
> Ore other Creatures . . .[84]

Milton is here drawing upon a tradition, ultimately Platonic, of the relation between soul and body, and of the power of the body to express the spiritual. And he is employing a fixed, objective symbolism. We need not commit ourselves to a full-blooded Platonism if we accept that people express themselves through their bodies in ways that go beyond consciously formulated intentions. Masculinity, for instance, is not simply a matter of the actual physical constitution of the male body, with, in addition, certain instincts and genetic factors which make this particular bodily machine behave in a masculine manner. Nor is it a matter of someone's simply choosing the masculine role; nor of a masculine soul's fortunately being associated with a male body. The way a man holds himself, moves, sits, speaks (the sexual differentiation of the voice is a natural fact, but also expressive)—all this expresses his masculinity, not only for others but for himself. In Proust when Marcel, unobserved, watches Charlus in his encounter with Jupien, he notices that when the force of Charlus's will has been withdrawn—when Charlus is unaware that he is being observed— his face seen thus in repose

and as it were in its natural state something so affectionate, so defenceless, that I could not help thinking how angry M. de Charlus would have been could he have known that he was being watched; for what was suggested to me by the sight of this man who was so enamoured of, who so prided himself upon, his virility, to whom all other men seemed odiously effeminate, what he suddenly suggested to me, to such an extent had he momentarily assumed the features, the expression, the smile thereof, was a woman.[85]

[84] Ibid., viii. 540–6.
[85] 'Cities of the Plain', pt. I, vol. ii, p. 626, in *Remembrance of Things Past*, trans. Scott Moncrieff, Kilmartin, and Mayor (Harmondsworth, 1983).

Later Proust describes

> some who, should we intrude upon them in the morning, still in bed, will present to our gaze an admirable female head, so generalised and typical of the entire sex is the expression of the face; the hair itself affirms it, so feminine is its ripple; unbrushed, it falls so naturally in long curls over the cheek that one marvels how the young woman, the girl, the Galatea barely awakened to life, in the unconscious mass of this male body in which she is imprisoned, has contrived so ingeniously, by herself, without instruction from anyone else, to take advantage of the narrowest apertures in her prison wall to find what was necessary to her existence.[86]

Despite his language about 'imprisonment' in a male body, Proust is describing homosexuality as typically involving the 'invert's' having a sense of himself as feminine through a sense of his own body as a woman's body. The poses he naturally falls into, the gestures he naturally makes, although they are spontaneous, are all significant for him and for his sexuality. So Proust goes on, describing the young homosexual in bed: 'No doubt the young man who sports this delicious head does not say: "I am a woman." . . . But let [his mistress] look at him as we have just revealed him . . . The pyjama jacket becomes a woman's shift, the head that of a pretty Spanish girl. The mistress is astounded by these confidences offered to her gaze, truer than any spoken confidence could be . . .'[87]

Proust's metaphor of imprisonment does correspond to the sense we have that people can be more and less at ease in their 'inhabiting' of their own bodies. Mental illness, for instance, frequently goes with dissociation from one's body (e.g. in catatonic states and anorexia nervosa). A sufferer may want to mutilate his own body or to kill himself. Schizophrenics are said often to have the sense that their bodies are 'unreal'. And there can be an ease in one's inhabiting of one's body—a grace—that expresses ease in the world, and an easy, confident relation with others. Conversely the shyness or shame of young people often expresses itself in gaucheness—hunched shoulders, stiff movements.

What makes this body my body is indeed that I move it at will. But this should be interpreted so as to include all those ways in which the human body is expressive. The way we hold ourselves, our comportment, the tone and pitch of our voices, the play of

---

[86] 'Cities of the Plain', pt. I, vol. ii, pp. 643–4.          [87] Ibid.

expression in our features, the sparkle, or lack of it, of our eyes—all these things express personality, character, consciousness. So does a masculine or feminine comportment. The body can be expressive in this way not through a conscious act of will, but through an accumulation of habit that may have become quite unconscious. Nevertheless, the human body expresses *character*; its range of expression, however habitual it may be, is voluntary to a very great degree. By contrast, the body of an animal expresses character only to a tiny degree, if at all; overwhelmingly, and quite involuntarily, it expresses the animal's species being.

Sexual expressiveness, which Proust describes, is of particular interest, because it is both voluntary—it reveals a picture which a man wishes to have of himself—and involuntary—a man habitually conceals from himself the role he is playing. Sexuality provides a particularly rich code, a particularly rich, if often ambiguous, system of physical signs. The ambiguity in the signs, the possible tension between the sign and the signifier—as when the homosexual whom Proust depicts imposes feminine behaviour upon a naturally male body—makes it easy for us to use the metaphor of a more or less easy 'inhabiting' of one's body, and for Proust to use the metaphor of the soul of one sex 'imprisoned' in the body of the other.

Is there any other area where we might find it illuminating to move from an abstract idea of character to talk of the body? Yes— the case of courage. We can certainly understand courage as purely a disposition of soul, or a disposition to choose and pursue certain ends. Yet if we are interested in the *phenomenology* of courage we will be interested in the way in which a brave man characteristically 'inhabits' his body. One could say that his intentions towards the world—the way in which he confronts it as a brave man—inhabit his body. He does not use his body as the instrument of a purely 'spiritual' courage. The brave man does not move his body 'at will' in one way, and the coward in another—if by that we understand the body as a sort of neutral instrument which can be used by people of different characters to their different ends. Equally, physical courage cannot be understood as produced by a certain sort of body—for instance, the male body. It is not a matter of 'brute facts', either about the body or (if one may so express it) the soul. Although the metaphor is by no means perfect, it is better to say of physical courage that the brave man inhabits his body in a particular way. What to another may be the last moment to which it is physically possible for him to hold out before revealing secrets to the torturer is to the brave man not the last moment. Sartre is again helpful. He is discussing a case of a man's being 'too tired':

I start out on a hike with friends. At the end of several hours of walking my fatigue increases and finally becomes very painful. At first I resist and then suddenly I let myself go, I give up, I throw my knapsack down on the side of the road and let myself fall down beside it. Someone will reproach me for my act and will mean thereby that I was free—that is, not only was my act not determined by any thing or person, but also I could have succeeded in resisting my fatigue longer, I could have done as my companions did and reached the resting place before relaxing. I shall defend myself by saying that I was *too tired*. Who is right? Or rather is the debate not based on incorrect premises? There is no doubt that I could have done otherwise without perceptibly modifying the organic totality of the projects which I am; or is the fact of resisting my fatigue such that instead of remaining a purely local and accidental modification of my behaviour, it could be effected only by means of a radical transformation of my being-in-the-world—a transformation, moreover, which is *possible*? In other words: I could have done otherwise. Agreed. But *at what price?* [88]

Sartre's contention is that fatigue is not to be understood simply as a state of the body—as being of a certain weight or of a certain musculature is a state of the body—but also, even primarily, as a mode of consciousness of the world. My fatigue is a way of seeing the hills as steeper, the roads as interminable, the sun as more burning.[89] This is an unreflective way of being fatigued—a fatigue manifested simply through one's consciousness of the world. However, one may then become reflectively aware of one's tiredness, and begin to suffer it: 'A reflective consciousness is directed upon my fatigue in order to live it, and confer on it a value and a practical relation to myself'.[90] It is only when I view my fatigue in this light that I think of it as either bearable or unbearable.[91] Fatigue, however, is not a thing which objectively is or is not too much for me. My attitude to my tiredness, my valuation of it, determines what sort of thing it is:

---

[88] *Being and Nothingness*, pt. IV, pp. 453–4. This passage is quoted and discussed by Mary Warnock, *The Philosophy of Sarte* (London, 1965), pp. 120–2.
[89] *Being and Nothingness*, p. 454.                                    [90] Ibid.
[91] Warnock, *Sartre*, p. 121.

Here is posited the essential question: my companions are in good health—
like me . . . They are for all practical purposes 'as fatigued as I am'.
Someone will say that the difference stems from the fact that I am a 'sissy'
and that others are not . . . but such a valuation cannot satisfy us
here. . . . To be a sissy is . . . is only a name given to the way I suffer my
fatigue . . . [A companion] will explain to me that he is fatigued of course,
but that he *loves* his fatigue; he gives himself up to it as to a bath; it appears
to him in some way as the privileged instrument for discovering the world
which surrounds him, for adapting himself to the rocky roughness of the
paths, for discovering the 'mountainous' quality of the slopes. . . . His
fatigue is nothing but the passion which he endures so that the dust of the
highways, the burning of the sun, the roughness of the roads may exist to
the fullest, his effort (i.e., this sweet familarity with a fatigue which he
loves, to which he abandons himself and which nevertheless he himself
directs) is given as a way of appropriating the mountain, of suffering it to
the end and being victor over it.'[92]

We might say something similar about the brave man. His
confidence that he will resist, that he will not reveal his secrets, is
not like a confidence that a rope will support his weight (based, say,
on an expert knowledge of the properties of the rope). But nor is it a
purely 'spiritual' confidence. It is a confidence in facing the world
that has its correlates and connections in the way a man may hold
himself, confront the world with a 'bold face', feel fundamentally at
home in the world, set an unconditional value on certain things, etc.
If a coward were to seek to become a brave man, it would not be
sufficient that he set himself to will certain ends; nor that he imitate
certain modes of behaviour of the brave man. He becomes a brave
man at a much greater price—just as the 'sissy' becomes more
manly only through a 'radical transformation' of his 'being-in-the-
world'.

So we can enlarge on the idea that what makes this body my
body is that I can move it at will. Schopenhauer's description of the
body as objectified will, or frozen will, is useful in pointing to the
expressiveness of the body. We can indeed see the body of another
as a set of signs—signs which arise from the natural constitution of
the body, but which bring it to life as expression. The most
dramatic example of the body as sign is the glance. In seeing the eye
as glancing I see not the eye but the intention. I see him. My original
sympathy with a man (as with an animal) is my sense that his body
is not simply an object amongst objects, but that around which, and

[92] Sartre, *Being and Nothingness*, pp. 454–5.

for which, space is organized. Space is organized around it just in that it has projects towards the world, and hence a point of view upon the world. My body inhabits a space of its own just in that it makes the world its object.[93] The body as a system of signs is important in our understanding of courage, temperance, pride, nobility, and numerous other traits of character. It takes its place in a system of mutually recognized intentions. A world inhabited entirely by disembodied beings who thought about each other would not be a world of mutual recognition, and would therefore be a world without self-consciousness.

In his *Aesthetics* Hegel suggests that the perfection of Greek sculpture has to do with each god's being presented fully and naturally in a particular physical form.[94] Greek sculpture is not 'symbolic', for it does not simply point to human spiritual qualities or human character for which the body 'stands'. Its not doing so is, indeed, part of its perfection. A figure of Apollo is not merely a symbol: his grace is the peculiar grace and serenity of Apollo, and at the same time a sublime representation of the human graceful and serene. A complete notion of the graceful and serene is concretely expressed in this figure and, indeed, in this god. Thus Greek sculpture can be religious, for polytheism is a naturally aesthetic religion, in that it seeks for a concrete representation of a set of human qualities, both in sculpture and in its actual pantheon. The fact that a complete expression of a set of spiritual qualities, a complete orientation towards the world, is captured and bodied forth means that what is represented is indeed the divine, lifted above suffering. This would apply even to the Laocoön (for instance), at least on the view of Winckelmann, who greatly influenced Hegel:

As the depth of the sea remains always quiet however much the surface may rage, the expression in the Greek statues shows a great and determined soul in spite of all passions. The more quiet the posture of the body is, the more apt it becomes to describe and express the true character of the soul. In all postures which deviate too much from the state of rest, the soul is not in its proper, but in a forcible and forced state. More recognizable and characteristic is the soul in violent passions. But it is great and noble in a state of unity and rest.[95]

[93] Cf. Sartre, *Being and Nothingness*, pp. 306–39.
[94] Trans. Knox (Oxford, 1975), pp. 481–2.
[95] Quoted by Paul Ferdinand Schilder, *The Image and Appearance of the Human Body: Studies in the Constructive Energies of the Psyche* (London, 1935), p. 271.

There is a perfect congruence between soul and body, but there is not a limited class of such gods, nor of such representations. We can think of the Greek religious and artistic tradition as one which laboured to set down each figure as complete, the definitive expression. The idea of the definitive expression suggests that each sculpted figure captures an essence.

We can, then, move naturally from the idea of persons as self-conscious, rational beings, to them as beings with certain emotions and attitudes, and with a certain apprehension of themselves and others mediated through their sense of their own and others' bodies. The body itself is importantly understood as a system of signs, incarnated intentions, which are, however, brought to life in a social context. In reading intentionality into physical appearances, one is not creating or acknowledging an arbitrary code. To use the musculature of the human face in order to smile is not to adopt a code which might well be private, for it is not an amazing coincidence that the smile is a universal mode of human expression and a universal human capacity. Again, one's ability to 'read' human sexuality is not something that has to be learned *de novo* by every human being in the way that everyone has to learn to read. Yet nor is it simply an instinct. It depends upon one's coming to see certain intentions as possible intentions for oneself, and hence to experience one's body as the natural medium of these intentions. This in turn implies membership of a social world. A sexual consciousness would be impossible as a sheer physical appetite detached from relations amongst persons. To 'read' human sexuality implies an ability to 'read' much else. A homosexual is not just someone with particular tastes but one who does not read the woman's body, and his own body, in the way the heterosexual does. He has perhaps a different sense of the role his own body may play in its appearance to others and in its influence over others. And hence he has a different sense of the role *he* plays.

In general our apprehension of the body depends upon our sense of ourselves in relation to others. The reduced sense that the 'psychopath' has that others are persons like himself very often goes with a corresponding lack of sympathy with their physical being. For even to see the body as a centre of sensation is to sympathize, to enter into its nature as the bearer of projects towards the world. For the 'psychopath' the body can become a mere thing, stripped of all that makes it significant. Conversely, the reverence one might have for an old man is not simply 'instinctive', but cultural—which means that it can be lost in a culture which has ceased to attach a meaning to the seasons of life.[96]

## V DEMANDS ON OTHERS

So our apprehension of others as persons includes our recognizing and responding to their claims and demands. Even our knowledge of our own bodies implies a recognition of others and a response to them. Our recognition of others, therefore, is not a matter of purely contemplative knowledge, but includes feeling, striving, and acting. We should now consider whether equally my sense of myself does not require me to seek recognition from others, to make analogous demands upon them, upon their feelings and attitudes. If it does, then my being myself might be something that I achieve rather than simply something I am aware of when I observe 'the internal operations' of my mind.[97]

According to the classical empiricist picture of the mind, my self-consciousness is a matter of introspection, a turning of an inner searchlight upon myself. It does not necessarily imply my being disposed to act. Therefore there is no necessary connection between my self-consciousness and my being able to move my body at will. So self-consciousness does not depend upon anything related to the will—feelings, attitudes, dispositions to action.

Not all consciousness is self-consciousness. Physical appetites, for instance, require consciousness, but not necessarily self-consciousness. A man might have become accustomed to living in a particular place, and to enjoying certain goods—food, water, and shelter. This does not mean that he regards these things as his. If he were dispossessed he might react with aggression, fear, and grief—yet that would not show that he had a sense of property. If his aggression were *anger*, if his grief implied reproach of his dispossessor, then we could say that he regarded these things as his

---

[96] 'Everything in man is a necessity . . . [but] this human manner of existence is not guaranteed to every human child through some essence acquired at birth, and in the sense that it must be constantly reforged in him through the hazards encountered by the objective body. Man is an historical idea and not a natural species.' Merleau-Ponty, *Perception*, p. 170.

[97] Cf. Locke, *An Essay Concerning Human Understanding*, ed. and abridged Pringle-Pattison (Oxford, 1924), bk. ii, ch. i, p. 43.

property. His sense of property must include the determination that another recognize these things as his. The sense of property does indeed imply self-consciousness, and this may dawn upon him only when his habitual possession has been challenged. Again, if a man laboured to produce crops, and if his response to dispossession were only fear and 'aggression' rather than reproach, anger, and indignation, then we could not say that he had taken possession of these things through his labour. Property requires not only that a man mingle his labour with things, but also that he look for recognition by others that he has extended his will over part of the world. The idea of his will, as distinct from his desires, implies a relation to others. Indeed, the notion of *his* will is of something that aims at recognition from others. It is not just another word for desire. Property, so understood, implies self-consciousness through a relation to other people. The claim to recognition that property implies is also a claim to respect. If one had no idea of the property of others beyond an awareness that one would be punished if one stole it, then it would be doubtful that one had a real understanding of property at all. In recognizing something as *his* one refrains from trespassing on *him*. Respect for property implies respect for the proprietor as proprietor. Simply to brush aside a proper claim to ownership is to commit a wrong against the person.

A man is not insulted when I do something to him that he does not like and does not expect, but only if I treat him in a way that he can claim to resent. I insult him by disregarding his claim to ownership, or his claim to be treated with courtesy. This implies that he has a certain picture of himself and a sense of what he can claim to be in the eyes of others. But the condition of his having such a picture of himself is that he can make a claim, that he can assert his rights.

Is there any general term for a person's readiness to make appropriate claims upon others, to extort from them a proper respect? Probably not. Yet we can perhaps say that someone with the general disposition to claim what is due to him, to show proper anger when he is slighted and a determination not to be treated as of no account, sets a value on himself. One's assertion of right to one's property, one's resentment of insult, both imply a self-valuation. A person who fails to make these assertions lessens his sense of what he is.

There is no neutral, passionless way in which one extorts

recognition. To fail in it is to be defeated in one's sense of onself. Success involves a large commitment, or is achieved (to use Sartre's words) at a cost. Indeed, it involves one's whole personality. We can make little sense of someone's having a disposition to claim appropriate recognition where this does not express what Hume called 'a steady and well-established pride and self-esteem'.[98] For the man who makes these claims sets a certain *value* on himself. Someone content with simple physical pleasures need have no vision of himself, or set any value on himself. To elicit recognition from others is to set a value on oneself. Nor is this simply having a certain opinion about oneself. It entails indignation at being undervalued; the sense that some actions would be beneath one or ignoble; that one merits a certain place in the world as a man. The best word for all this is 'pride'.

## VI PRIDE

Pride is the self-regarding version of respect for others. The man who is incapable of attempting to elicit for himself the recognition that he knows he should extend to others is defeated in his sense of himself as a person. There are no good grounds for accepting an asymmetry between oneself and others in this respect. The same connection which exists between apprehending others as persons and acknowledging their claims, taking their anger seriously, respecting their property, exists also between asserting one's own claims and being conscious of oneself as a subject. We inherit from Christianity a very strong prejudice (which in Christianity itself is something other than a prejudice) against all those forms of self-affirmation that we may sum up under the heading 'pride'.

One form this prejudice takes is a refusal to distinguish between pride and vanity. A vain man has something that resembles self-esteem in that he envisages a certain place for himself in the world, and demands from others what looks like respect. And indeed a well-founded vanity may look for a proper respect, and is not necessarily to be condemned.[99] But in general we may doubt that

---

[98] *Treatise*, p. 599.

[99] '. . . vanity is tiresome only when the person pretends to be modest. Some of my best friends have been kept permanently happy and good-natured by the attractive picture constantly reflected from their looking glass . . .'. Harry Daley, *This Small Cloud* (London, 1986), p. 84.

respect from others is what the vain man really seeks. Vanity resembles envy in being somewhat passive, and in having no certain limit on its demands.

> That casting weight Pride adds to emptiness,
> This who can gratify, for who can guess?[100]

is a description of vanity rather than of pride. As envy, like hatred, can have any and every object, so vanity can attach itself to anything and everything. Vanity may set no limit on the flattery that it either seeks or is pleased to receive, however trivial or unrealistic. Although one may have a pretty good idea of the settled objects of a particular man's vanity, it can characteristically be seen as a sheer demand for praise, flattery, and reassurance. The vain man is notoriously a slave to flatterers, and we might even say that vanity turns a man into an object for others, abjectly dependent on their judgements. Vanity can remain intact however degraded the behaviour of the vain man. Shame and the desire for honour are not essential to vanity. The 'pride that licks the dust'[101] is, again, a description of vanity. Vanity essentially looks to other people and their attitudes, but need not involve a 'steady and well-established pride and self-esteem'. Or we might say, vanity is the self-directed version of flattery, whereas pride is the self-directed version of respect for others.

We can scarcely criticize someone by saying that he has no vanity as we can criticize him by saying that he has no pride. In criticizing someone by saying that he has no pride we may suggest that he is willing to do what is degrading, that he has no sense of honour; or that he is willing to allow something degrading to befall those whom he loves or to whom he owes loyalty, or for whose honour he should be jealous. A man who refuses to do something because he is too vain may be moved entirely by his appearance in the eyes of others—in the sense of the figure he cuts. A man who refuses to do something out of pride may be moved by a sense of what he is, what is due to him, what it would be shameful or dishonourable to do. His pride may be a loyalty to others (which vanity scarcely is), a generous care for the respect which is their due. So a man may be— should be—proud of his son's achievements and may resent any depreciation of them. Indeed, pride may be a moral obligation; and

---

[100] Pope, 'Epistle to Dr Arbuthnot', ll. 177–8.
[101] Ibid., l. 333.

my not being proud may be evidence of a mean spirit, pusillanimity, or jealousy. It may also be that one should be proud of a larger community, that one should have that 'respectful pride' in one's own country, 'in Latin called *pietas*, in English patriotism'.[102] Pride may indeed give me my sense of the larger community, may express my belonging to my country.

Since pride is active and demands the most fundamental sorts of recognition, it is best to think of it as a passion. Although there can be a calm and cold pride, reflecting a massive sense of superiority, pride characteristically finds expression in passionate behaviour. Indeed, the truest pride, reflecting a well-founded self-esteem, may be implied in the highest courage. We can think of the greatest courage—courage in the face of death—as a man's greatest triumph over his natural being, his natural wishes and fears. It may be that the fullest understanding of this sort of courage will have to take into account the sort of picture men wish to have of themselves and value most profoundly. Perhaps to cleave to such a picture in such circumstances is related to being proud.

These are, however, as yet merely speculations, and moreover speculations which—given our inheritance from the Christian tradition of a prejudice against all 'self-regarding virtues', especially pride—may be regarded as simply provocative. Pride will be an underlying theme of this book, a theme that has been implied in much that has gone before. At this point, therefore, there is no need to do more than mention it.

## VII CONCLUSION

This chapter began with the abstract notion of a person as a self-conscious rational being, and moved to a more concrete picture of what it is to be such a being. Human emotions, appetites, and embodiment, and human social existence can all be seen as expressions of rational agency, rather than as adventitious additions, or even obstacles to it. Clearly my suggestion is that the best, and perhaps the only, way of giving a concrete picture of what it is to be a person and to apprehend others as persons is to say something about human beings. It is to be hoped that this is an

[102] J. Enoch Powell, 'A Conservative Estimate', *The Cambridge Review*, 100 (Nov. 1978), 52–4.

unexciting conclusion. Nevertheless it does lead to thoughts that are not uncontentious. If all these things illuminate rational agency, and express concretely what it is to be a person, then it is extremely difficult to draw a clear line between those human phenomena which express rational agency and those which do not. Hegel, whose ambition to trace reason's (or Mind's) expression in the human world is unequalled, never tried to draw such a line. On the contrary, he believed that only the fullest history of human culture, institutions, religion, and thought could illuminate what it is to be a self-conscious rational being. My aims are considerably more modest. The systematic study of the virtues dropped out of modern moral philosophy essentially because of the influence of Kant. There is no doubt but that the virtues—including the four cardinal virtues of courage, temperance, wisdom, and justice—are concerned with much that is accidental, or (as Kant would say) 'pathological'. They assume the emotions and appetites, and the possibility of ordering them. They assume man's physical nature. As we shall see, when we reflect on the virtues we also reflect upon man as a social being. An ethic of the virtues is, in Kant's sense, 'heteronomous'. It is concerned with much that is contingent. Furthermore, it is indeed very difficult, and perhaps impossible, to decide in advance what sorts of contingency are to be ruled out of consideration. Does the truest courage demand not only qualities of mind and spirit that many people simply do not possess, but also physical prowess, and even political opportunities which only a small minority are blessed with? Does practical wisdom demand unusual intelligence? Does temperance imply a 'harmony' of qualities that it is extremely difficult to attain? Does justice assume a certain sort of society?

Like Plato, the Stoics, St Augustine, and most Christians, but unlike Aristotle, Hegel, and Nietzsche, Kant wanted to make the essential good for man as far as possible independent of circumstance. Modern men have inherited, and are profoundly loyal to, the conviction that the moral life ought to be available to all, that man's essential good should not be thought of as the preserve of those with special skills and talents, or—still more—of exceptional luck. Yet at the same time modern men are also influenced by traditions of thought—including Utilitarianism and Marxism—which bring circumstance to the centre of their understanding of the human good. I shall not be attempting to find a clear way out of the confusion in which we find ourselves. I assume, indeed, that there is no way out. Yet I shall be trying to suggest that it is possible to think of the virtues as not depending upon contingency in any simple way. And in so far as they do depend upon it, I shall suggest that this does not mean that an ethic of the virtues may not substantially overlap with what the Kantian tradition understands as morality. I have already suggested[103] that the study of the virtues, even in the idiosyncratic (and syncretic) form in which it appears in the following chapters, will be found to coincide to a surprising extent with an ethic that takes the idea of persons and their relations as its starting-point.

Yet it will not wholly coincide. This may mean that the enterprise of this book involves irresoluble tensions—perhaps contradictions. The reader will decide whether that is simply damaging, or also a virtue in our present situation. If the net result is to persuade readers that an ethic of the virtues, as it will be sketched here, is at any rate less mysterious than one which tries to avoid contingency altogether, then something will have been gained.

[103] Preface, p. vii.

# 2

# COURAGE

WE all agree that courage is a necessary virtue, and we all admire it. We are not all agreed about what courage is, nor what we admire about it. People commonly distinguish between 'moral' and 'physical' courage and often feel (or at least say) that 'moral' courage is the truest sort. Yet at the same time, daredevil exploits, flamboyant boldness, have never lacked an appreciative audience. Again, many people would say that courage is essentially a matter of someone's intentions and efforts. People living quiet, private lives, who have never had the opportunity of showing striking boldness, or ever been obliged to do so, may nevertheless possess a fortitude in no way inferior to the courage of those who win the Victoria Cross for gallantry on the field of battle. They may reveal it by stoicism in the face of painful illness or grievous disappointment. Yet at the same time most people—especially those who are not intellectuals—are capable of being moved by the great public ceremonies honouring those who die in battle, even if they cannot easily find words to describe or explain their feelings. Many people too, even if they are embarrassed about patriotism, find themselves deeply impressed by the patriotism of others—by Polish cavalry charging German tanks, Afghan guerrillas resisting Russian invasion, the French Resistance. What we might call 'political courage' is something we seem to understand in practice, if not in theory.

There is a tradition of thought about courage, which runs from Homer to Aristotle, through Roman writers, through Aquinas, to Machiavelli and the theorists of Republican virtues of the Renaissance. This tradition confidently understands courage as being preeminently a public virtue, the chief motives of which are patriotism and the love of honour. For Aristotle, most like true courage is that shown by citizen soldiers facing dangers, because of the penalties of the law and the reproaches they would otherwise incur, and because of the honours they would win by their courage.[1] We show courage where there is an opportunity of showing prowess or where death is noble.[2] For Machiavelli, courage is the highest expression of *virtù*, and *virtù* is the possession of whatever qualities are needed 'to save the life and preserve the freedom of one's country.'[3] More recently there have been creeds—Jacobinism, Leninism, Maoism—which have cultivated an ideal of revolutionary heroism which is not completely alien to these classical and Renaissance traditions. And the Islamic *Jihad* is still taken seriously by millions.

Aristotle and other writers thought as they did about courage because they understood man as essentially a political animal, whose virtues must finally be understood in a political context. It may well be that what makes such a view alien to many moderns is that it flies in the face of the spirit of liberal individualism. Indeed, the idea that courage displayed in greats deeds on a public stage, and pursued for the sake of honour, is a greater and better thing than a 'subjectively' equivalent fortitude shown in, say, patiently bearing sickness and obscure suffering, will strike many people now as not only misguided, but revolting.[4] Our inheritance from both Christianity and Kant makes us uncomfortable with the idea.

Despite these difficulties, I shall discuss courage in an essentially Aristotelian spirit. I shall take seriously that ancient and Renaissance tradition which starts from the assumption that man is above all a political being. I shall not be arguing that the 'truth' about courage (or any other virtue) is to be found in any of the writers in this tradition, or that we have to accept their metaphysics. Rather I shall be reflecting upon why and how we could find such writers, and such an assumption, persuasive now, and what sense such a view of courage might make of our own experience.

---

[1] *Ethics*, 1116ª15–20.

[2] *Ethics*, 1115ᵇ1–10.

[3] *Discourses*, trans. Walker (London, 1970), p. 515. See also Quentin Skinner, *The Foundations of Modern Political Thought* (Cambridge, 1978), vol. i, p. 184.

[4] Presumably an additional reason Aristotle had for exalting active courage over passive fortitude was metaphysical. In the Aristotelian metaphysic activity is higher than passivity, and pure activity—e.g. intellectual contemplation—the highest state of all. It is interesting that Socrates in the *Laches* (191 C 7–E 7) mentions courage on a sick-bed in the same context as courage in the field of battle.

## II FEAR

The first duty of a man is still that of subduing *Fear*.

(Carlyle)[5]

Human beings face a multitude of difficulties and dangers which must be confronted and overcome if they are to live a human life. The human body is extremely vulnerable, always exposed to the possibility of accident, illness, pain, and death. Yet people are not usually obsessed with these undoubted dangers, and life would scarcely be possible if they were. All pleasure in life would be lost were we overwhelmed by all the actual and possible dangers that surround us. Valetudinarianism—like that of Jane Austen's Mr Woodhouse, who thought that a lightly boiled egg *might* not be harmful[6]—suggests a neurotic inability to live. Countless decisions in life—even including what career to follow, and what philosophy of life to give one's settled allegiance to—require a steady confidence that is not always vulnerable to doubt. Confidence and faith are indeed essential in life; and confidence and faith imply the control and overcoming of fear.

As well as being beset by difficulties and dangers from without, human beings have to contend with various biases and warps within themselves. Not only fear has to be overcome, but other appetites and passions—greed, lust, and softness—which, if they prevailed, would also prevent men from living a fully human life. Our sense of the human growth to maturity is not that of a natural process, which will proceed well if nothing interferes with it, but much more one of education and training which imposes a control that would otherwise be lacking. This education also restrains that boundless egoism which is another human characteristic.

If we think like this we will have a clear, simple, and quite plausible picture of the moral education of man. He has to learn to deal with particular obstacles and difficulties in the outer world, and with defects in his own nature. He has to acquire, by education, a 'character', a sort of second nature, which will enable him to cease to be simply natural, a prey to all his passions and appetites. In this way he will develop his truly human potential, his self-command,

---

[5] *On Heroes, Hero Worship, and the Heroic in History* (London, 1891), p. 29.
[6] *Emma*, ch. 3.

practial intelligence, resolution, and sense of justice, qualities which will be essential if he is to live in a human society. This picture would accord quite well with Aristotle's description of moral education, and with Hegel's account of human nature as dialectical—man as needing to strive to possess his own essence. Those capabilities which are inherent in people to face danger and overcome fear, to regulate and control passions and appetites, to take seriously the claims of others, and which are realized in education, might be thought of as particular powers or *virtues*. It will be natural to think that the overcoming of fear will require its own special virtue. If this account is not entirely satisfying, that is not, surely, because it is inherently implausible. On the contrary, it is highly plausible so far as it goes. However, it tells us nothing of the way in which fear is to be overcome, and it perhaps leaves the impression that the pervasiveness of fear in human life is a simpler thing than really it is.

Fear in human beings is both more pervasive and more mysterious than in animals. With animals we can give a functional account of fear. An animal fears when it scents danger; its fearful behaviour is obviously related to self-preservation. In those species which we colloquially call 'timid' their fearfulness will almost always help them to survive. It is true that some animals—for instance, horses—seem to be just nervous, and that we often cannot account for what frightens them. And with the apes there are fears that seem very like human 'phobias'. However, we can in general say that fear in animals is a response to actual or apprehended danger.

Many people would wish to say the same about human beings. However, since it is notorious that human beings often fear what is not dangerous, the 'functional' account of fear is readily amended, so that human fear is thought of as a response not only to 'real' but also to 'imaginary' dangers. Yet not everything we fear comes into the categories of either real or imaginary dangers. Fear seems intertwined with the human condition in a way that resists easy explanation. Almost every stage of human development is accompanied by fear. A child may have to overcome fear in learning to walk. Most stages of life, including growing from childhood to youth, from youth to a maturity which includes sexual initiation and accepting the need to make one's own way in the world; the accepting of family responsibilities; facing old age, and, finally, death—all these require the subduing of fear. It is a very remarkable feature of human life that it is pervaded by fear. In many—perhaps nearly all—of these cases we cannot explain the fear by the apprehension of either real or imagined harm. A baby may be fearful at being separated from its mother; it demands the breast with a mixture of rage, determination, and fear. We cannot confidently say that its separation from its mother, its lack of the breast, seems harmful to the baby. All we can say is that both can cause fear and anxiety. And if we must talk of harm, we can only say that separation and lack of immediate gratification seem harmful to the child just in that it fears them. But that is to use the notion of fear to explain the notion of harm, rather than the other way round. The sexual relation can also produce fear as well as desire. It is possible to speculate—as psychoanalysts do—about 'unconscious beliefs' that explain this fear. The question is not whether such speculations might sometimes be right, but whether we can understand such fear only in the light of these speculations. Yet it seems that we can understand what it is for a sexually inexperienced young man to fear women without having to invoke conscious or unconscious beliefs about how they might harm him. Bashfulness, a desire to appease, a desire to please, are all forms of fearing that go with awe, or respect, or simply desire. They imply a depreciation of the self in comparison with someone else. Again, if a young man feels apprehension or melancholy at the prospect of having to make his way in the world, this need not be because he actually believes that this will be difficult. He may none the less shrink from it, feel anxious, dispirited. This also is fear. Above all, we fear death: and no arguments from Epicurus, Lucretius, or Plato have ever convinced people that they fear it because they falsely believe it to be a harm.

How is fear subdued? I can sometimes rid myself of a fear by being persuaded that what I fear does not actually exist. So Lady Macbeth tried to rid Macbeth of his fear of Banquo's ghost by insisting that the dead do not return. And I might possibly rid myself of my fear of spiders when I am convinced that they can neither bite nor sting. But my coming to see that a fear is unfounded is not the only way in which I may subdue it. I also remove fear by acquiring confidence in myself, by setting myself, as it were, against what I had feared. One way in which I may do this is by feeling and expressing anger.

I have already suggested[7] that the angry man claims attention of a personal sort, claims a certain respect, succeeds in expressing himself. In failing to feel or show anger one may suffer an inner defeat. I suggested that anger has an active quality.[8] A man may fail to be properly angry through poor-spiritedness, rather as he may fail to have the heart to carry through a course of action which he intended. A man may need to learn anger: and this is not like learning to have a passion—as he might learn to love women by coming to know many. Rather one may learn to be angry rather than simply dumbly mortified in the way in which one may learn to articulate an emotion which until then one had only inarticulately suffered. In learning to articulate an emotion one may give it an active quality, and make it part of one's intentional attitudes. To learn anger may be a moral achievement. One may be learning to assert oneself, to show something better than poor-spiritedness. And this may be a way of learning how to be courageous. That is not just because to show anger may sometimes be dangerous, but also because anger is in the nature of self-assertion. As I have already suggested,[9] anger involves a readiness to confront another person, to rebuke, punish, seek justice or revenge, and consequently requires self-esteem.

As we saw, Aristotle includes 'proper temper' amongst the virtues: the man who is angry with the right things, and the right people, and as and when he ought, is praised.[10] A sheer passion cannot be commanded; but it can be morally right to show the active quality of anger because it answers to certain moral imperatives. To be angry may be to see what is the right thing to do. Anger can transform one's relationship with another person, introducing equality where before there was only a relationship of inferior to superior.

Quoting Macrobius, Aquinas mentions the following dispositions as 'parts' of courage: confidence, perseverance, and freedom from anxiety.[11] Someone who has these qualities has certain attitudes towards difficulties and dangers. Where something can be done, the attitude will be one of confronting them with the practical expectation of surmounting them, of not being daunted. Such a man does not just have certain feelings, but actually sees the

---

[7] See ch. 1, p. 13.    [8] See ch. 1, p. 12.    [9] See ch. 1, pp. 12–13.
[10] *Ethics*, 1125$^b$30–5.                    [11] *Summa*, 2a2ae, 128, 6.

situation differently from one who is habitually daunted, oppressed by circumstance. His confidence will be confidence in himself, perhaps self-assertion, some sense of superiority. So if the qualities of confidence, perseverance, and freedom from anxiety go with (are the 'parts' of) a particular virtue, that virtue will not be (for instance) temperance. In being confident that one will be able to overcome gluttony, one does not have the sort of confidence that may dispose a man to set himself against something threatening or painful. One may be confident simply in that one knows oneself well. The confidence that seems to go with courage can involve pitting oneself against something threatening, perhaps even making oneself superior to pain. This does not mean that a courageous man does not feel fear, but that he has spirit, and therefore overcomes his fear. (Or, he does not feel fear, not because he is insensible, or simply confident in the way that a skilled professional—say, a tightrope-walker—is confident, but because he has spirit.) The control of fear is related to capacities such as anger, and hence to the 'spirited' part of the soul, and to courage. The 'spirited' is not shown only in anger, of course. When Hector leaves Andromache in order to fight, despite her pleas that he not go, he is not angry.[12] He goes to fight despite what he knows of his fate, rather than despite fear of pain. And he steadily foresees his (and Andromache's) fate—how he will be killed and she led into captivity. His courage includes his steady acceptance of the inevitability of death—'No man, whether brave or a coward, has escaped his doom, when once he has been born.' But Hector's stated *reason* for fighting is shame, and the desire for honour which has been bred in him: '. . . wondrously have I shame of the Trojans, and the Trojans' wives with trailing robes, if like a coward I skulk apart from the battle. Nor doth mine own heart suffer it, seeing I have learnt to be valiant always and to fight amid the foremost Trojans, striving to win my father's great glory and mine own.'[13] Shame and the desire for honour are also 'spirited' elements.

To talk of a 'spirited' element is not simply to assume Aristotle's tripartite soul, but to see why that picture of the soul is attractive. There really does seem to be an analogy between the way in which a man capable of proper anger has a practical sense of certain possibilities of action being open to him that is denied to the man

[12] Homer, *Iliad*, trans. Murray (London, 1924), vi. 405–502.
[13] Ibid., 441–6.

capable only of dumb resentment or melancholy, and the way in which the brave man has a sense of possible courses of action that is denied to the coward. To be angry rather than frightened may itself be a decision to resist, to struggle, rather than to flee or surrender. It is difficult to imagine a courage which does not include such things as the decision to be angry rather than afraid on particular occasions. (But to be ashamed of the temptation to flee may also be to see what is the courageous thing to do.) Similarly those dispositions which Aquinas thinks are parts of courage—confidence, perseverance, and freedom from anxiety—may be related to self-assertion, superiority to obstacles and pains, and ability to banish, or at least confront, anxiety—dispositions that are themselves related to anger. And a further exploration of these connections—of anger with self-assertion, and of both with courage (which Aquinas includes among the 'irascible' capacities of the soul)[14]—will help to show why it is plausible to connect anger with pride. It will also bear upon Aquinas's assertion that *magnanimitas* (Aristotle's *megalopsychia*) is 'a part of courage'.[15] Aristotle also says that the brave man is supported by anger in his acts.[16]

### III CHOICE

Aristotle says that courage is a disposition 'to be confident in aiming at an honourable end, the end itself being pleasant, but the pleasure being concealed by the attendant circumstances'.[17] He says also that courage is concerned with feelings of confidence and fear[18] and 'chooses and endures things because it is noble to do so, or because it is base not to do so'.[19] Again he writes: the brave man 'endures and acts for a noble end as courage directs'.[20] Aquinas contrasts courage with temperance: temperance curbs the bodily pleasures and passions, when they seek to draw us away from rational behaviour; but the emotions 'may in another way drag us away from the course which reason dictates, by fears of perils or hardships; it is then that a man must be firm in what is rational and

---

[14] *Summa*, 1a2ae, 46, 3.  [15] *Summa*, 2a2ae, 129, 5.
[16] *Ethics*, 1116$^b$30–5 (the word Aristotle uses is *thumos*); Aquinas, *Summa*, 2a2ae, 123, 10.  [17] *Ethics*, 1117$^a$35–1117$^b$5.
[18] Ibid.  [19] *Ethics*, 1116$^a$10–15.  [20] *Ethics*, 1115$^b$20–5.

should not retreat; and the virtue here is courage'.[21] Later Aquinas quotes St Ambrose: 'Rightly is it called courage when a man conquers himself, and does not weaken or waver by any entice-ments.'[22] He also quotes an opinion that courage is 'a disposition of the soul to stand firm to what is in accord with reason amid the sundry assaults of passion and of the hardships of practice'.[23]

These accounts of courage have in common the idea that courageous behaviour cannot be simply a matter of passion or desire; rather courage can somehow stand against passion and desire, and can therefore be described as action in accord with *reason*. Let us explore this emphasis upon reason and choice by considering the difficulties that would arise were we to insist upon regarding animals as brave.

Some animals—lions, for instance—have traditionally been used to symbolize courage. Or we might call a dog brave that fought a lion which was attacking its master, and was killed in consequence. However, there are things that we could not reasonably say about the dog. We could not say that it 'overcame its fear' or that it acted 'without regard for its own safety', or that it 'sacrificed itself'. It may well be that what is wrong in saying things of this sort is also what is wrong in calling the dog 'brave'.

Since most of us are sentimental about dogs, and since anyway dogs are trained to mimic some sorts of human behaviour, it might be better to take an animal which we are less tempted to regard as brave. We are told that a male rat seeking to mate with a female is prepared (this being observed in laboratory experiments) to run over electrified plates, suffering considerable pain, in its eagerness to reach the female. We perhaps would not want to describe the rat as 'brave' on the grounds that it is prepared to undergo, or put up with, something in order to satisfy its desire. Indeed it would be rather misleading to describe the rat as 'being prepared to put up with something in order to satisfy its desire'. What in the rat's behaviour shows that it is 'prepared to put up with the pain in order to . . .'? Certainly what the rat is doing is pursuing the female—that is why it goes in the direction it does—and it does this despite the pain. It might show both its dislike and fear of the pain—through hesitancy, turning back and so on—and yet still eventually get to the female over the electrified plates. But we do not have to describe

---

[21] *Summa*, 1a2ae, 61, 3.    [22] *Summa*, 1a2ae, 61, 4.    [23] Ibid.

it as 'being prepared to put up with pain in order to gain pleasure' or 'gain the female'. There is a conflict of two passions—fear and the mating instinct; and the mating instinct proves to be the stronger passion (or 'drive') of the two. We could say that the urge to mate overcomes the fear.

We do not have to bring a reference to the pain into our description of the rat's intentional behaviour. The reference to pain that we might make would be extensional rather than intentional.[24] If I say that the rat runs over the electrified plates, despite the pain, then this remark would have to be understood in such a way that someone could infer from it that the rat is putting its left foot before its right, despite the pain, or moving towards the far wall, despite the pain, or moving away from the experimenter, despite the pain. There is no unique description of what it is that, *despite the pain*, the rat is doing. We could say, noting an interesting fact about the creature: 'Look! It goes over the electrified plates despite the pain.' This, along with 'It is trying to get to the female', would be a sufficient description of its intentional action. The reason why the context 'it is doing . . . despite the pain' is extensional rather than intentional is that the rat is not 'putting up with the pain in order to reach the female'. Such a locution has its full point only where it is possible to say 'its reason for putting up with the pain is that it wishes to reach the female'. That is to say, its course of action is one which, out of possible courses of action, it *chooses* in order to reach an end which it desires. If we say of the rat, 'it put up with the pain because it wanted to get to the female', the 'because' has the force of the giving of a reason. Once we have introduced the concept of 'reason' then we also allow for the concepts of 'motive' and 'choice'; and hence of the idea of virtue. As Jonathan Bennett says: '. . . if the concept of "reason" or "motive" could be brought to bear upon the behaviour of ants which march straight into the fire, they would have to be applied in such a way as to justify describing that behaviour as brave, self-sacrificing, etc.'[25] For the rat to act for reasons and from motives, it would have to be capable of forming universal judgements—i.e. of being rational. Only rational beings act from motives and for reasons, and hence choose what they do.

---

[24] That is to say, 'doing X despite the pain' is not the object of the rat's mental attitude; that the rat is 'doing X despite the pain' is an object of the experimenter's mental attitude.     [25] *Rationality*, p. 45.

A man may do something extremely dangerous, inspired by passion. He knows all about the danger, but in his passion he fails to take it into account, does not think of it. At the time, in fact, he might as well not know about the danger, for all the awareness he has of it. His action cannot be truly brave, for he does not take the danger into account, does not deliberate about it. The fact of the danger would enter into our description of his action only extensionally and not intentionally. To take something into account is not just to know about it and not to have forgotten. One may know about something, not have forgotten it, and yet still have to be reminded of it when it comes to action. The man who acts passionately, or rashly, or negligently, is in this position. His actual knowledge does not enter into his action: he does not deliberate. Hence he acts (to use Aristotle's distinction) not *from* ignorance, but *in* ignorance. In the practical sense of 'know' he acts not knowingly.[26] Courage implies knowledge, and even where an emotion—such as anger—assists courage, it does so only in so far as it helps one to know, to deliberate. Blind rage would reduce the element of knowledge and choice, and would make the action rash rather than courageous.

In the case of rash action we may be reluctant to praise the agent for the good consequences that fortuitously flow from it. We may be unwilling to include these consequences in an account of what he did. But someone who acts deliberately has the good consequences of a brave action attributed to him: they are what he *did* and he can be praised on account of them.

This is simply to apply the concept of voluntary action to courage. However, it also suggests that a courageous action which is truly voluntary involves deliberation, awareness of possible dangers, correct assessment of possibilities. And all this may suggest the connection of courage with another virtue: *phronesis* or practical wisdom.

So courage at least involves trying to carry through a course of action despite fear of pain or danger. The action must be genuinely chosen, and the agent must be practically aware of what there is to be feared. Action simply from blind passion is not courageous; but passion can support courage. 'Now brave men act for honour's sake, but passion aids them ...'[27] This suggests that courage

[26] Aristotle, *Ethics*, 1110$^b$20–30.
[27] Ibid., 1116$^b$30–5.

expresses the person, as distinct from his emotions or appetites, and
that if we praise courage we praise the person.


## IV  GREATNESS OF MIND

Most people would agree that courage is necessary. But we do not
value bravery in ourselves or others simply as useful. We are proud
of it in ourselves (or at least, ashamed of the lack of it) and esteem
and admire it in others. It may be that courage is attractive in itself,
as well as necessary or useful.

The philosopher who most memorably insisted on the intrinsic
attractiveness of courage was Hume. Having divided the virtues
into those which are useful and those which are 'immediately
agreeable' he says that courage, as well as being socially useful, is
immediately agreeable to ourselves:

The utility of courage, both to the public and to the person possessed of it,
is an obvious foundation of merit. But to anyone who duly considers of the
matter, it will appear that this quality has a peculiar lustre which it derives
wholly from itself and from that noble elevation inseparable from it. Its
figure, drawn by painters and poets, displays in each feature a sublimity
and daring confidence which catches the eye, engages the affections, and
diffuses, by sympathy, a like sublimity of sentiment over every spectator.[28]

A little earlier Hume had connected 'sublimity' with 'greatness of
mind':

Who is not struck with any signal instance of greatness of mind or dignity
of character, with elevation of sentiment, disdain of slavery, and with that
noble pride and spirit which arises from conscious virtue? The sublime,
says Longinus, is often nothing but the echo or image of magnanimity; and
where this quality appears in anyone, even though a syllable be not uttered,
it excites our applause and admiration, as may be observed of the famous
silence of Ajax in the Odyssey, which expresses more noble disdain and
resolute indignation than any language can convey.[29]

For Hume our response to courage in another is a sympathetic
identification with certain qualities of mind and character—with
nobility, confidence, generous pride—all of which he sums up
under 'sublimity' and 'greatness of mind'. The sublimity of

[28]  *An Enquiry Concerning the Principles of Morals*, sect. vii.
[29]  Ibid.

sentiment that the courage of another calls forth in ourselves is directed not only at his disposition to act courageously, or at his spiritual or mental qualities, but at all these as expressed in his gesture, his posture, that which 'catches the eye' and 'engages the affections'.

Hume's 'greatness of mind' is obviously a translation of Aristotle's *megalopsychia*; and Aristotle, like Aquinas, thought that the *megalopsychos* would be unsparing of his life in the face of great dangers.[30] I shall be discussing Aristotle's account of greatness of mind, or magnanimity, later.[31] For the moment we might note that the *megalopsychos* thinks himself worthy of great things, and claims respect and honour on account of his worthiness. But can we find any connection between courage and greatness of mind? And how is such a connection to be understood?

We might first ask whether we can take the idea of greatness of mind seriously at all. Certainly human beings are sometimes capable of remarkable feats of endurance, initiative, and daring, which show some superior power or energy that we might as well call 'greatness of mind'. But the greatness of mind to which Hume refers goes with that 'disdain of slavery, and with that noble pride and spirit which arises from conscious virtue'.

Virgil's Aeneas is a man of 'greatness of mind'. His magnanimity and his courage are not depicted by Virgil just as a sort of natural force. (There is more natural force in the character of his rival, Turnus.) In Aeneas, Virgil wishes to represent a hero whose greatness can in the end be understood through his loyalties. Aeneas introduces himself on one occasion with the words 'Sum pius Aeneas';[32] and it is indeed his *pietas*—towards his father, his wife, his city, the gods—that is at the centre of his *virtus*. The courage of Aeneas is not intelligible apart from the ends to which he is committed. These ends reveal the inner nature of his courage. We understand his courage and his greatness of mind through understanding his sense of his place in the world, and hence his values. Aeneas identifies himself with his family, his city, his gods, and, above all, with his destiny (*fatum*). Therefore he is *pius Aeneas*, as he says he is.

---

[30] *Ethics*, 1124$^b$5–10. Aristotle says that the magnanimous man is not *microkindynos*—one who risks his life for trifles—but *megalokindynos*—one who risks his life for great things.
[31] Esp. in ch. 6, pp. 199–203 below.  [32] *Aeneid*, i. 378.

Of course Virgil's portrait of Aeneas is idealized. He so completely identifies his hero with fate and political loyalties that he reduces our sense of him as a person. For many this makes Aeneas a rather chilling hero—especially by comparison with, say, Odysseus, or Achilles. But Virgil does give us a picture of a greatness of mind and the courage that goes with it, which is not to be understood as some mysterious force or energy, but as self-value, loyalty to the Roman imperial destiny, and a sense of his place in the world.

This gives a picture of courage somewhat more complicated than I have so far considered. We could give a purely formal account of courage as a disposition to aim at an end, using deliberation, confronting the difficulties and dangers. Most people would agree that such a disposition is necessary to human beings, and that we necessarily have a reason for cultivating it. But can we understand courage simply as a disposition to act? Or must we also allow that the brave man sees things differently from the way in which the coward sees them? Aristotle thinks that courage involves shame and the desire for honour, and aims at a noble end. For him courage has a certain end, and is not just a way of acting. (I shall be discussing the idea of 'the noble' later.[33]) But even a formal account of courage implies a cognitive element. For if courageous action implies deliberated action—and if courage is connected with *phronesis* (practical wisdom)—then we may conclude that the brave man does not simply have different feelings from those of a coward, but that he sees the world differently. He sees possibilities of action differently from the coward, and hence he knows (in the practical sense of 'know') things differently from him. He also sees things differently from the rash man, for he does not put difficulties and dangers out of mind.

An understanding of what the brave man knows can go much further than this. Alasdair MacIntyre writes of 'heroic societies':

[The structure of heroic society] embodies a conceptual scheme which has three central interrelated elements: a conception of what is required by the social role which each individual inhabits; a conception of excellences or virtues as those qualities which enable an individual to do what his or her role requires; and a conception of the human condition as fragile and vulnerable to destiny and to death, such that to be virtuous is not to avoid

---

[33] Below, pp. 67–83.

vulnerability and death, but rather to accord them their due . . . all three elements find their places only within a larger unitary framework . . . the narrative form of epic or saga, a form embodied in the moral life of individuals and in the collective social structure. Heroic social structure *is* enacted epic narrative.[34]

Hector and Achilles are both such men, and the courage of each does go with a readiness to face steadily his fated death. Hector is not self-conscious, however, and does not dramatize his sense of his fate. Achilles is the only hero in the *Iliad* who is self-conscious in that sense. Hume turns the idea of the brave man's being able steadily to confront his destiny into a picture of self-conscious nobility (a picture influenced by Stoicism and Longinus). The brave man is conscious of his virtue, and confronts his destiny with a certain style. Hume suggests that courage is an echo of sublimity, and that through the power of sympathy we feel elevated at the manifestation of courage. He sees courage as containing elements of pride and self-awareness. It is indeed, among other things, a performance, the acting of a role. There is even the suggestion that acting the role of the brave man is part of the brave man's *motive*.

To the modern mind this will seem implausible, if not actually repellent. If 'to act like a brave man' is one's motive for brave action, then will not this be essentially theatrical, role-playing? Surely if courage is to be a virtue it must essentially be directed at a good which is not necessarily the good of the agent; and, when it is directed at the good of the agent (when, say, it helps him to preserve his life), it need not involve his thinking well of himself.

I suspect that most modern people are attracted more to unselfconscious, Homeric courage than to the conscious nobility of Aeneas, or of the Stoics. At any rate they may, in this respect, feel the charms of 'naïve' art above those of 'sentimental' art.[35] In Homer courage, like anger, is something which flares forth inexplicably, almost miraculously. *Thumos* ('soul') can mean anger, wrath, spirit, courage. The pride Homeric heroes feel in their courage is also without self-consciousness; it is not a matter of 'conscious virtue.' It is more like a sensation. And it certainly is possible to understand courage in this 'naïve' way. The Virgilian, or the Stoic, or the Longinian picture of courage (which Hume adopts)

---

[34] *After Virtue* (London, 1981), p. 121.
[35] See Schiller, 'On Naïve and Sentimental Poetry', *German Aesthetic and Literary Criticism*, ed. H. B. Nisbet (Cambridge, 1985), pp. 192–3.

has indeed an element of *comportment*, which is absent from Homer.

I do not think it possible to argue decisively for a preference for the later picture of courage over the earlier. We can try to preserve the phenomena of courage, and to find the truth in both pictures. And the truth surely lies in the matter of pride and shame. Hector does not fight in order to have a certain picture of himself as a brave man and valiant fighter. Nevertheless, he would be ashamed before the Trojans if he did not fight. That a man would be ashamed of a cowardly act, rather than that he acts from the conscious motive of honour, is what is important.

This points to a crucial problem in our understanding of courage, and, indeed, of the other virtues. It is often thought—and is sometimes taken to be typical of the procedures of analytical philosophy—that we can define a concept by appealing to common usage. Yet there may well be divergencies and contradictions within usage. If a man rescued his child from a burning house without regard for his own safety, everyone would think that brave. His motive was love for his child, and that is good enough. When an aeroplane crashed into the Potomac, a passenger, whose identity has never been established, helped half a dozen other passengers into helicopter rescue-harnesses before being drowned as the plane sank. He did not know any of the people whom he helped. The question of his motive seems irrelevant. His action was entirely selfless. We do not think of him as acting from a sense of 'how the brave man acts'. Most people would not think that the question of what view either of these men took of themselves would be relevant to whether their actions were 'truly brave'.

Conrad's Lord Jim is an interesting case. He is the mate of a ship full of pilgrims, which he deserts thinking (wrongly) that it is about to founder. He is tormented ever afterwards by shame for his action. And yet we are not sure what sort of shame it is. Is it because he was cowardly? The question cannot be answered, because Jim never really distinguishes between courage and heroics. He behaved as a seaman should not, essentially because there was no audience to witness an act of courage. But it is important that Conrad does not dismiss Jim's agonized desire to think well of himself.[36] Rather he treats it as a difficult question; Jim is very like

[36] *Lord Jim*, chs. 5–13.

a hero, very like a brave man. His shame is like the shame of a decent man, but not *exactly* like it.

It is probable that most people uneasily combine both these attitudes. They both recognize and honour a courage which does not seem self-conscious, and at the same time consider that courage and cowardice are intrinsically grounds for praise and blame, pride and shame.

Both the Aristotelian and Stoic traditions stress the connection between courage and a picture of himself which the brave man wishes to have. (Stoicism, indeed, particularly as dramatized in Seneca, sees the courageous man as performing in a certain role.[37]) This does not of itself show that the Homeric understanding of courage is at odds with this later tradition. The 'naïve' and 'sentimental' are styles in art, rather than different theories of virtue. The self-consciousness that goes with the Stoic picture of virtue is generally lacking in Homer.

## IV THE NOBLE

We can try to imagine a people who in circumstances of hardship and danger—in hunting and warfare, for instance—show endurance, persistence, indifference to pain, and an unflinching readiness to accept death. Yet it may be that these qualities have no important place in their picture of themselves. Their hardiness is something they take for granted, and it does not go with any social practice of praise and blame, pride and shame, admiration and contempt. They are not proud of their toughness, nor ashamed when it fails them. Do they have the virtue, and, indeed, the concept of courage?

These people might be very glad that they are hardy and dogged, just as we are very glad of having healthy bodies. People without these qualities might be regarded as defective, or ill, or as simply unfortunate. They might even grade each other on this basis, judging the hardiest to be the most useful members of society. They might reserve the army for such people, and richly reward them for their service—in land, for instance. This class might be an

---

[37] It is worth noting that courage as a sort of self-conscious posing is to be found in Pindar, as is the connection of courage with sublimity and with the noble.

aristocracy—indeed, it might not be utterly unlike actual aristo-cracies in European history. Would all this show that the virtue of courage was being valued?

If courage is valued simply for its utility, then this would look very much like courage. And if people said that this was how they understood or valued courage, we could not convict them of a mistake about the meaning of the word. Aristotle mentions several sorts of behaviour to which the term 'brave' is commonly applied. (1) People with experience with regard to particular facts are called brave. Professional soldiers have experience, and are therefore good in attack and defence. But they run away when the danger becomes real. (2) 'Passion is sometimes reckoned as courage.' Pain, fear, and hunger lead wild beasts to attack; and 'lust also makes adulterers do many daring things'. He adds that this passionate 'courage' seems the most natural, and would be courage if choice and motive be added. (3) Sanguine people seem brave, because past success has given them confidence. But they are not really brave, for they run away when they fail. (4) People ignorant of the danger appear brave, but are not. So, most like the truest courage is (as we have seen) that of the citizen soldier.[38]

Aristotle really seems to think that the first four sorts of courage are really examples of *false* courage. They merely look quite like courage, but lack what is essential to it. For instance, they lack the right motive. Professional soldiers, unlike citizens, have no honour-able love for their cause. 'To the latter flight is disgraceful and death is preferable to safety on those terms.'[39] And he distinguishes the brave from the sanguine man as one who will not run away because to do so would be disgraceful.[40] Aristotle's picture of the brave man is clearly a picture of a man who has certain loyalties and values. If we were to ask what reason there could be for preferring this picture of courage over (say) a purely utilitarian one, what would be the answer? One answer would be that Aristotle's way of understanding courage relates it to other values. In sketching the truly brave man he is, surely, sketching the citizen, the free man with genuine and steady loyalties, who also values himself and his own honour in a way that only free citizens can. He is driven to fight not by fear of the lash, but by fear of disgrace. But disgrace, for him, would be failing to have and to show true loyalty

---

[38] *Ethics*, 1116ᵃ15–1117ᵃ30.    [39] *Ethics*, 1116ᵇ15–20.
[40] *Ethics*, 1117ᵃ15–20.

to his city. Therefore if one wishes to commend Aristotle's picture of courage, one can do so only indirectly, by eliciting sympathy for the political vision which informs it.

Hume's picture of the sublimity of courage, although very different in tone and language, and in its emphasis on sentiment, from Aristotle's, is not finally at odds with it. As a Sentimentalist, Hume wishes to turn honour and shame into objects of feeling. What Aristotle sees as essential to courage, Hume describes as overwhelmingly attractive.

Hume and Aristotle together suggest a way of thinking about the virtue of courage that connects it with a certain sort of deliberate choice, with a certain sort of motive, and hence with honour, pride, shame, and self-value. It would allow us to see it as commanding admiration, and also a respect that goes beyond, or at least is not the same as, the respect that Kant thinks we are constrained to feel towards the morally good man.

Furthermore, courage so understood is not a virtue that can be thought of purely in terms of good intentions, or the good will, since it also includes success in acting upon the world, a particular appearance in the eyes of others, perhaps even a style of behaving— comportment. It suggests both a public role and a social practice.

The brave man, thus understood, would indeed have a certain sense of himself, and this would be part of the motive of his courage. Aquinas says that the brave man has two ends in his acts. The 'final end' is to achieve a certain good. However, he also has an 'immediate end', which is 'to express the reflection of his quality in his acts'.[41] It is not simply that he wants certain good ends which his courage can bring about. Nor does he merely feel confident that he can do certain things. He also sees himself as a certain sort of person—and it would seem that he *values* himself as this sort of person. He therefore wants to 'express the reflection of his quality in his acts'. In Virgil this is reflected in Aeneas' 'Sum pius Aeneas'— he wishes to be identified by his virtue. Hume's description of courage has about it something of Stoic role-playing. The conception of courage that we find in both Hume and Aristotle connects it with demands for recognition and respect, and with such practices as paying honour. The honour to which courage lays claim, in both the ancient and the Renaissance tradition, could probably not be

[41] *Summa*, 2a2ae, 123, 7.

offered by an inner assent of the mind independent of any customs of recognition, of *honouring*. And for Aristotle the end of courage, which is also its motive, is, as we have seen, the *noble*.

## i *The Idea of the Noble*

A straightforward idea of courage is of desiring an end and pursuing it intelligently despite hardships, overcoming fear, and being prepared to accept pain. So understood, courage is not necessarily a morally good quality. A man may pursue a wicked end determinedly, intelligently, and boldly. This is why Kant said that moderation in the affections and passions, self-control, and calm deliberation are not unconditionally good, although they have been esteemed so by the ancients, for a cold villain might have all these qualities and hence be even more villainous.[42] Most people—and certainly most philosophers—would say that courage can indeed be employed to bad ends, since it is simply determination in the face of dangers and difficulties. So although it is usually a good quality, since its absence would make life impossible, it is not *necessarily* good. There is nothing paradoxical in Clarendon's summary of Cromwell as 'a brave, bad man'.[43]

One way of countering this opinion is to insist upon the unity of the virtues. Courage on its own (it might be said) could be used for evil purposes. So also could courage informed by self-control and intelligence. But courage accompanied by justice must necessarily be a good quality.

The trouble with this is that it does not tell us anything specific about courage. In describing a man with all the virtues, including justice, we are very likely to be describing a good man. What would be more interesting would be the possibility that the good end of courage is not simply a matter of its fitting into a list of the virtues. In taking seriously Aristotle's remark that the end of courage is the noble—which posits a good end as part of the specific nature of the virtue—I shall be exploring that possibility.

If we start from the idea that courage is essentially a matter of desiring an end and aiming at it pertinaciously, we will obviously never make sense of what Aristotle says, or of any similar claim that courage has a good end. Yet we can start from another simple

---

[42] *Fundamental Principles of the Metaphysic of Ethics*, sect. 1.
[43] *History of the Rebellion*, ed. W. Dunn Macray (Oxford, 1888), bk. xv.

picture of courage which also appeals to common sense. Why should we not say that the best 'primitive' model of courage is of a small boy who hurts himself but refuses to cry? He refuses to cry because he is proud, because he does not want to seem a baby, because he is ashamed to cry. (In *Vanity Fair* young Rawdon Crawley, aged five, being flung playfully into the air by his father, hits his head violently on the ceiling and '[makes] up his face for a tremendous howl.' ' "For God's sake, Rawdy, don't wake mamma," [his father] cried. And the child, looking in a very hard and piteous way at his father, bit his lips, and clenched his hands, and didn't cry a bit.'[44] Could we not teach a child to be brave by encouraging such pride? It is very likely that in deciding what are the best simple examples of courage we will be influenced by our understanding of how we can best describe the concept in its most developed, most fully realized form. Our choice of 'paradigm cases' will reflect a certain view of courage—one which we prefer because it seems coherent, or fits with a synoptic view of human nature. I do not suggest that our larger picture of courage can be adopted arbitrarily, or as the straightforward expression of certain values, but that it may be part of a picture of human conduct which will as a whole be found plausible, or explanatory, or traditional, or charming.[45]

In fact we do not characteristically teach children courage by urging them to persevere in trying to get what they have set their hearts upon. We talk about doing what is right; we encourage a child to think that it is silly to scream every time it hurts itself; we encourage, however implicitly, feelings of shame and pride. Courage understood in this way essentially involves one's having a picture of oneself in relation to others, having a sense of one's place in the world, taking seriously one's reputation. It is odd that philosophers who have thought about courage have often left all this out of account. And it all bears upon the idea of the noble.

But do we need the concept of the noble? Can it really play an important role in ethics? Those who would answer 'No' and who would argue that the notion of nobility, supposing it to be

---

[44] Vol. ii, ch. 2.

[45] 'Many of these explanations are adopted because they have a peculiar charm. The picture of people having subconscious thoughts has a charm.' Wittgenstein, *Lectures and Conversations on Aesthetics, Psychology and Religious Belief*, ed. C. Barrett (Oxford, 1970), p. 25.

intelligible at all, is at best marginal in helping us to understand human moral goodness, would be influenced above all by the Kantian tradition in moral philosophy. The traditional idea of the noble seems to run together so many ideas—morality and manners, the individual and the social, that which is in the power of every man to will, and that which is within human power only contingently. It blurs—what Hume wished to blur, and Kant to emphasize—any sharp distinction between moral and non-moral excellences.

There is no great problem in deciding what qualities of character constitute nobility. Generosity of spirit (Spinoza's *generositas*, which he connected with *fortitudo*),[46] a disdain of the petty, a tempering of egoism that is not poor-spiritedness but rather a *contemptus mundi* which springs from the contemplation of 'whatsoever is grave and constant in human suffering'[47]—all these entered into the ancient and Renaissance idea of the noble. We can still understand what these things are whether or not they seem relevant to the conditions of our own lives. The problem arises where certain morally good qualities—for instance, the Good Will—pass over into something else. The noble does not coincide with the Kantian picture of the man of Good Will. It does not place all its weight upon intentions, since it also takes into account success in acting upon the world. It assumes that certain admirable personal qualities may depend for their realization upon contingencies—particular gifts, or particular worldly circumstances. Aristotle seems to think a slave is by nature incapable of the cardinal virtues.[48] It would presumably follow that he who pursues noble ends cannot be a slave. (The Homeric hero who was enslaved actually lost much of his *arete* by that very fact.) And it is notorious that in his picture of the man of greatness of mind Aristotle includes qualities that seem purely accidental: he moves slowly and has a deep voice.[49]

The connection traditionally assumed between courage and nobility adds to the difficulty that modern men have in taking the idea of the noble seriously. The traditional idea of the noble has put the highest value on courage, and has done so because it is in brave

[46]  *Ethics*, pt. III, prop. 59.
[47]  Joyce, *A Portrait of the Artist as a Young Man*, p. 209.
[48]  *Politics*, 1259$^b$20–1260$^a$25.
[49]  *Ethics*, 1125$^a$10–20.

action that the greatest human achievements lie. Courage can encompass the highest, greatest things in practical life. The brave man faces death in battle on behalf of his city. If courage is to be valued partly on account of the greatness of its end, then it will follow, as Aristotle thought it followed, that courage with what might be thought of as a lesser end—the fortitude, for instance, which endures sickness patiently—will be a lesser thing, even though it require as great a subjective effort by the sufferer.[50] (And it would probably be an Aristotelian argument that temperance is a lesser virtue than courage since it resists an evil rather than actively aims at the highest good, or actively confronts the greatest terrors.) This relates to the self-value of the brave man. His self-respect, or pride, with its implicit claim on the respect of others, is based not only on the purity of his intentions, but also on what he actually achieves.[51]

So a central problem about the idea of the noble, if it is to be understood in anything like its traditional form, is that it seems to be both an ethical quality, to involve dispositions that every human being necessarily has a reason for cultivating, and at the same time to characterize superior people, what we might call those who are favoured with exceptional qualities and advantages. To be like these people cannot be an obligation for everyone.

We should notice a problem that might be thought to arise from a distinction between primary and derivative uses of words. We can talk of noble actions and a noble character. We can also talk of a noble piece of music (Elgar regularly includes the direction 'nobilmente'), and a noble building. Indeed 'noble' as an aesthetic term is most often used of buildings in the classical style. (Lutyens tried to see how a noble expressive tradition could be continued with a considerable modification of the inherited classical vocabulary of architectural nobility.) We can also talk of a noble face. The human body itself can also be thought of as noble; and yet we may think that this is a matter of how one can imagine it, or even of a tradition of representing it in art. The nobility of the human body may be an artistic discovery.

[50] What Aristotle actually says is that the brave man would not seem to be concerned even with death in *all* circumstances, e.g. at sea or in disease. See *Ethics*, 1115a.

[51] For Nietzsche, this stress on the value of an intention, rather than consequences, is 'an inversion of perspectives' and 'a fateful new superstition'. *Beyond Good and Evil*, trans. Hollingdale (Harmondsworth, 1973), sect. 32.

One—simple—solution would be to say that there are two or three uses of 'noble' each denoting a different concept. There is noble character and action, which is the primary concept. Then there is the noble face, and finally aesthetic nobility proper, these being derivative concepts.

I shall in fact be trying to see how a noble character may indeed be intimately related to a noble appearance, or nobility of comportment. So I shall simply assume for the present that these various uses of 'noble' express the same concept, and that the term is not being used in several senses.[52]

There is another important aspect to the idea of the noble. Nobility is something that can be presented directly to the eye. It can appear (to use Hegelian language) 'in concrete form'. The seated statues of Lorenzo and Giuliano de' Medici in the tomb of San Lorenzo visually express two aspects of the noble. One is the noble as active; the other the noble as contemplative. In neither case do we infer a quality of mind or character from outward signs. The statues do not *symbolize* nobility, or make us think of nobility. It would be truer to say that the nobility of the two figures is something that we can actually see, and not something we infer, any more than we infer the expressive qualities—say, the plangency—of a piece of writing, or the sadness or gaiety of a piece of music. For Hegel, 'symbolic art' is a particular style or phase of art, distinct from and probably inferior to full and true representation.[53] We might apply what Hegel says to a common phenomenon: I recognize an old friend whom I have not seen for many years. At first the face is unfamiliar, but then it suddenly becomes familiar. In Wittgenstein's words, 'I see the old face in the altered one.'[54] What is this phenomenon of recognition? It is not just that the face before me brings the thought of my old friend to mind. For I might be thinking of him precisely at the moment when I am looking at him (as Gloucester thinks of Edgar just as he looks at 'Poor Tom'),[55] and still not recognize him. Rather I must somehow incarnate him in the face before me: I must see the old face in the altered one. The

[52] For further discussion of this point in relation to 'sincerity' the reader is referred to my 'The Autonomy of Art', *Royal Institute of Philosophy Lectures*, 6 (1971–2), 65–87.

[53] *Aesthetics*, p. 317.   [54] *Philosophical Investigations*, p. 197.

[55] 'I' th' last night's storm I such a fellow saw, | Which made me think a man a worm. My son | Came then into my mind; and yet my mind | Was then scarce friends with him.' *King Lear*, IV. i. 32–5.

act of recognition is immediate and not an inference from an experience to an idea. The 'idea' of my friend is present in the act of recognition. This immediacy is, for Hegel, present in all our experience of art. In the case of the mimic we do not make an inference from the present experience to the absent man. For Hegel this would be a paradigm of art. All art involves the presentation of ideas in sensuous form. In understanding a work of art we do not make an inference from what we see to the ideas that are being conveyed. When a figure is designed (as Hegel thought Egyptian figures were designed) merely in order to stand as a symbol of the human mind, reminding the spectator of things that are in no way intrinsic to his perception of the figure itself, then we do not have true art. In Greek sculpture, by contrast, we find an 'appearance' that is alive with the idea of the human mind. The spectator sees in the sculpted figure a representation of qualities of mind and soul that is distinctively Greek. The sculpture is not a mere step in a process of inference, but a concrete embodiment of ideas; and our perception of the sculpture cannot be described without some reference to these ideas.

Our admiration of the Michelangelo statues will not, on this view, be simply a response to certain abstract ideas that the statues symbolize. We will somehow see the noble as a visual representation. The Medici statues visually represent greatness of mind, and at the same time suggest what I can only call a peculiar consonance between these men, as represented, and the world. Their nobility includes not only something inner or spiritual, but also comportment, a sense of how they are to be looked at, how they are to appear. The serenity of mind that these statues express seems to imply a unity with the world, a sense that their subjects have a secure, recognized, and pre-eminent existence in the world. A public world is, for Lorenzo and Giuliano de' Medici, somehow the fulfilment and condition of their sense of themselves. Honour, and indeed glory, is what is demanded by their deepest sense of what they are. This vision is something that we can see, and which enters into our aesthetic appreciation of these sculptures.

It could be objected that all this amounts to treating the noble as a matter of *style*—indeed of a style that may be possible only at certain historical periods. But this is exactly what I wish to suggest. On the one hand we can see the human body as noble; and yet we can also think (as perhaps Hegel thought) that the noble aspect of the human form was a stylistic and spiritual discovery of the Greeks and their sculptors. It may be difficult to see the body as noble outside such a tradition. We might even consider that the human form in pre-classical art—even in Egyptian art—is not 'noble'. Alternatively we might say that *our* idea of the noble human form cannot be detached from its origins in Greek art, and that it is therefore difficult for us, as Europeans, to find an equivalent nobility in, say, Aztec sculpture.

The noble involves not only a disposition of mind or spirit but also certain expectations of social and material conditions. The serenity which Hegel finds in the sculpted figures of Greek gods is not simply a state of mind outwardly symbolized by a physical pose. The statues are of the nobly human, an idea that is captured in the vision of the human body that they express. If there is a particular philosophy or religion that envisages man as noble, then these sculptures are not propaganda for it but concrete expressions of it.

There is a particular difficulty, for us as modern men, in taking this idea of the noble seriously. This arises from different conceptions of the self. The characteristic modern view of the self (given philosophical expression by Descartes) is of a centre of thoughts and sensations. One is not essentially a man or a woman, a Frenchman or Englishman, a Christian or a Muslim, but something—a person—which is essential and which transcends these accidents. Many people in other societies—the ancient Greeks, for instance—included in the idea of a man's self much that we would exclude. They included not only his social role, but even his fate. 'His early death is *part* of Achilles, as much constitutive of his identity as his great prowess and invulnerability.'[56] One way in which people have expressed their identity with a social world is in looking for honour from their city—as Aristotle says that brave citizen soldiers do. People can find that their real self is the self which finds pride in, looks for honour from, something that transcends the individual—a group, city, or state. It is not that no modern people can feel in this way—soldiers probably still do, and so do people engaged in resistance movements against foreign occupiers. But it is not at all characteristic of that important ideology of our time—liberal individualism.

[56] See Charles Taylor, *Hegel* (Cambridge, 1975), p. 501.

So the idea of the noble which I have been trying to capture includes something like the following: it is an idea of being-in-the-world, of one's self being fulfilled in a social role or function, and of an identification of oneself with the public world which is revealed in feeling and action. This is an understanding of 'noble' which blends elements of Aristotle and Hume, and fits into something that we can, with some looseness, call a 'tradition'. Admittedly, this is not the only way the term 'noble' can be used. It states neither the necessary nor sufficient conditions of a concept. There is the Stoic doctrine that 'virtus sola atque unica est nobilitas';[57] there is the Noble Savage; there is Nietzsche's vision of the 'noble soul', who is much too much of an individualist to identify himself with the State. There has to be some doubt whether these conceptions of the noble overlap sufficiently to be considered parts of the same idea. Yet it is not unreasonable to think of them as representing a continuing debate about the nature of the noble.

All this may look like the insinuation of an unreconstructed Renaissance ethic into the modern world. In fact it is intended as a rational reconstruction of, or at least a rough approximation to, the most intellectually powerful account of the noble which exists—that given by Hegel in *The Phenomenology of Spirit*.[58] The noble consciousness is, for Hegel, one which identifies itself with the State, and with state wealth and power. The noble consciousness finds the State, in its universality, to be the reality of itself; it finds itself in the State. This means that it finds itself in a service to the State that will go as far as the most complete self-sacrifice—in death.[59] Hegel calls this 'the heroism of service'.[60] This would allow for an identification with the public realm that could give rise to feelings that are as intense and as real as those of private life. Notoriously patriotism can express the most intense human attachments, which include attachment to language and culture as well as to place ('Thus, love of a country | Begins as attachment to our own field of action').[61] So grief for the misfortunes of one's country can be no less revealing of what one is than private grief. Hegel also suggests that the noble consciousness, in thus identifying itself with what we have been calling (weakly) a public realm, but

---

[57] Juvenal, Satire viii. 20.      [58] Sect. 500.

[59] *Phenomenology*, sect. 506. In fact Hegel suggests that this readiness to die is actually insincere.      [60] *Phenomenology*, sect. 503.

[61] T. S. Eliot, 'Little Gidding', iii.

which he calls 'state power', 'acquires reverence for itself, and gets reverence from others'.[62] What Hegel seems to be saying is that we have here a picture of the self that achieves its reality, its realization, through the State; and at the same time *ipso facto* the State becomes 'real' for the self. Power, and indeed wealth, becomes 'essential' to the noble consciousness.

I do not wish to dwell on the details of Hegel's fascinating account of the noble consciousness, but merely to notice how it could help fill out an account of the noble. The same can be said of another very fine account of the same topic that draws explicitly upon Hegel, and in particular upon Hegel's treatment of Diderot's *Rameau's Nephew*—that given by Lionel Trilling in *Sincerity and Authenticity*.[63] Trilling points out[64] that the term 'noble' is not traditionally used as part of a polarity of 'good and evil', but so that the polar opposite of the noble is the 'base'. The values that have historically gone with the noble—such as the aristocratic and martial virtues—are essentially self-regarding: 'The noble self is not shaped by its beneficent intentions towards others; its intention is wholly towards itself, and such moral virtue as may be attributed to it follows incidentally from its expressing the privilege and function of its social status in mien and deportment.'[65] Trilling goes on to associate the noble consciousness depicted by Hegel with the vision given supreme expression in the late plays of Shakespeare, 'the ones we call romances'.

. . . the norm of life which they propose is one of order, peace, honour and beauty, these qualities being realised in, and dependent upon, certain material conditions. The hope that animates this normative vision of the plays is the almost shockingly elementary one which Ferdinand utters in *The Tempest*—the hope of 'quiet days, fair issue, and long life'. It is reiterated by Juno in Prospero's pageant: 'Honour, riches, marriage, blessing, | Long continuance and increasing.' It has to do with good harvests, full barns and the qualities of affluent decorum that Ben Jonson celebrated in Penshurst and Marvell in 'Appleton House', and that Yeats prayed for in his daughter's domestic arrangements.[66]

---

[62] *Phenomenology*, p. 527, trans. Baillie, (London, 1910).

[63] Oxford, 1972, ch. 2. This passage and its relevance for my argument was drawn to my attention by Christopher Edwards.

[64] Recapitulating Nietzsche, without mentioning him.

[65] Trilling, *Sincerity and Authenticity*, p. 37.

[66] Ibid., pp. 39–40.

## ii *Nietzsche*

Nietzsche opposes to Kantianism something that he sometimes calls 'the master morality' and sometimes 'the noble morality'. It was Kant who (following the Stoics) asked the question: 'What can be called "good" without qualification?' and answered it in this way: 'It is impossible to conceive of anything in the world, or indeed out of it, which can be called good without qualification save only a good will.'[67] In the *Critique of Practical Reason* Kant went on to explain under what conditions the will is good. The will is good only when whatever it wills it wills as a possible law for all mankind. This doctrine—the Categorical Imperative—is, for Kant, a law of pure practical reason. It is not a well-tried means to a certain end—for instance, happiness—but is necessarily, and a priori, the fundamental moral law, not just for human beings but for all rational creatures (e.g. angels). If we try to discover a moral principle that will accord with our deepest intuitions of what morality is like, this is what we will eventually hit upon.

This a priori principle is not advanced by Kant as the expression of any *particular* morality, but as the precondition of any genuine morality whatsoever. However, it can also tell us in advance (as it were) what morality must be like. For Kant deduces certain psychological consequences from his principle. First of all, not only is the categorical imperative not based upon 'empirical' or 'pathological' desires—it is quite opposed to them. The categorical imperative expresses itself in the form of a moral law that is the ground of determination of the will; it thwarts our natural inclinations, and 'hence must produce a feeling which can be called pain'. At the same time this law, since it conflicts with and overcomes our inclinations, must be an object of respect. So it strikes down, or humiliates, self-conceit: 'Therefore, the moral law inevitably humbles every man when he compares the sensuous propensity of his nature with the law.' When we perceive the moral goodness of another, we are inwardly humbled before it, even if we refrain from showing our respect outwardly.[68] So for Kant the

---

[67] *Fundamental Principles of the Metaphysic of Ethics*, trans. Abbott, 10th edn. (London, 1965), sect. 1.
[68] *Critique of Practical Reason*, trans. Beck (Indianapolis and New York, 1956), pt. 1, bk. i, ch. 3.

good man wills universally, rather than egoistically, and feels pain and humility in apprehending a universal moral law which, being universal, is intrinsically at variance with, and in authority over, his own particular inclinations.

We might divide (artificially) Nietzsche's riposte to Kant into its historical and analytical components. The historical component is Nietzsche's interest in tracing 'the genealogy of morals'. He suggests, in effect, that when a moral philosopher thinks that he has formulated the timeless requirements for a morality, he almost inevitably shows ignorance of the history of moral concepts, and simply hypostasizes the morality of a particular epoch, or a morality framed with certain specific intentions, and hence imagines himself and pretends to others that he has discovered the a priori requirements of any morality whatsoever.

The 'analytical' aspect of Nietzsche's argument is this: whatever a philosopher, in his historical ignorance or unconscious moral commitment, lays down as necessary to morality, he settles nothing. It always remains possible to show that his a priori moral principles actually embody substantive moral teaching, and it always remains possible plausibly to recommend a morality that is ruled out by his a priori principles. So Kant tries to show that any genuine moral consciousness is necessarily humble and necessarily universal (i.e. that its humility is the necessary consequence of an awareness of the contrast between the universal moral law and the particular ('pathological') desires of the average man): Nietzsche in reply argues for a morality that is essentially proud and essentially particular. The difference between a moral scheme that is essentially proud and particular, and one which is essentially humble and universal, is not the difference between something that is not a morality at all and something that is a *genuine* morality, but the difference between a 'master' or 'noble' morality, and a 'slave' morality:

The essential thing in a good and healthy aristocracy is . . . that it does not feel itself to be a function (of the monarchy or the commonwealth) but as their *meaning* and supreme justification—that it therefore accepts with a good conscience the sacrifice of innumerable men who *for its sake* have to be suppressed and reduced to imperfect men, to slaves and instruments.[69]

---

[69] *Beyond Good and Evil*, sect. 258.

Again:

Life itself is *essentially* appropriation, injury, overpowering of the strange and weaker, suppression, severity, imposition of one's own forms and, at the least and mildest, exploitation—but why should one always have to employ precisely those words which have from of old been stamped with a slanderous intention?[70]

On the requirement that any moral duty, if it is truly to be *moral*, must be universal, Nietzsche writes: 'Signs of nobility: never to think of degrading our duties into duties for everybody; not to want to relinquish or share our responsibilities; to count our privileges and the exercising of them among our *duties*.'[71]

Nietzsche's man of noble soul is an *egoist* (the very type whom Kant's philosophy of morals would seek to rule out a priori), not in the sense that he is 'selfish', but in the sense that he feels himself to be a standard, and creator of values. Nietzsche buttresses his idea of the noble soul with an account of what we might call the natural satisfactions of the aristocrat. He describes the 'aristocratic value equation' as 'good = noble = powerful = happy = beloved of God'. The noble morality, with its aggression, cunning, strong drives, its pride, is something to be *feared*. Nietzsche is not describing the 'good' man, at least in any sense which Kant would recognize, but rather the superior specimen, the 'great man'. He is not a good man because he obeys the moral law, but is a source of values, a superior man, a man born to command, to inspire fear and awe, a man whose sense of his own power is a cause of both pride and nobility:

The noble type of man feels *himself* to be the determiner of values, he does not need to be approved of, he judges 'what harms me is harmful in itself', he knows himself to be that which in general first accords honour to things, he *creates* values. Everything he knows to be part of himself, he honours: such a morality is self-glorification.[72]

The chief outcome of the noble ethic is that the man of noble soul has reverence for himself and looks for honour from others.[73] The respect which others feel for him is not directed at his good will but at all those dispositions which both make possible and are the

---

[70] Ibid., sect. 259.  [71] Ibid., sect. 272.
[72] Ibid., sect. 260.  [73] Ibid., sects. 265 and 287.

outcome of his successful action upon the world. He 'takes pleasure in willing'[74]—but this must be not only because of an inner power, but also because he objectifies this power in actual life. Nietzsche insists that the noble ethic concentrates upon action, what is achieved, rather than on motive.

This gives us a notion of human excellence that is deeply involved with contingency, in which the qualities we most admire in people are qualities of their being-in-the-world. They will include spiritedness, aggression, fierceness. For Nietzsche only the self-affirmation, pride, self-reverence that goes with these qualities can make *persons* the source of values, and can make values intelligible.

The idea of the noble has always contained discordant elements. I have stressed Hegel's account of the noble soul identifying himself with the State. Nietzsche's idea of nobility is largely a rejection of that 'slave morality' which constitutes (in his eyes) the modern way of identifying with the State. In rejecting a morality which links man to man essentially by oppressing all that is vital in individuals, Nietzsche also rejects any picture of man as a social being. His ideal types (such as they are) can only be thought of as solitary creative geniuses. Or, as MacIntyre puts it: 'Nietzsche replaces the fictions of the Enlightenment individualism, of which he is so contemptuous, with a set of individualist fictions of his own.'[75]

But there is something analogously discordant in Aristotle himself. Aristotle's magnanimous man certainly pursues noble ends, and demands a respect and honour that is intelligible only within a civil context. Yet the portrait Aristotle gives of him makes it difficult to imagine him really having what were later called the 'civic virtues', or even having friends.[76] (That despite Aristotle's saying of him that he will not make his life revolve around anyone, except a friend.[77]) Aristotle has an ideal of human self-sufficiency, and the magnanimous man seems to approach this ideal. Whether a self-sufficient man is truly a 'political animal' must be a matter for debate. For Aristotle, self-sufficiency (*autarkeia*) is a mark of the *polis*,[78] and we could perhaps see the magnanimous man's relative self-sufficiency as an image of political association. But we can say that Nietzsche's individualism brings to the surface a tension in Aristotle himself; or that Nietzsche rediscovers that opposition

---

[74] *Beyond Good and Evil*, sect. 208.          [75] *After Virtue*, p. 122.
[76] *Megalopsychos* later comes to mean 'arrogant'.
[77] *Ethics*, 1124$^b$30–1125$^a$1.                        [78] *Politics*, 1152$^b$25–40.

between the individual and the political order which some of the Sophists had proclaimed,[79] but which both Plato and Aristotle were at pains to deny.

### VI POLITICAL COURAGE

Aristotle lists five sorts of courage, of which the first 'is most like true courage'. This is the courage of the citizen soldier: 'Citizen soldiers seem to face dangers because of the penalties imposed by the laws and the reproaches they would otherwise incur, and because of the honours they win by such action; and therefore those people seem to be bravest among whom cowards are held in dishonour and brave men in honour.'[80] He adds that this is the sort of courage which Homer depicts. Aquinas interprets Aristotle as talking here of *political* courage, in virtue of which men act courageously through fear of dishonour or punishment.[81] For Aristotle the reason why political courage is most like true courage is that to act from motives of honour and shame shows that one pursues a noble end; and 'courage is noble'.[82] (It is interesting that Socrates, generally charged with undermining these ideas, is credited with great courage—which is indeed that of the citizen soldier—by Alcibiades in the *Symposium*.)[83]

The idea of honour clearly underpins and gives intelligibility to 'political courage' and also to the idea of the noble. It is striking that whereas today the notion of honour finds almost no place in the thought of moral philosophers, it was a central, indispensable idea of ancient and Renaissance ethics. One reason for this is that honour begins by being related to social status: to be 'honourable' is to possess a certain rank, and 'dishonourable behaviour' might be thought of in the first place as behaviour not suitable to a Roman senator, or to a feudal lord. In such a context it will be doubtful that there are actions which simply are dishonourable for *any* man to do—a slave, for instance.

However, even if we consider that the concept of honour (and other cognate ideas such as the noble, and the gentleman) originate in social roles, it is important not to give only a superficial meaning

[79] e.g. Callicles in the *Gorgias*, 482 E ff.  [80] *Ethics*, 1116ᵃ15–20.
[81] *Summa*, 2a2ae, 128, 1.  [82] *Ethics*, 1115ᵇ20–5.
[83] 219 D 2–221 C 1.

to social roles themselves. To a Homeric warrior, his social role, as warrior and as noble, is also his character: it is *him*, he identifies himself with his role, and does not understand himself in any different way. He may also understand himself as a husband, a father, a Greek, the subject of a king. But if we abstract all these 'roles' in order to find the true self, there is nothing we can find.[84] The Enlightenment and modern idea of the self which transcends its roles, its nationality, even its culture, seems to have no place in the Homeric system. Hence although the honour that might be claimed by the warrior will, in one sense, be 'conventional', in that it will be determined by a social role, in another sense it will be for him an appreciation of what he finally is.

It is worth thinking of honour apart from some of the social roles which have traditionally claimed it, even if in the end it cannot be entirely separated from them. For it may be that the notion of honour, neglected though it now is, is indispensable, and that an ethical scheme without it would leave a gap in our understanding of ourselves and others.

Honour is something we give to others, and which others may choose to bestow upon us. Honour may be necessary to us not just because we like having it—although everything suggests that it is what human beings like having more than anything else—but because it really is part of how we understand ourselves. At any rate, people who have consciously cared about honour—and cared in a way which suggests that for them it was not simply 'conventional'—seem to have felt that honour was somehow deeply connected with the meaning of their actions as a whole, the meaning of their whole course of life. How can we understand this?

To begin with a truism: we ought to think of people in a way that is appropriate to what they are. Yet if that is a truism, it is nevertheless not obvious why it is true. For if we should think of people as they really are, and if we should do that irrespective of any result of our thinking—irrespective, for instance, of their knowing how we think of them—then it seems that we should appreciate, or assess, or sympathize with the lives of others. A man's honour involves others having an attitude to him which he has merited. Most people have thought it vital to their self-respect, or happiness, or fortune that others recognize their merits.

[84] See MacIntyre, *After Virtue*, ch. 10.

Let us approach the question of honour by considering another claim that human beings are naturally driven to make: that they be remembered:

> 'ricorditi di me, che son la Pia;
> Siena mi fe', disfecemi Maremma'[85]

Remember me who am la Pia; Siena made me, Maremma unmade me

But how is it possible to have a duty to the dead?

In these lines from Dante, a woman of whose life all reliable tradition has been lost, but who was born in Siena and perhaps murdered by her husband in the Maremma region of Tuscany, begs to be remembered. Above all, perhaps, she wants the poet to record her name. After the long account of the death by violence of two famous men earlier in the canto, the few lines of this unknown woman who wishes simply to be remembered have a particular quality of desolation. To remember the dead would seem to be the simplest duty we could have towards them, and the one which we might most easily imagine them wishing to lay upon us if they could. In the *Odyssey*[86] Odysseus's mother, Anticleia, appears to him and tells the story of her death, how she died from longing for her son, for his counsels and tender-heartedness. And she ends by saying: 'Haste thee to the light with what speed thou mayest, and bear all these things in mind, that thou mayest hereafter tell them to thy wife.'[87] She wishes her story to be known and remembered in the world of the living, and especially by another woman, who will more fully understand her grief.

We perhaps find it as natural as did Homer and Dante to imagine that the dead would, if they could, lay upon us the duty to remember them. We unreflectively think that to be remembered after death is a human good, and to pass soon into oblivion a human evil: 'And some there be, which have no memorial; Who are perished as though they had never been, And are become as though they had never been born.' These words convey not only the idea of a human evil, but also something like a rebuke. For being remembered after one's death is taken to be a reward for righteousness, even a sign of it: 'But these were merciful men, Whose righteousness hath not been forgotten. . . . Their bodies are buried in peace, But their name liveth for evermore.'[88]

[85] Dante, *Purgatorio*, v. 133–4.
[86] xi. 150–224.
[87] Trans. Murray (London, 1919), p. 403.
[88] Ecclus. 44: 9.

It is as natural for us as for the writer of Ecclesiasticus to think that to be remembered after death is a human good, and to think also we might have a duty to the dead—to some of them at least—that we remember them. But although it is natural, is it right? Can we really have a duty to the dead? For we must remember that there is a tradition of thought, deeply embedded in our intellectual (one might almost say, our spiritual) tradition, which holds that such feelings, although natural, are seriously mistaken. The arguments are simple, but cogent, and go back to antiquity. What they ask is this: how can the absence of a possible good count as an evil for anyone, unless someone *mind* about this deprivation, unless someone consciously suffer from it? But the dead do not mind: they feel neither pain at our neglect, nor pleasure in our dutifulness. The dead cannot be harmed; neither can they be benefited. And for me to fear that I will be forgotten after death, that I shall perish as though I had never been, is irrational. For even apart from the fact that the most famous men are not thought of as often after their death by those who admire them as they were during their lifetime by those who loved them, it is also true that after death one will have no experience of this neglect, and so no one who has died will mind it. It will be utterly different from being neglected and lonely during one's lifetime.

This consideration, that the dead cannot be harmed, since they can have no experience of what happens after their death, and hence cannot mind it, stands behind the most celebrated attempt in antiquity to prove that death itself is not an evil. Lucretius argued that it is as irrational to think with horror of the eternity of time after one's death in which one will not exist, as it would be to think with horror of the stretch of time before one was born in which one *did* not exist. So long as a man is alive, then he was not died, and so does not experience the evil of death. Once he has died, then he no longer exists, and so does not experience the evil of not existing. Hence there can be nothing about the state of being dead that is itself an evil; and being dead for a future eternity after death is no different from, and no worse than, not having existed for an eternity before one was born. And that no one will think of us at some time after our death is no more terrible than that no one thought of us before we were born.

This line of thought is powerful, and it perhaps strikes modern men especially as containing the truth, of showing that feelings that are indeed natural to us may none the less be deluded or self-deceived. A very persuasive philosophical picture stands behind these arguments and gives them their plausibility, a picture which centrally expresses a modern view of the human person. According to this picture, what is good and evil for human beings can in the end only be what human beings can actually experience as pleasant and painful. For a person is in the end a mind, a centre of consciousness. The story of a man is the story of his conscious experiences. Those things only can be good and evil which can be the pleasant and painful experiences of a conscious mind. Therefore nothing bad can happen to a person which it is quite impossible that he could experience as unpleasant and therefore think of as bad. This flows from the conviction that to be a person just is to be conscious, to think—a conviction that has been dominant in our culture since the seventeenth century.

The conclusion is that the dead cannot be benefited, and that therefore we cannot truly be said to have a duty towards them. For what is it to have a duty? What is it, for instance, to have a duty towards the living? Is it not to acknowledge a claim of service, or gratitude, or love? But if the living were completely unconscious of these claims, unaware of whether we fulfilled them or not, unmoved by our neglect, and untouched by our dutifulness, then surely duties even to the living would lose their meaning. For a moral obligation can only be understood if it has some palpable effects upon other conscious beings.

Yet now let us consider some consequences of this line of thought.[89] Imagine a brilliant man just entering upon a career of distinguished intellectual achievement. He is injured in a motor accident and reduced to the mental condition of a contented two-year-old. We call this a tragedy and pity him. But he cannot regard it as a tragedy, he is quite contented. Where, then, is the tragedy? Yet our natural instinct is to pity him, to find it a tragedy for *him*—and not just for the world that will lose his contribution.

Or consider the case of someone who is calumniated behind his back: he does not know of the wrong, and his career (we may suppose) does not suffer from it. Our instinct is to think that this is an evil none the less, that a wrong has been done. It is not just the

[89] I am much indebted in this section to Thomas Nagel's article 'Death', in *Mortal Questions*, pp. 1–11.

fact that he would be unhappy if he found out about it that makes it an evil. He would be unhappy if he found out because to be calumniated is itself an evil—an evil because it is wrong, and a wrong because it is an injustice.

The truth is that there is much in human life that we rightly regard as good and evil quite apart from how someone experiences it at the time. Much that is important in the story of a man transcends what happens to his body, and even what he thinks and feels. We naturally think that whether someone is honoured, whether his motives are justly assessed, whether after his death his will is set aside, or works that he has written are wrongly credited to another—all these things are part of the story of a man.

For many, and perhaps most of the obligations we have, transcend what people care about and are conscious of. Parents have an obligation to their children to do them good that the children cannot know about at the time, and may never know about or care about. Indeed, people may feel an obligation to unborn generations, and hold that it would be wicked to destroy what these would otherwise inherit.

Obligations can transcend caring and knowing. So we are convinced that to set aside a man's will is a wrong done to the dead, that justice is outraged. Justice may be outraged also in the killing of an unborn infant who in the nature of things cannot know that its life has been cut off. Justice is to be done, and the doing of justice does not simply depend upon those whom it benefits caring about it.

If we think along lines such as these, we find it natural to try to understand the human person as something other than just a thinking soul, a purely individual centre of consciousness and sensations. Our intuitive feelings about remembering the dead, our disposition to think that, in a sense, the dead *can* be harmed, cannot find a rational support in the isolated Cartesian soul or self which is capable of detaching itself from all roles, from custom, history, and culture. The characteristic ancient Greek view of the human person was that he was a man with ancestors, with descendants, the citizen of a particular city, someone who has done certain deeds, and who has merited a certain reputation, perhaps a certain honour. In his funeral oration Pericles says: 'For the love of honour alone is untouched by age, and when one comes to the ineffectual period of life it is not "gain" as some say, that gives the greater satisfaction but honour.'[90] A person is someone who essentially has a history. We cannot get at the idea of a person unless we think of his life as a history, one which begins in the womb, perhaps, or at birth, or at the age of reason. The life of a man is the story of a man (in the way that the life of an animal is not the story of an animal), and this means also that every life has a significance, a meaning, offers itself for interpretation and assessment. It was a characteristic vision of the ancient world, and again of the Renaissance, that a human being was not just the sum total of his thoughts and feelings, but the whole pattern taken by his life, his reputation, the true assessment of his deeds, his glory after death, his inheritance of a particular form of life, his citizenship of a particular city. The ancient Athenian view, expressed for all time in Pericles' funeral speech, was that the hero was one who identified himself with his city, lived beyond himself in the life of the *polis*, and hence lived beyond death in his fame among his people.[91] Therefore human happiness (*eudaimonia*) is only complete in reputation and glory after death— a glory owed to the dead hero by the city which he has benefited by his death.

So honour is to do with belonging and identity; and happiness can be understood objectively. That is to say, happiness may be connected with the assessment of a life that only a rational being can make; but this may also mean that happiness may entail a pattern in a man's life that is to be seen by others, whether or not he can still see it himself. In that sense the dead can be harmed or benefited in so far as they are accorded or not accorded the reputation that is their due.

A man's sense of his own honour derives from that to which he can feel a loyalty, or which expresses what he takes to be his deepest self. Honour must be integral to one's sense of the meaning of what one does. In Wordsworth's *Michael* a father finds himself convinced that the deepest significance of living is to be found in a task handed down and carried on, the continuance of a life in one place. Hence his pain in his son's defection is a deep grief, a sense of betrayal. One must feel a deep respect for this man, for his convictions, and for his *task*. Indeed the insistence on *work* as a basis of honour is an important theme in Hegel: 'In the State, the

---

[90] Thucydides, *The Peloponnesian War*, trans. Marchant (London, 1923), bk. ii, ch. 44.　　　　　　　　　　　　[91] Taylor, *Hegel*, p. 190.

citizen derives his honour from the post he fills, from the trade he
follows, and from any other kind of working activity. His honour
thereby has a content that is substantial, universal, objective, and
no longer dependent on an empty subjectivity.'[92]

Hegel understands honour as the respect which a man merits
through that activity which most profoundly defines him as a man.
For him this is the life of work. The dignity of labour derives from
the fact that it is through work that man most profoundly expresses
his nature as a social being. Hence it is only through finding the
labour appropriate to him that the individual realizes himself. The
man who never comes to identify himself with an already existing
world of human labour will remain adolescent or infantile. '. . . the
youth . . . must learn to see that . . . the world is the substantial
element and the individual merely an accident, and that therefore a
man can find his substantial occupation and satisfaction only in the
world which pursues its own course independently in face of him,
and that for this reason he must procure for himself the skill
necessary to accomplish his work. Reaching this standpoint, the
youth has become a *man*.'[93]

It may seem that we have strayed from the subject of courage.
Yet reflection on courage does lead us naturally to think of those
ways in which men attach themselves to a larger world, to their
deepest loyalties, their pride, and sense of honour. And one way in
which men can become consciously courageous is precisely in
coming to see themselves as political beings.

Consider this exchange in Shakespeare's *Henry IV, Part II*
(Falstaff, having embezzled the money with which he was to recruit
soldiers for the King, is reduced to encouraging the least likely
warriors to buy themselves off. They all do, until he encounters
Feeble, a tailor):

FEEBLE. By my troth I care not, a man can die but once, we owe God a
    death. I'll ne'er bear a base mind—and't be my destiny, so; and't be not,
    so. No man's too good to serve's prince, and let it go which way it will,
    he that dies this year is quit for the next.
BARDOLPH. Well said. Th'art a good fellow.
FEEBLE. Faith, I'll bear no base mind.[94]

The scene is (of course) funny: Feeble completely fails to understand that Falstaff *wishes* him to buy himself off, and responds with

[92] *The Philosophy of Mind*, trans. W. Wallace (Oxford, 1971), sect. 432.
[93] Ibid., sect. 396.                                    [94] III. ii, 229–35.

a quite unexpected spirit. And he expresses himself entirely in saws and proverbs. Yet he does, in a comic way, see himself as something other than just a tailor. He is also a subject of his prince, and therefore refuses to be 'base'.

There is such a thing as the birth of courage, and one way in which it is born is when someone sees himself as acting in a certain role. One role might indeed be 'subject of a prince'. Others might be 'citizen patriot' or 'revolutionary'. How does one come to adopt and to identify oneself with one of these roles? It is difficult to give a general answer. But it is certainly possible to stop thinking of oneself as someone with purely private concerns, in one's role as merchant or tailor or farmer, and to begin to think of oneself as citizen or subject. When the French Revolutionary regime instituted universal conscription this was intended as a recognition that all citizens participated in the same way in the State. There was not to be a warrior class, alongside a peasantry and a clerisy. We can understand what it is for the individual to find courage in an identification with a group. We might consider that people who understand their relations with others purely in economic terms— who understand society simply as facilitating the exchange of commodities, for instance—profoundly misunderstand what they are. To discover a sense of solidarity with others—by coming to think of themselves as *citizens*, and not simply as tailors or lawyers—may indeed be to discover a truth that had previously eluded them.

The acts by which people identify themselves as political beings are infinitely various. They include the comic persistence of Feeble, Leopold Bloom's proud recollection that he had handed back Parnell's hat to him after it had been knocked off his head in a brawl, for which Parnell had thanked him,[95] and the Parisians uniting before the Bastille in 1789.[96]

## VII VIRTUS

In his *Life, of Coriolanus*, Plutarch writes: 'Now in those dayes, valiantness was honoured in Rome above all other virtues: which

[95] Joyce, *Ulysses*, (London, 1960), pp. 761–2.
[96] See Sartre, *Critique of Dialectical Reason*, trans. A. Sheridan-Smith (London, 1976), bk. ii, pp. 351–63.

they called *Virtus*, by name of vertue selfe, as including in that general name, all other special vertues besides.'[97] The root of *virtus* in the word *vir*, of course, denotes 'manliness', and in its primary meaning the word *virtus* includes strength and manly excellence. (The Italian term *virtù* has a similar meaning.) The word came to denote excellence in general.[98]

Many people would not now see any special connection between 'valiantness' and 'manliness'. What seems so obviously true to Aristotle that he simply asserts it—that the courage of a man differs from that of a woman, and that a man would be thought to be cowardly if his courage were only the same as that of a courageous woman[99]—seems obviously untrue to many people now. Among the reasons why its untruth seems so obvious is that women are now found in roles that were exclusively male—for instance, in the armed forces (although not in combat duties). And many people would assume that apparent differences of character which coincide with differences of sex are usually to be explained by inherited social roles and expectations. But it may be that there is another reason which lies deeper, and which takes us away from current debate about sexual 'stereotypes'. This is the widespread modern conviction that 'moral' courage is more genuine than 'physical' courage, and the accompanying idea, that whatever depends upon something so clearly accidental as the superior physical strength of one sex cannot be a matter of moral merit. In other words, the notion that a virtue could be connected with anything as 'biological' as sex offends against our Kantian prejudices in favour of original moral equality. The most general version of this prejudice would be that a virtue cannot depend upon something as accidental as anyone's physical endowments.

Of course, as soon as one tries to put any weight at all upon the popular distinction between moral and physical courage, it collapses. The physical courage of rugby players is obviously a matter of psychological attitude as much as physical strength and fitness. But this psychological attitude would not exist without the fitness. A man habituated to physical buffeting is physically brave

---

[97] Plutarch, *Life of Coriolanus*, trans. North (London, 1899), p. 2.

[98] Of course the root of the Greek *arete* also applies originally to the masculine. But no argument is to be based on etymology.

[99] *Politics*, 1277[b]20–5. Aristotle says that both the temperance and the courage of a man differ from those of a woman in much the same sort of way as the same virtues in a ruler differ from those in a subject.

just because of his habituation. The sort of boldness that is displayed in hard games, hunting, fighting, is both physical and psychological. Indeed, even if one thinks that such activities are useless, or overrated, it would be a prejudice to assume that this sort of courage has nothing of the moral about it.

If we think of courage without thinking about physical boldness, the passion men have shown in combat, fierceness, exuberance, the 'wrath' and *thumos* that Homer attributes to his heroes in battle, then we will have only a one-sided and anaemic picture of it. There are many reasons—some of them good—why people are unhappy about connecting courage with physical aggression and fighting spirit. Any suggestion that a virtue, which we all have a reason for cultivating, might find its fullest expression in martial valour, is so contrary to the spirit of the age that it seems pointless even to attempt to take it seriously. Yet a courage which was entirely passionless, entirely abstracted from our physical being, would, I suggest, be unbelievable. Hume gives us an aesthetics of courage; Addison in his stoic *Cato* gives us a courage which is essentially a matter of moral declamation. Is it possible to think about courage so as to restore a sense of its physicality, and at the same time preserve a picture of it as a public or political virtue?

The question is a difficult one, and I shall answer it only tentatively, with what may well be regarded as another exercise in the 'aesthetics of courage', in reflecting upon some examples from Shakespeare. Shakespeare portrays several heroes whose sense of 'the nobleness of life'[100] is an identification with a role which necessarily entails danger, and hence a noble courage. Othello does this. For him his role in the world—which is the role of a warrior and ruler in the service of Venice—is part of what he is, so that in losing that he loses what is essential to himself. Othello's conviction that he has lost Desdemona expresses itself as a farewell to his 'occupation' as a soldier:

> I had been happy if the general camp,
> Pioners, and all, had tasted her sweet body,
> So I had nothing known: O now for ever
> Farewell the tranquil mind, farewell content:
> Farewell the plumed troop, and the big wars,
> That makes ambition virtue: O farewell,

[100] *Antony and Cleopatra*, I. i. 36.

> Farewell the neighing steed and the shrill trump,
> The spirit-stirring drum, the ear-piercing fife;
> The royal banner, and all quality,
> Pride, pomp, and circumstance of glorious war!
> And, O ye mortal engines, whose wide throats
> The immortal Jove's dread clamours counterfeit;
> Farewell, Othello's occupation's gone![101]

Othello is moved by the sadness of his own fate. This is not simply self-pity: war and its glory are bound up with his love for Desdemona, and hers for him. Othello is a warrior, and in losing that 'occupation' he loses himself. Similarly in *Antony and Cleopatra* Cleopatra's love for Antony cannot be separated (at least when Antony is absent) from her sense of his greatness, his glory. Antony's magnificence—and we should think here of the Aristotelian virtue of magnificence (*megaloprepeia*), which includes greatness of mind, imagination in display, and bounty—is also the object of her love.

But the play of Shakespeare that most repays our attention as a study of *virtus* is *Coriolanus*. Shakespeare's Coriolanus is a man who has a conception of what is noble, and of what is courageous. He too identifies himself with 'state wealth and power', and in the play we see this identification branch out into a consciousness of even the body itself as expressing an impersonal ideal, becoming thing-like, an adamantine instrument, an 'engine' related to a state that has also become palpably a thing, a juggernaut. Coriolanus as an engine: '. . . when he walks, he moves like an engine, and the ground shrinks before his treading: he is able to pierce a corslet with his eye; he talks like a knell, and his hum is a battery'.[102] This goes well with the juggernaut state:

> . . . you may as well
> Strike at the heaven with your staves as lift them
> Against the Roman state, whose course will on
> The way it takes; cracking ten thousand curbs
> Of more strong link asunder than can ever
> Appear in your impediment.[103]

Of course, the description of Coriolanus is partly humorous; and the picture of the Roman state is not without irony. But the irony of

---

[101] *Othello*, III. iii. 351–63.      [102] *Coriolanus*, v. iv. 19–23.
[103] I. i. 64–9.

the play does not entirely undercut our sense of Coriolanus', and Rome's, greatness.

Coriolanus pursues honour as an end in itself. His exclusive attachment to honour means that he in effect takes seriously some mocking words of Menenius and divides Rome into the honoured and honourable patricians, and the plebeians who are scabs, curs, rats, who do not belong to 'the fundamental part of the state'—but who must *therefore* give honour to those who are worthy of receiving it. Coriolanus's honour is undoubtedly an identification with Rome, whose perfect instrument he is to be, an identification with a perfect fighting role that in its rejection of all human weakness becomes something like an attempt to cut free from all human relations—an attempt which must fail at the very moment when he most explicitly commits himself to it.

> I'll never
> Be such a gosling to obey instinct, but stand
> As if a man were author of himself
> And knew no other kin

He says this immediately before he surrenders to the importunities of his mother.[104] Coriolanus' attachment to honour 'as an end in itself' becomes pride and egotism, a pride that the tribunes seriously or hypocritically see as inhuman:

> You speak o' the people
> As if you were a god to punish, not
> A man of their infirmity.[105]

Coriolanus' attachment to honour is indeed expressed in the strangely insistent physicality of the play. Not only is his honour deeply involved in physicality, but his sense of courage is a sense of the body which becomes either a thing or an emblem of the state. His body is identified with the state in becoming its sword—his very body is to be made a sword by the soldiers, an apt expression of his proud dedication to the honour of the warrior: '. . . [*They all shout, and wave their swords; take him up in their arms, and cast up their caps.*] O me, alone, make you a sword of me?'[106] And his mother sees him as Rome's instrument, her weapon killing men, in a splendidly sinister conceit:

> Death, that dark spirit, in's nervy arm doth lie,
> Which, being advanc'd, declines, and then men die.[107]

---

[104] v. iii. 34–7.  [105] III. i. 80–2.
[106] I. vi. 75–6.  [107] II. i. 151–2.

His sense of his own honour is a sense of his masculinity and manliness. When he agrees to humble his pride and abase his honour by speaking gently to the plebeians, he sees his setting aside of his natural disposition, his pride, as an abnegation of his manliness:

> Well, I must do't.
> Away my disposition, and possess me
> Some harlot's spirit! My throat of war be turned
> Which choired with my drum, into a pipe
> Small as an eunuch or the virgin voice
> That babies lulls asleep.[108]

The flesh in *Coriolanus* is never seen *as* flesh, except when he is suddenly overcome by it, as when he kisses his wife, Virgilia. His pride in what he understands as the highest value—*pietas* towards the state—calls for a transformation of ordinary human feeling, of the ordinary weakness of the body into something rigid, unfleshly, adamantine. It is to become a thing, an emblem, something that incarnates all that '*virtus* or valiancy' which Plutarch (in North's translation, which was, of course, used by Shakespeare) says was honoured in Rome above all other virtues, and which can finally be understood only as service to and an identification with the state. Aufidius, the rival of Coriolanus, also sees his body as something of superhuman hardness:

> Let me twine
> Mine arms about that body, where against
> My grained ash an hundred times hath broke
> And scarr'd the moon with splinters.[109]

And he inspires in Aufidius that 'sublimity of sentiment' which Hume says the actual representation of the 'figure' of courage inspires 'by sympathy':[110]

> Know thou first
> I loved the maid I married; never man
> Sighed truer breath; but that I see thee here,
> Thou noble thing, more dances my rapt heart
> Than when I first my wedded mistress saw
> Bestride my threshold.[111]

---

[108] III. ii. 110–15.                         [109] IV. v. 109–12.
[110] See p. 62 above.                         [111] IV. v. 116–21.

Volumnia sees her son as destined to exist and exert himself in the public realm:

... when youth with comeliness plucked all gaze his way ... I considering how honour would become such a person—that it were no better than picture-like to hang it on the wall, if renown made it not stir—was pleased to let him seek danger where he was like to find fame. To a cruel war I sent him, from whence he returned his brows bound with oak. I tell thee, daughter, I sprang not more in joy at first bearing a man-child than now in first seeing he had proved himself a man.[112]

This public realm can be understood only as the polar opposite of something else—the ignoble, scurrying world of the plebeians. Hence for both Coriolanus and his mother genuine virtue is inseparable from genuine pride. His love of Rome must involve pride because it has become something self-contained and complete in itself, an attachment to a certain image, which includes himself and his own role. This goes naturally with a series of oppositions between man as a creature of flesh and blood and man as embodying the Roman state.

We might notice, incidentally, the part played in all this by images of blood. As the body itself becomes simply an instrument of Rome, so the *wounded* body is turned into an emblem: as part of the instrumentality of the body Coriolanus' blood is seen by his mother as sharing in the beauty of courage:

VOLUMNIA.                    His bloody brow
  With his mailed hand then wiping, forth he goes,
  Like to a harvest-man that's tasked to mow
  Or all or lose his hire.
VIRGILIA. His bloody brow? O Jupiter, no blood!
VOLUMNIA. Away, you fool! It more becomes a man
  Than gilt his trophy. The breasts of Hecuba,
  When she did suckle Hector, looked not lovelier
  Than Hector's forehead, when it spit forth blood
  At Grecian sword, contemning.[113]

Speaking to his soldiers before Corioli, Marcius himself exults in his blood:

                    If any such be here—
  Which it were sin to doubt—that love this painting
  Wherein you see me smeared; if any fear

[112] I. iii. 6–18.          [113] I. iii. 35–44.

Lesser his person than an ill report;
If any think brave death outweighs bad life,
And that his country's dearer than himself . . .[114]

Blood in *Coriolanus* is an image of all that is overcome in
courageous action. The wound itself means nothing: it is only
where blood can be taken as the accompaniment of and the
counterpoint to the sacrificial action that it has meaning. The
images of honour and glory in the play cover over the weakness of
the flesh: blood shed in battle is a symbol of all that is passive
in man being overcome in the exercise of martial courage—it is all
that spontaneous life that is controlled or transcended in the service
of the warrior. It is only the 'honourable wound' that we see in this
way. We do not understand menstrual blood, or blood from
internal bleeding, nor even the wound of Amfortas in *Parsifal*,
which expresses private, unaccepted suffering rather than noble
sacrifice, in the same way. In *Coriolanus* the body seems to attain
significance in a political world, a world of honour and sacrifice.

Yet it must be remembered that the play is full of irony.
Coriolanus' honour is destructive, and leads him to betray his
loyalty to Rome. His courage and pride have meaning only as what
later came to be called 'civic virtues'. Yet they have become
detached from the loyalty to the city that makes them virtues. And
the emblematizing of the body in the play is frequently hyperbolic,
often produces conceits, and is often entirely rhetorical. This is to
be expected in a work of the poetic imagination. Nevertheless,
*Coriolanus* is not essentially ironic, but tragic, and the protagonist
is a tragic hero because his wholly serious convictions lead him into
actions which horribly contradict his own deepest loyalties.
Although the play achieves its political vision through poetry and
rhetoric, and qualifies it with irony, and even comedy, it does take
seriously (at the very least) the idea of courage as a mental and
physical unity, and as fulfilled in the political sphere.

The play certainly does see courage in terms of masculinity. We
might say that it transforms the idea of masculinity, as conven-
tionally conceived, from that of a sexual kind to that of an ideal of
conduct. This imaginative connection of courage with manliness
has both a social and a phenomenological component. The social
component relates to all that corporate activity which can be

[114] I. vi. 68–73.

identified with a political realm. It would include all that willingness to risk one's life that is experienced as an obligation, arising from one's sense of oneself as a citizen, and going with motives of shame and honour. The phenomenological component involves a perception of masculinity as bound up with certain potentialities of the body, potentialities which cannot be simply read off from the sheer form of the body, but are connected with our sense of a man as an agent who has rational motives for overcoming pain, privation, and fear. This is not the mere perception of the body. It is rather the perception and understanding of a certain kind of rational agency.

None of this entails that there could not be an imaginative depiction of political courage based on an ideal of femininity. Indeed, I am using the terms 'masculine' and 'feminine' distinctly from 'male' and 'female', to name not sexual kinds, but cultural and moral ideals. Such ideals deeply influence our sense of what is natural—whether it is 'natural' (for instance) for males to set a particular store on a particular sort of physical courage. But ideals are, of their nature, always open to revision. An imaginative picture of feminine political courage would give us a sense of what is natural very different from what we find in *Coriolanus*.

### VIII CONCLUSION: FEAR OF DEATH

It may well be objected that no conclusive, or even powerful, arguments have yet been advanced why we should think of courage in this way at all. There is no doubt but that for most practical purposes we can understand courage in far simpler terms. To say that courage includes motives such as pride and shame, that it has a connection with a noble end, and that it is seen at its fullest in public or political life, may or may not be interesting as an exercise in cultural nostalgia, but it cannot compel anyone.

That is quite true. I have not, in fact, been trying to establish indisputable connections among ideas—between for instance, courage and the noble. Nor do I think it possible to prove that 'the concept of courage' includes all the elements that have been discussed in this chapter. Clearly the picture I have given will seem persuasive only to someone who can sympathize with its emphasis on man as a political animal. But that idea is itself an ideological battleground, and can hardly be used to demonstrate the rest of the argument.

All I can hope is that this picture of courage may be seen, on reflection, to correspond to our experience at more points than at first sight it may seem to do. It may help us to relate the idea of the virtue of courage to other virtues and values, and to other human activities, more suggestively than a simpler, more commonsensical picture might. That it attempts a modest amount of excavation of a long-lost tradition of thought on the subject may also be in its favour. But in the end, the only success that will matter will be that the reader find it attractive, or natural, to think along lines such as these.

There is one further idea which needs to be touched on. Most ancient and Renaissance writers on courage thought that it was especially concerned with facing, and controlling, one's fear of death. Aristotle and Aquinas both say this.[115] Both also think that courage is above all shown in facing death in warfare.[116] The arguments for this are plain: courage regulates fear, and death is the most terrible thing we have to fear. So the highest courage is that which enables men to face this most terrible of perils. As we saw, Aristotle thinks that the noblest deaths are in battle, 'for these take place in the greatest and noblest danger.'[117]

Most of us would probably feel that this is all a bit too brisk. Such a bald argument will convince only those who are already sympathetic to the scholastic style. But it would be a pity were we therefore to decide that there is nothing in the idea that courage is especially concerned with death and the fear of it.

In *After Virtue* Alasdair MacIntyre sketches a picture of courage as it is understood in heroic societies: 'To be courageous is to be someone on whom reliance can be placed. Hence courage is an important ingredient in friendship. The other ingredient in friendship is fidelity. My friend's courage assures me of his power to aid me and my household . . .'.[118] MacIntyre observes that we might expect to find a contrast in heroic societies between the expectations of a man who possesses courage and its allied virtues, and who has kinsmen and friends, and the man who lacks all these things:

Yet one central theme of heroic societies is also that death waits for both alike. Life is fragile, men are vulnerable and it is of the essence of the

---

[115] Aristotle, *Ethics*, 1115$^a$20–30, and Aquinas, *Summa*, 2a2ae, 123, 4.
[116] Aristotle, *Ethics*, 1115$^a$30–5, and Aquinas, *Summa*, 2a2ae, 123, 5.
[117] *Ethics*, 1115$^a$30–5.  [118] p. 116.

human situation that they are such . . . The man therefore who does what he ought moves steadily towards his fate and his death. It is defeat and not victory that lies at the end. To understand this is itself a virtue; indeed it is a necessary part of courage to understand this.[119]

This would suggest that the courageous man has a deeper, more serious sense of life than other people. He would show this in his actions, rather than simply in his sentiments. For it does not seem difficult to imagine someone who has a sense of human vulnerability, and who is also an arrant coward. Or a man's contemplation of such things might make him so detached that he might never set himself to do anything bold. He might be like Aristotle's old men who 'are cowardly, and are always anticipating danger . . . old age has paved the way for cowardice.'[120] It is not only the *coward* who lacks this grave sense of life, who is fatuously optimistic, who is full of hope because he was never experienced adversity, and feels that life will last for ever. Aristotle says this of young men: 'They look at the good side rather than the bad, not yet having witnessed many cases of wickedness . . . They are sanguine . . . they have as yet met with few disappointments . . . Their hot tempers and hopeful dispositions make them more courageous than older men . . .'.[121]

Furthermore, frivolity need not exclude someone's being courageous. The daredevil courage of many Battle of Britain pilots often went with an apparent frivolity. Was it therefore less genuine than the courage of Japanese kamikaze fighters who solemnly dedicated themselves to their homeland before taking off on their last missions? They may not have talked about it, but we assume that most Battle of Britain pilots were moved by patriotism. This would be true even if they thought only that they were doing their job. *Esprit de corps*, the *élan* of fighting men, are forms of local patriotism. If we knew of a pilot who cared for none of these things, or who fought only 'for love of slaughter',[122] then we might be uncomfortable with his 'courage'. For we certainly are concerned with motive, even where, from the outside, his actions look exactly like those of a brave man.

The assumption underlying all this is clearly expressed in the

---

[119] *After Virtue*, p. 117.      [120] *Rhetoric*, 1389$^b$25–35.

[121] *Rhetoric*, 1389$^a$.

[122] 'some for love of slaughter, in imagination, | learning later . . . some in fear, learning love of slaughter.' Pound, 'Hugh Selwyn Mauberly (Life and Contacts)', *Selected Poems*, ed. T. S. Eliot (London, 1959), pp. 173–87.

concept of 'civic virtue', in the writings of the Italian republican humanists of the Renaissance. In Machiavelli, for instance, courage is the highest expression of man's *virtù*; and *virtù* is above all man's civic spirit, his disposition to be active for the common good, or, more specifically, for civic glory and greatness.[123] Accordingly, attachment to one's city is an attachment to something that is necessary to complete one's private concerns. Civic virtue negates natural selfishness, an attachment to private interest. Hegel is writing in this tradition when he defines courage, first, as a formal virtue 'because . . . it is a display of freedom by radical abstraction from all particular ends, possessions, pleasure and life . . .'.[124] And the idea that this 'radical abstraction' is best understood in political loyalty corresponds to the second, substantive part of Hegel's definition: 'The intrinsic worth of courage as a disposition of mind is to be found in the genuine, absolute final end, the sovereignty of the state. The work of courage is to actualise this final end, and the means to this end is the sacrifice of personal actuality.'[125]

So the dominant theme of courage relating especially to man's being as a political animal gives us at least some purchase on the idea that courage has a particular relation to death. It is not that the brave man will *think* about death, but that he will (to use a phrase of Heidegger's)[126] have a 'being towards death', in the very fact of his loyalties.

The idea of *virtù*, especially in Machiavelli, brings out tensions, and perhaps contradictions, in my account of courage. For on the one hand the assumption will be that the loyalty that goes with courage will be to an established polity, and can be described in terms of *pietas*. But on the other hand, zeal for the glory and greatness of one's city can go with instability, including policies of aggressive expansion. In the *Discourses* Machiavelli devotes himself above all to analysing Livy, whose whole history is an account of the growth of the power of Rome through war. So the conflicting ideals of Classical republicanism are perhaps being invoked because they come close to reconciling the conflicts in my account of courage.

---

[123] Cf. Skinner, *Foundations*, i. 175–80.
[124] *The Philosophy of Right*, sect. 327.
[125] Ibid., sect. 328.
[126] *Being and Time*, trans. Macquarrie and Robinson (Oxford, 1978), div. ii, sect. 1.

My account does indeed contain unresolved contradictions. 'Political' courage includes both patriotism, or loyalty to the state, *and* the emphasis on 'noble egoism' of Nietzsche, and, we can even say, of Coriolanus. Indeed, *Coriolanus* throws the problem into relief. In that play we feel conflicting loyalties, and conflicting attitudes towards the hero. Rome is presented as a scene of conflict between the classes, not as a setting of the *Sittlichkeit* that Hegel imagined as existing in the Greek *polis*. In other words, I have wanted to understand courage both as a virtue involving political loyalty, and as something potentially subversive. In Coriolanus it exists in both forms. For modern man, as for Renaissance humanists (if not for Hegel), the State cannot be seen as entirely stable, the object of an unproblematic loyalty. Our experience makes such a vision only something we can entertain with a certain ironic detachment. This may mean that courage, for us, strives towards a form which it cannot attain.

# 3

# TEMPERANCE

FOR Aristotle and Aquinas temperance is the virtue that governs those pleasures which arise from the sense of touch.[1] Excessive pleasures arising from sight and hearing are not, strictly speaking, intemperate. For both, even the pleasures of smell and taste are to be resolved into the pleasure of touch.[2] To subordinate sensual pleasures to reason is necessary if we are to be truly human; and temperance is the rational control of our physical appetites. Aristotle draws a distinction between temperance and continence: the temperate man is not at all drawn to what is brutish in human pleasures, whereas the continent man controls his appetites where they are bad.[3]

If temperance deserves its traditional place as a cardinal virtue, then we must be convinced that someone who lacked it could not possibly be a good man. Aristotle and Aquinas say much that supports that opinion. Can we go further and say that someone without temperance is actually *evil*? The Aristotelian tradition is not really concerned with what is evil—as distinct from being defective—in people. The self-indulgent man is seriously bad—for instance, he will be vicious with *conviction*[4]—but he is not exactly evil. I shall be interested in how far it is fruitful to see intemperance as actually evil. This will involve supplementing the Aristotelian picture of the need for reason to control the passions and appetites with some thoughts drawn from the Augustinian / Christian tradition. This, together with the fact that I shall largely ignore Aristotle's temperance / continence distinction, means that I shall not really be discussing his concept of temperance at all, but what a true Aristotelian would regard as a strange hybrid.

[1] Aristotle, *Ethics*, 1118ᵃ20–30, and Aquinas, *Summa*, 2a2ae, 142, 4.
[2] *Aristotle, Ethics*, 1118ᵃ30–5, and Aquinas, *Summa*, 2a2ae, 141, 5.
[3] *Ethics*, 1119ᵃ10–15, 1114ᵇ10–15, and 1151ᵇ30–1152ᵃ5.
[4] i.e. he will not repent, and is therefore incurable: *Ethics*, 1150ᵃ20–5.

### I SLOTH AND GRACE

#### i *Sloth*

Could we think of temperance as a quality which some people have just by nature? It seems so. Some people just seem naturally less given to gluttony and lechery than others. Some *peoples* seem temperate in some things: Mediterranean races are much less given to drunkenness than are northern peoples.

We could perhaps imagine a child who without any teaching or good example shows all the signs of temperance. He has no temptation to overeat; he is active and industrious; he never shows childish petulance and rage. This paragon is simply a *lusus naturae*, or perhaps a precocious saint.[5] We could think of these habits as just facts about the child, on a par with its being dark and brown-eyed.

Surely there is something wrong here. For there is no doubt but that this naturally temperate child is also a *good* child. His temperance cannot exist alone without other qualities. That a man can whistle melodiously tells us nothing about his character. Musical talent can just exist on its own. Virtuous (and vicious) dispositions are not like that. They do reveal character, and they go with certain ways of thinking and of valuing. We can ask ourselves whether this naturally temperate child would be disgusted at the thought of wallowing in drunkenness, stuffing himself with food (in the Roman manner) until he vomits, so that he can eat again. If he felt no abhorrence at this sort of behaviour, no shame if (for once) he indulged in it, then I wonder why we would want to call him 'temperate'.

Temperance refers to a wide range of behaviour that is rooted in attitudes and values. A man might be naturally abstinent with wine, but a glutton. Or he might eat sparely, but throw himself into sexual pleasures to the point of mania. Temperance has traditionally been thought of as covering all these, and other pleasures. If there really is such a virtue, then a man cannot have it just because he has a set of individual tastes (and distastes) unrelated to each other. Indeed, to think about a virtue is to reflect upon the ways in which people's habits, tastes, and feelings are connected, and how they

---

[5] That remarkable infant, St Nicholas of Bari, abstained from his mother's breast on fast-days of the Church, and from both breasts on the most solemn fast-days.

express values. Temperance is important—or 'cardinal'—if it points to what is central to the good life.

I shall begin with sloth. Is this a disposition that shows a failure of temperance, and which is therefore a serious moral defect? We could think of sloth as just a state of the body. Some people are active, others sluggish. At some times and in some moods we are active and energetic; at other times we just feel like doing nothing. All sorts of things can make us slothful—climate, health, diet. Tropical climates have often been blamed for the slothfulness of whole peoples. (Sturdy hill-peoples sweep down and conquer the effete inhabitants of the plains, and become in turn soft themselves because of the enervating effects of the lowlands, etc.) Yet we do not need to think long about sloth before we also find it necessary to think of the states of mind that go with it.

Could we imagine a man who actually enjoyed a totally slothful existence? It is not just that he has a frequent disinclination to act vigorously, but rather that he enjoys a state of something as close to complete inactivity as will allow life to continue. We can easily imagine the delights of sloth which follows vigorous activity—indeed, that is one of the greatest human pleasures. Tribes of hunters spend as much of their time as they can in slothful ease, like lions, interrupted with the intense efforts of the chase. But a pleasure in ease which is not a rest from effort is a different thing.

Would a totally inactive man enjoy his existence? It would not be enough that he said he did. For us to believe him we would have to have some understanding of his pleasures. He would have to be pleasurably absorbed, not bored, not dulled. He would have to be enjoying himself, elated, amused, never wanting to talk about anything else, and talking about this with spirit or conviction.[6] Yet it would be as difficult to imagine this as it would to see how someone could take a constant delight in a lifelong itch or tickle, or in one musical note endlessly prolonged.

I suggest that we naturally regard a complete indisposition to act as pathological, in the sense that it shows a disturbed mental attitude. Can we say that someone in this state has a particular way of seeing himself in the world? He experiences his body as a sort of dead weight, and this means that he does not see the world as to be acted upon. This is actually how one does feel in a state of severe

---

[6] See Gilbert Ryle, *The Concept of Mind* (London, 1949), pp. 107–8.

depression. Sartre gives an account of 'passive sadness' which is relevant to this. He says, in effect, that the sad man sees the world as 'bleak', as not offering or demanding courses of action, as seeming to be 'of undifferentiated structure': 'there is muscular relaxation, paleness and cold at the extremities; one turns away to some corner to sit there motionless, making the least possible contact with the world'.[7] This is a way both of experiencing one's body and of having an attitude towards the world—it is both physical and mental. To desire to act, to see the world as the field for one's action, is at the same time (assuming that one is not suffering from paralysis, for instance) not to feel one's body as an alien object. Correspondingly, slothfulness involves a shrinking from activity, a melancholy, a lack of attachment.

This description of the mental attitude which sloth contains corresponds to what Aquinas calls *acedia*, or 'spiritual apathy'.[8] He defines it as a sin against charity, and quotes Damascene that 'it is a kind of oppressive apathy (*tristitia aggravans*) which so oppresses the soul of man as to prevent him wanting to do anything.'[9] *Acedia* is a kind of sorrow over spiritual good; it shrinks from spiritual good as laborious or irksome to the body.[10] Later he quotes Isidore, saying that despondency (*tristitia*) engenders 'spite, pusillanimity, bitterness, and despair', whereas spiritual apathy (*acedia*) engenders 'idleness, drowsiness, uneasiness of mind, restlessness of body, instability, verbosity, idle curiosity'.[11]

One must be struck by the confidence with which Aquinas lists the mental states that go with sloth. I want to suggest something weaker and more tentative: that sloth does entail an attitude towards the world, and cannot be thought of simply as a physical state; and that it is an intrinsically joyless condition.[12]

Aristotle makes an interesting remark when he talks of 'a certain gourmand' who 'prayed that his throat might become longer than a crane's, implying that it was the contact that he took pleasure in.' He goes on:

To delight in such things and to love them above all others, is brutish. For even of the pleasures of touch the most liberal have been eliminated,

---

[7] *Sketch*, pp. 68–9.

[8] *Summa*, 2a2ae, 35, 2.

[9] *Summa*, 2a2ae, 35, 1.

[10] *Summa*, 2a2ae, 35, 2.

[11] *Summa*, 2a2ae, 35, 4.

[12] I should emphasize that my discussion does not follow Aquinas at all closely, for he discusses sloth entirely under the heading of charity, and not of temperance.

e.g. those produced in the gymnasium by rubbing and the consequent heat; for the contact characteristic of the self-indulgent man does not affect the whole body but only certain parts.[13]

Aristotle is not talking about sloth, and the passage is not easy to understand. Yet it may be useful to think about pleasure in the *whole* body rather than in certain parts only.

We feel pleasure when our bodies are in good muscular tone. The glow of a healthy, well-toned body can certainly be thought of separately from the activities which produce health. Indeed, the 'glow' often comes when we rest immediately after exertion. But can we think of the pleasure of a well-toned body, or even the pleasant glow of health, as *both* a physical sensation *and* a disposition to action? An athlete who takes pleasure in his feeling of physical fitness is able to do so only because he has trained hard. It is not just that hard training is one way—at the moment the only way—to achieve this sensation, but rather that the sensation is necessarily related to what brings it about. Can we think of this feeling of fitness as a form of practical knowledge? The ability to ride a bicycle is necessarily related to having learned to ride and having ridden bicycles. It is a habit that is acquired only in performing these particular actions. Similarly an athlete is not fit simply because his muscles are in a certain condition, but because he has acquired the habit of muscular tautness and physical endeavour. Although it seems obvious that a drug could not produce one's ability to ride a bicycle or play the piano, because these sorts of practical knowledge obviously depend upon learning, it may not seem obvious that a drug which produced large muscles could not produce the 'practical knowledge' of the athlete. But the body of an athlete or of a gymnast, with its special muscular development, can support what he does only because it has been trained, i.e. he has acquired certain habits. Obviously a crippled body could not be the body of an athlete, and so the cripple could not acquire these habits. But the physical state of the athlete or the gymnast is at the same time his endurance, endeavour, and concentration upon learning certain skills.

We can say of athletes and gymnasts that they have a sense of the power of their bodies. This does not mean that they simply believe that their bodies will do their bidding or fulfil their wishes. An

[13] *Ethics*, 1118ª30.

active, energetic man is not someone who wishes a lot, but someone who is practically aware of the power of his body, and does not experience it as recalcitrant, as a sort of dead weight which has to be overcome. So we might say that the athlete's pleasure in his well-toned body, his sense of power, is less like a belief that something is the case, than a pleasurable readiness to act upon the world.

Yet there is a sense in which his body is not the object of his pleasure, or not the object of his attention. Rather his pleasure is a disposition to act which is conditioned by the state of his body. Sartre says that when I am writing, I do not focus on the hand which holds the pen. I do not use my hand in order to hold the pen: 'I am not in relation to my hand in the same utilizing attitude as I am in relation to the pen; I *am* my hand.'[14] So when I know that I can write, and am about to write, it is writing that I concentrate on, not my hand, even though it is my having learned the physical skill of writing that allows me to do that. We can also recall Sartre's contention that fatigue is not just a state of the body, but also, even primarily, a mode of consciousness of the world, of seeing the hills as steeper, the roads as interminable, the sun as more burning.[15] To use Sartrean language, the athlete's being-in-the-world differs from that of the flabby man, for his training of his body is at the same time an acceptance of fatigue, pain, physical endeavour. A man's sense of what his body can do, of what he can do through his body, is mediated through a sense of the world as to be acted upon. To the experienced rider a horse offers itself to be ridden, rather than as a wayward beast whose hooves are to be avoided.

So we can say that the man who experiences his body as fit, well-toned, and resilient has a disposition to act, and has acquired the habit of acting. His physical state is indeed a matter of habit, but of habit which includes an attitude towards the world. Slothfulness is indeed a shrinking. The slothful man has a different being-in-the-world from that of the energetic man. Not only is his sense of his body different, but *ipso facto* his sense of the world is too. The dispositions which Isidore sees as being engendered by *acedia*— 'idleness, drowsiness, uneasiness of mind, restlessness of body, verbosity, idle curiosity'[16]—if rather confidently specific, do not seem all that far-fetched. For a slothful man, shrinking from action,

---

[14] *Being and Nothingness*, p. 323. See also p. 34 above.
[15] Ibid., p. 454. See also pp. 40–41 above.
[16] Aquinas, *Summa*, 2a2ae, 35, 4.

does not see any particular place for himself in the world, in that he does not see particular tasks beckoning him. This suggests a certain aimlessness, which could indeed produce something like the vices in Isidore's list. It seems intuitively right to say that the man who forms a coherent pattern of wishes and intentions, and vigorously carries them out, is unlikely to be restless, verbose, and idly curious. To the man afflicted with these and the other vices listed, the world is a very different place from what it is for the confident, energetic man. His experience of his body is also different.

For Aquinas, then, *acedia* is a morbid state of soul. Aquinas has given an interesting argument in favour of the proposition that most of us would accept intuitively—that a man could not delight in sloth, just because sloth is a form of *tristitia*, and hence an intrinsically unpleasant state of mind. Considerations like these help to show why sloth is a very serious vice—and, indeed, why it has been considered to be a capital sin. Aquinas expresses his sense of its seriousness by calling it a sin against charity, because it is a sorrow over spiritual good precisely as the divine good.[17] If my discussing sloth under the heading of intemperance rather than uncharity has a certain arbitrariness, we can nevertheless see that what at first might look like a simple and harmless physical state does indeed point to deeper disorders.

It has to be admitted that this way of thinking can have repulsive applications. It seems, for instance, hostile to any idea of 'negative capability'.[18] Coleridge certainly was 'slothful', but it would be a man of narrow sympathies who could see no value in a man who took delight in the excessive 'plasticity' of the world, its being infinitely malleable into new forms. True, Aristotle thinks that he can distinguish the virtue of 'playfulness' (*eutrapelia*, or 'ready wit') from buffoonery, which is the excess, and boorishness, which is the defect—but it is a pretty dull thing. Our modern pleasure in sensibility, in the free play of imagination, is not easily captured by this scheme, which has a rather strong note of *discipline*. Indeed, it is unsympathetic to what we have come to value as the inner life.[19] I register this objection, without attempting to dispose of it.

---

[17] *Summa*, 2a2ae, 35, 3.
[18] See Keats, *Letters*, vol. i, no. 45, p. 193.
[19] Irish Murdoch trenchantly attacks something like this underplaying of the inner life in 'The Idea of Perfection', *The Sovereignty of Good* (London, 1970), pp. 1–45.

## ii *Grace*

In his account of temperance, Aquinas draws an analogy between bodily and spiritual beauty: '. . . beauty of body consists in a man's having well-proportioned limbs with a certain proper radiance (*claritas*). And similarly spiritual beauty consists in this, that a man's conversations or acts should be well-proportioned according to the spiritual radiance of reason.'[20] Discussing 'modesty in the external motions of the body', he quotes with approval St Ambrose's remark that 'a seemly gait has the stamp of authority, the trend of gravity, and the step of tranquillity, yet without being studied or affected but pure and simple.' He also mentions Ambrose's disapproving description of 'a voice too shrill and bodily gestures too awkward and uncouth. Let nature be our model, and her likeness the pattern for learning and the form of gracefulness.'[21] Aquinas comments: 'Hence there is a moral virtue at work in composing our physical movements.'[22] And he quotes Ecclesiasticus: 'The attire of the body and the laughter of the teeth and the gait of a man show what he is.'[23]

Underlying all this is the idea that temperance denotes not a mere disciplining of passions and appetites, but a harmoniousness of soul that will naturally find its expression in bodily comportment. This makes it possible to see grace of behaviour, of manner, of movement, as expressing moral character. Needless to say, such ideas are not current in modern ethics, which, preoccupied with distinguishing sharply between 'moral' and 'non-moral' qualities, would dismiss 'gracefulness' and the 'composing of our physical movements' as a matter of (at best) aesthetics.

Yet grace in human beings is something we do recognize, and it is an expressive quality. Some animals strike us as graceful, for instance, cats, antelopes, and gazelles. And we often think of graceful animals in describing the grace of human beings ('Two girls in silk kimonos, both | Beautiful, one a gazelle').[24] Yet a man or woman who literally moved like a gazelle would be a horrible sight. The grace we may discover in an animal does not express a

---

[20] *Summa*, 2a2ae, 145, 2: 'Whether the honourable be the same as the beautiful'.
[21] *Summa*, 2a2ae, 168, 1 (citing Ambrose, *De officiis*, 1. 18, *PL*, 16, 49).
[22] *Summa*, 2a2ae, 168, 1.                                    [23] 19: 7.
[24] Yeats, 'In Memory of Eva Gore-Booth and Con Markeiwicz', in *Collected Poems* (London, 1950), p. 263.

mental attitude. Grace in a person is always a quality of expression. The movements of a ballet-dancer are graceful as part of an expressive whole. Without music, and without our sense of the pattern of the dance, and perhaps also of the drama, they lose nearly all their gracefulness. And a single gesture may have grace entirely because of its dramatic context, as when the Count kneels to ask pardon of his wife in *The Marriage of Figaro*.

Grace is an aspect of beauty—as Aquinas implies when he relates beauty to qualities of spirit and character. Grace can be disrupted by whatever is discordant in expression. The beauty of a face can be spoiled when an ugly expression crosses it. Clearly Aquinas and the writers he quotes think that what shows itself as ugly in expression is especially connected with disordered feelings and desires. In *Paradise Lost* Satan betrays himself to the watchful Archangel when his angelic beauty is darkened by the passions of rage and envy passing over his face.[25] We all have had the experience of seeing an apparently plain face light up and become beautiful with a smile that expresses a noble character.

We can at any rate see how the idea of grace in people is not of something purely 'aesthetic', but suggests qualities of spirit and of character. And in so far as beauty in human beings—of face, especially—is an expressive concept, then beauty also can be seen as the expression of spirit and character. It is plausible to discuss this, as Aquinas does, under the heading of temperance, since this is the virtue concerned with producing emotional harmony, and tempering the will and appetites.

In seeing someone as graceful we can be aware of what goes beyond purely personal expression. Proust writes of Saint-Loup:

. . . there were moments when my mind distinguished in Saint-Loup a personality more distinguished than his own, that of the 'nobleman', which like an indwelling spirit moved his limbs, ordered his gestures and his actions; then, at such moments, although in his company, I was alone, as I should have been in front of a landscape the harmony of which I could understand. He was no more than an object the properties of which, in my musings, I sought to explore. . . . In the moral and physical agility which gave so much grace to his kindnesses, in the ease with which he offered my grandmother his carriage and helped her into it, in the alacrity with which he sprang from the box when he was afraid I might be cold, to spread his own cloak over my shoulders, I sensed not only the inherited litheness of

[25] iv. 114–19.

the mighty hunters who had been for generations the ancestors of this young man. . . . I sensed in it above all the certainty or the illusion in the minds of those great lords of being 'better than other people'.[26]

This body is, as it were, owned and given meaning by a tradition of behaviour and self-esteem. Saint-Loup's physical grace is redolent of a social role of which he is largely unconscious. He lives his body in such a way that it is an emblem, whether he will or no, something in the service of an ideal.

In thinking about grace, then, we are thinking about the relations between physical beauty, comportment, and qualities of character or spirit. We do not have the confident beliefs about these relations that are to be found (for instance) among Platonists of the Renaissance. Yet we surely are disposed to find connections between the physical grace of some people and how they see themselves in the world. Proust sees Saint-Loup's grace as expressing a sense of himself in the world that he inherits from his ancestors, and of which he is barely conscious, or which he would consciously disavow. We find in grace of comportment something in the spirit of people that we might want to call 'harmonious'. And gracelessness in manner and comportment often goes with those defects of character that suggest lack of temperance. Wilfulness, childishness, uncontrolled passion very often show themselves in graceless behaviour, and even in sheer ugliness of physical gesture.

In all these passages there is the idea that we recognize grace and beauty in people neither as a simple fact about how their bodies naturally move and look, nor as the revelation of some hidden spiritual quality. Rather they manifest character in essentially the same way that virtuous actions do. Aquinas finds it possible to relate much that we are inclined to see as purely accidental to the virtues. Style, manners, bodily comportment, and grace can be seen to be relevant to virtuous activity. Just as aggression and physical strength might be the natural foundations of courage, so some sort of 'natural grace' might be a natural foundation for the 'true graciousness' (*decor honestatis*) that pertains to virtue.[27] Perhaps we can say that even the natural beauty of the face is (as it were) waiting to be completed by the virtue of temperance, which will confer true grace upon it.

---

[26] Proust, 'Within a Budding Grove', vol. ii, pp. 791–2.
[27] *Summa*, 2a2ae, 168, 1.

## II UTRUM INTEMPERANTIA SIT PUERILE PECCATUM ('WHETHER INTEMPERANCE BE A CHILDISH SIN')[28]

Aristotle and Aquinas both say that intemperance is a childish fault. Aristotle likens the intemperate man to a child who has not been chastened: He is *akolastos*.[29] I began by doubting that temperance could be a purely natural quality, rather than one produced by moral education. Another way of putting this is that the temperate man is not just someone with certain tastes and desires, but someone whose will has been chastened—that the notion of wantonness having been overcome is inherent in our idea of temperance. In this temperance differs from courage: for although courage overcomes fear, it does not (as it were) carry within it fears which have been overcome. But temperance, so understood, corresponds to Kant's picture of *all* moral goodness as the overcoming of our disordered human nature by the moral law. In thinking about the chastening of the will, it will be useful to supplement these Aristotelian reflections with insights from the Augustinian / Christian tradition.

We are wilful, and are so from infancy. We may think that when a baby cries and screams for the breast this shows that he is the helpless victim of his physical needs. Yet we do not have to think that. Do we really know that a baby's physical needs are objectively greater and therefore more overwhelming than those of adults, and that the baby is simply overcome by his needs? We could equally think that a baby *values* his needs in an infantile way. What is overwhelming is the baby's peremptory will, his desires, his demands. Hegel tends to come down in favour of the second opinion:

At first . . . the child is much more dependent and in much more need than the animal. Yet in this, too, the child already manifests its higher nature. It at once makes known its wants in unruly, stormy, and peremptory fashion. Whereas the animal is silent or expresses its pain only by groaning, the child makes known its wants by screaming. By this ideal [!] activity, the child shows that it is straightway imbued with the certainty that it has a right to demand from the outer world the satisfaction of its needs, that the independence of the outer world is non-existent where man is concerned.[30]

---

[28] Aquinas, *Summa*, 2a2ae, 142, 2.  [29] *Ethics*, 1119ᵃ.

[30] *The Philosophy of Mind*, sect. 396, *Zusatz* (trans. W. Wallace and A. V. Miller).

How we understand the behaviour of babies will be influenced by how we understand adults. With adults we have few doubts. A childish adult is often greedy, and cannot accept that anything should come between his needs and their immediate gratification. What to others might be small irritations are to him occasions of anguish. He hates to be thwarted, and sees attempts to thwart him as outrages upon his rights. We are often quite confident in judging the childish adult, and in believing that his own assessment of his needs, his suffering when thwarted, is unreliable as a guide to how he *really* is, precisely because it has all the impatience and egoism of a child. Yet to him his desires, his rages are overwhelming: he has no idea of restraining them. We can see in the cries of a baby the presence of powerful will, and we can trace much adult behaviour to sources in childish wilfulness. This does not *prove* that a baby is wilful, rather than overcome by his physical needs. But we might remember the pre-Romantic picture of children as evil, wilful beings who cease to be monstrous only when they are 'chastened'. One modern philosopher has forthrightly taken the traditional view: 'Anyone who listens to a child's crying and understands what he hears will know that it harbours dormant psychic forces, terrible forces different from anything commonly assumed. Profound rage, pain and lust for destruction.'[31] We may feel that we 'understand what we hear' when we sense the presence of a powerful will. There are many natural and man-made noises that are unpleasant, but the human voice has a power to irritate (as well as to please) beyond anything found in nature or machines. The screams of a small child have a power to irritate or enrage beyond most other sounds. (Only the reader can judge whether that observation is true to experience.) I suggest that the reason for this is that we hear the child's cries precisely as a peremptory demand. One's dislike is a hostility to the child, rather than to his noise, an antagonism to his unfettered determination to have his demands met. The unchastened quality of the child's cries has something hateful and hating about it. One does sense a 'dormant' egoism in the child, a readiness to treat others as the instruments to the gratification of his own will. Obviously the last thing the child can do is recognize that there are others who have wishes as deserving of consideration as his own. If the child's will is *akolastos*, this is because he has not yet learned to

---

[31] Wittgenstein, *Culture and Value*, trans. Winch (Oxford, 1980), p. 2.

acknowledge the wills of others. Of course we contain our irritation, either out of patience, or (if we are the parents) out of love. But in doing this we restrain a natural reaction of hostility to a being who tries so brazenly to bend us to his demands. We also know that the child can *only* express his desires in the form of blind will, because his desires, without ability to achieve, result in the pathos of frustration. Therefore a hostility to the wilfulness of children is tempered by compassion for their inability to attain their desires. That a child's desires need to be 'chastened' does not mean that they must simply be curbed, but that they need to be turned into practical knowledge (*bouleutike orexis*). But faced with an adult who behaves like a monstrous child, we are much more willing to find his behaviour hateful, and are more justified in doing so.

There is very much in the external world which is recalcitrant to a child's will. But the only thing that *chastens* his will is his encounter with the wills of others. One's sense of the untempered will of an adult is characteristically the sense of a will which has not been resisted by others, and which therefore does not take into account or respect the will of others. What in a child seems like a blind or helpless determination to have his wishes met is, in a childishly wilful adult, a lack of respect for others.

To learn self-control is to learn respect for another person, to recognize that he too can make claims. The beginning of this respect is fear and obedience. Obedience remains an element in self-control in that the respect we feel for another includes a certain humility, a readiness to abase one's own claim in the face of the other. Self-will is not simply following what one desires (the determined self-will of the child is never that), but the preference of one's own will over that of another. (Augustine talks of 'the perverse will' and of the spirit 'that wills to delight in its own power.'[32]) The pleasure of self-will is above all a pleasure in manipulating or avoiding, or cancelling, the will of another. Without the existence of the other, one's self-will would dwindle and die. The child who overcomes self-will simply is the obedient child. The temperate man, then, is *tempered*; he is a chastened character; he is not *akolastos*. It is as though what produced the tempering enters into the virtue, enters into the character as we

[32] Augustine, *De libero arbitrio*, trans. Benjamin and Hackerstaff (Indianapolis, 1964), bk. iii, chs. 17 and 25.

perceive it. We have a vivid sense of certain vices of egoism and wantonness being held in check. (I have said that I shall not be placing stress upon the Aristotelian distinction between temperance and continence. For Aristotle the 'tempered' man is not simply *enkratikos*—the continent man who has suppressed his bad desires—but rather someone who has directed his desires in general.)

Wilfulness, then, like pride, vanity, anger, and love, requires the existence of another person if it is to exist. Can we go further and say that for this very reason unrestrained wilfulness contains a practical contradiction? In asserting his own will against that of others, the wilful man affirms his own freedom. But he implicitly denies the freedom of those whom he wishes to treat as the instruments for the fulfilment of his desires. Yet if those whom he manipulates really were merely objects, then his pleasure in his own will would be lost. In other words, it is only as agents whom he knows to be free, and to have projects of their own, that he wishes to manipulate them. Or we could say, his pleasure in treating them as means arises only from his knowledge that they are ends. Is there any resolution to this contradiction? The resolution for the child is for him to come to identify his will (which includes his desires and values) with that of his parents. He experiences their point of view as impersonal and disinterested, when compared with his own anarchic egoism. Indeed, his growing obedience and love is what gives him the idea of what is disinterested. In accepting rebuke he comes to understand what it is to have preferred his own private will over something more impersonal. For Augustine the true description of this subordination of the will is of an obedience to God, and therefore of being in accord with its own nature. '. . . a wicked will is the cause of all evil. If the will were in accord with its nature, it would maintain that nature, not harm it; and therefore it would not be wicked. From this we gather that the root of evil is this: not being in accord with nature.'[33] And perhaps we can say that the 'obedience' of temperate adults takes the form of their identifying their private wills with (for instance) those institutions which have a claim on their loyalty and duty. This is a line of thought—which we might see as a secular version of St Augustine— that is fully developed in Hegel's theory of the truly free, and hence

---

[33] *De libero arbitrio*, bk. iii, ch. 17.

good will, being the will which has aligned itself with 'the ethics of actual life in family, civil society and State.'[34]

But although wilfulness is rooted in our relations with other people, it also manifests itself in less obvious ways, for instance, in the sorts of belief we have. Wilfulness can reduce our sense of reality, and prevent us from taking an objective view of ourselves. The untempered man is excessively ready to see the world in the way he *wants* to see it. The man of unbridled wrath is not the same person in a rage that he is when calm. The lustful man gives an illusory significance to his desire. Don Giovanni is not really a cold seducer, but a fantasist. When he desires a woman she seems at the time the most important thing in the world. People with untempered wills derive pleasure from their disordered beliefs and desires, but only by a certain detachment from reality. One's pleasures and emotions can heighten or reduce one's sense of reality. To develop this thought it is worth reflecting further upon emotion.

### III EMOTION AND IMAGINATION

#### i *Emotional Consciousness*

In his *Sketch for a Theory of the Emotions*, Sartre argues that an emotion is a specific manner of apprehending the world,[35] one that involves a 'magical' transformation of it.[36] In emotional consciousness we seek to change the world upon which we have to act by a ceremony or conjuration that essentially simplifies the task before us, renders the inherent difficulty of the world more amenable. It transforms the world by massively transforming our consciousness of it. Hence the emotional consciousness is something inferior to an unemotional consciousness, even though it is 'one of the ways in which consciousness understands . . . its Being-in-the-World'.[37] Sartre's sense of how it is inferior comes out in a number of things he says, some of them general remarks, some anecdotal. For instance: 'A consciousness becoming emotional is rather like a consciousness dropping asleep';[38] 'We do not take flight to reach shelter: we flee because we are unable to annihilate ourselves in unconsciousness. Flight is fainting away in action; it is magical

---

[34] *The Philosophy of Mind*, sect. 487.        [35] p. 57.
[36] pp. 63, 65.        [37] *Sketch*, p. 91.
[38] *Sketch*, p. 78.

behaviour which negates the dangerous object with one's whole body . . .'.[39] He gives an example of a man lifting his hand to pluck a bunch of grapes. He cannot do so; they are beyond his reach; so he shrugs his shoulders, muttering: 'They are too green', and goes on his way.

The gestures, words and behaviour are not to be taken at face value. This little comedy that I play under the grapes, thereby conferring this quality of being 'too green' upon them, serves as a substitute for the action I cannot complete. They presented themselves at first as 'ready for gathering'; but this attractive quality soon becomes intolerable when the potentiality cannot be actualized. The disagreeable tension becomes, in its turn, a motive for seeing another quality in those grapes: their being 'too green', which will resolve the conflict and put an end to the tension. Only, I cannot confer this quality upon the grapes chemically. So I seize upon the tartness of the grapes that are too green by putting on the behaviour of disrelish. I confer the required quality upon the grapes magically. In this case the comedy is only half sincere. But let the situation be more critical; let the incantatory behaviour be maintained in all seriousness: and there you have emotion.[40]

Sartre's aim, as he describes it, is to study the 'significance of emotion'; and 'every human fact is of its essence significant. If you deprive it of its significance you rob it of its nature as a human fact.'[41] In Sartre's theory, emotion is not a mere extra feature of human consciousness—an addition to the human repertoire—but the whole of consciousness in one particular mode of apprehending the world. This is its essential significance. For the purposes of this discussion I shall accept much of the Sartrean theory whilst at the same time trying to find ways of modifying his account of emotion as an inferior mode of consciousness.

In being aware of an emotion I am not aware of a state of myself which I proceed to correlate with an event or object in the world. It is essential to an emotion that it be directed at an object, and that it be a mode of consciousness of an object. So if I am afraid, I am afraid of something; if I am amused, I am amused at something. I necessarily know what is the object of my fear and my amusement, and in feeling an emotion I bring the object of it under a certain description. If our model of my emotion and its object is of an inner impression which I correlate with a cause, then it would seem to

[39] *Sketch*, p. 67.  [40] *Sketch*, pp. 65–6.  [41] *Sketch*, p. 27.

follow that I judge that this state of myself is produced by that particular state of affairs in the world. In that case my consciousness of my emotion would seem to be a reflective consciousness of a state of myself. My self would necessarily be the object of my consciousness when I am conscious of an emotion. Yet it is characteristic of an emotion that I am conscious of *an object* under a certain description—'to be fled', 'to be attacked', 'to be kissed'—and that this consciousness of the object is not mediated through a consciousness of myself. In other words, my emotional consciousness is a consciousness of the world as 'to be *x*'d'. Sartre expresses this by saying that fear does not begin as consciousness of being afraid, 'any more than the perception of this book is consciousness of perceiving it. The emotional consciousness is primarily consciousness *of* the world.'[42] It is because 'the emotional subject and the object of the emotion are united in an indissoluble synthesis'[43] that the emotion is a specific manner of apprehending the world.

## ii *Magic*

If we are to consider what might be meant by 'inferior consciousness' we might begin by again thinking of some of the activities of children. We might reasonably assume that we have reason to be glad for having grown out of the childish consciousness. Perhaps we can describe why that is a good thing, at least in outline. We can start by noticing what in the behaviour of children seems to be a 'magical' transformation of the world, how it relates to transformations that it would be better to describe with some other adjective even though they do not represent an actual working upon the world (i.e. a 'transitive' attitude towards it), and whether there might be any natural passage from one sort of activity to the other. There is obviously much in common between the play of children and the serious activities of adults. Nevertheless they are different. Yet it is possible to pass naturally from childish to adult activities without an extraordinary and dramatic break intervening.

Here are some things we might notice about the play of children. First, it offers to them a pleasure that they find absorbing. Secondly, it contains a good deal of pretending, fantasy, acting, and imagining. Thirdly, it is very often repetitive: indeed, repetitiveness as such often seems attractive to children. Fourthly, the pretending,

---

[42] *Sketch*, p. 56.          [43] *Sketch*, p. 57.

imagining, often seems to have an extraordinarily schematic quality. Lastly, children's play (as distinct from playing with children by joining in their play) has for the normal adult an emptiness that would make it profoundly unattractive to go back to being a child.

First, the schematic quality of much childish play: a small child can find a pin-man a suprisingly satisfactory representation of a man, and can be satisfied that in drawing a pin-man he has represented a man. He can also be satisfied that he has represented his mother in a daub that no others would recognize as her.[44] We could say that accurate representation does not play the same role for a child that it does for an adult. That is presumably true, in that a child cannot intend by his drawing what an artist intends by his. (It would probably be wrong, though, to say that the child has no grasp of representation: children are well able to recognize what is represented in proper pictures, even when they equate their own efforts with them.)

An adult may remember with nostalgia the many happy, carefree hours he spent playing as a child. If he remembers the detail of what he actually did—or if he overcomes his nostalgia sufficiently to bring this out in mundane clarity—it is doubtful whether his mood of nostalgic recall would remain intact. What is interesting about that sort of nostalgia is the excess of sentiment over actual, remembered detail. Indeed, precise, remembered detail seems to war against the mood. Nostalgia tends to involve a deliberate cultivation of a feeling, and a recall of just those images that support the feeling. It is not just a remembering of the past; it is a style of remembering it.

This style of remembering has a schematic quality. There is a relative sensuous poverty in the images or phrases I use to summon up the nostalgic feeling. Nostalgia of this sort is very unlike the remembering we find in Proust. The taste of the madeleine brings back the whole of Combray—'all the flowers in our garden and in M. Swann's park, and the water-lilies on the Vivonne, the good folk of the village and their little dwellings and the parish church and the whole of Combray and its surroundings, taking shape and solidity, sprang into being, town and gardens alike, from my cup of tea.'[45]

---

[44] Cf. Joyce Grenfell: 'Oh Samantha what a lovely purple triangle. Oh . . . it's mummy! . . . Aren't you going to give mummy a nose?'

[45] 'Swann's Way', p. 51.

This is not nostalgic recall, but reality. When one recalls nostalgically one aims at having a certain feeling by means of the images one summons up, and the relative poverty of sensuous recall goes with a simplicity of the emotion. It is the partiality of the reverie that one wants; a complete recall would spoil this, just as a joke would disrupt a self-consciously solemn ceremony.

There seems to be a relation between the wilfulness of the feeling and the simplicity of the means to it, between my *indulging* it and the fact that its expression is peculiarly schematic. And the language of nostalgia tends to have a vagueness that goes with the voluntary simplification of the feeling.

Children often seem to be absorbed in play in a way that, to an adult, can seem mysterious. A child can spend hours pretending that his sand-castle is under assault from an imaginery enemy. If you hear him describing this to himself, it is often not a very good story, and often extremely repetitious. This does not stop him enjoying himself immensely. Yet there is a poverty in this pleasure, a poverty correlated with the banality of the story, and (although it is priggish to *say* this) adults ought to be pleased that they have got beyond it.

There is point in using the Sartrean category of 'magic' to describe the play of children, and even the world of children. There is obviously a great deal of pretending and make-believe in their play, and they are ready to believe in wonders. Sartre uses the term 'magic' to describe not a set of beliefs, but a particular consciousness. Magic has a particular connection with the exercise of the will; it is a particularly direct and unmediated working of the will upon the world. If the child's world is magical, this does not mean that he has a set of irrational beliefs, or that he does not understand causal connections. From a very early age he shows a rich awareness of causal laws; he can find his way about the world very successfully. But although a child may be quite able to separate make-believe from belief, he also finds it easy to pass from imagining to believing, from pretending to invoking.

This is particularly true of the emotional behaviour of children. A child who is enraged, frustrated, or disappointed will often put on a performance which is uncannily grief-stricken, even tragic. Yet we know that he does not suffer tragically, that when he weeps with rage or disappointment, he is not grief-stricken. This is just one of several 'tragedies' that may occur during a day at the seaside.

Indeed, what is most remarkable is that although a child can express grief—can give an expression of the tragic that is like a Greek tragic mask—he usually cannot actually *feel* grief. An actual grieving sorrow is usually beyond a child's capacity either to feel or to express, although he may respond with grief-stricken behaviour to, say, a rebuke. To feel a grief that is commensurate with the expression of grief—a grief that enters into the texture of his life— that is beyond him. And when a child suffers a bereavement he characteristically does not grieve. That is to say, he does not put on a 'tragic' performance. He may become silent, withdrawn, unreachable; or later he may become wild and unruly.

The problem is this: there is much in a child's behaviour which suggests a subjective intensity of suffering—his face wears a tragic expression, and he weeps passionately. Yet the behaviour with which he surrounds these tragic performances also suggests that he really does not take it very seriously. An adult who wept passionately, but was all smiles half an hour later, would not be thought truly to suffer. But can we distinguish between the subjective intensity of suffering and how it really is?

I have already suggested that in the weeping of children we frequently detect a powerful presence of will. The presence of will and determination in the baby crying to be fed shows itself in the crying's being frequently on the edge of rage. He is determined to make the world accord with his will. Our sense of the insincerity of a child's tears comes from our strong sense of this determination. He intends to achieve an effect by his performance. The excess of his apparent sorrow over the occasion for it suggests that he is putting on a performance or ceremony which aims to make the world what he wishes it to be.

This childish consciousness does not arise from absence of knowledge, or the child's inability to reason. It perhaps has more to do with a schematic approach to the world, and that in turn with the presence of determination. The child who says—apparently sincerely—that his pin-man 'is Daddy' shows that he *intends* it as his father, and that for him the wish is as good as the deed. Magical consciousness consists in a child's willingness to take an extremely schematic representation as bodying forth what is to be represented. He has represented his father not by a labour of looking and drawing, but by a piece of magic that short-cuts all that. His relation to the world is immensely affective, a matter of conjuring it to correspond immediately to his wishes. A child sees a piece of stuff on the stairs and is very frightened because his nurse said it was 'a piece of Satan'.[46] She had in fact said 'a piece of satin'. The difficulty of understanding how a child can believe that the stuff is a piece of Satan is one with the difficulty of understanding how he can fear a piece of stuff lying on the stairs.

Here we might talk of 'phobias' to refer to those strange fears of childhood that seem to have a psychic content beyond what can possibly be justified by the object. They are certainly very characteristic of childhood, and do not show intellectual incompetence. In becoming prey to a phobia a child does seem to enact an attitude towards the world: there is much in a phobia that is not like real fear and does not seem to embody a real belief.

A child may do something that seems to express a real belief—a false belief in certain causal relations—but at the same time seems very like a magical ceremony. Two children put pieces of broken glass on top of a very small sand-heap 'in order to bring down German bombers', they say. Did they believe it would do this, or did their action rather embody a will, and hence a magical ceremony for changing their world? Magic is not a special sort of belief, but a particular relation between belief and will. The world is influenced by the ceremony, as a parent is conjured up by the act of scrawling a few lines on a piece of paper; or as a bit of cloth can be the devil.

The child's enactment of the tragic is also magical. It shows a strong will to change the world by the ceremony of grief. The tragic performance is turned on at will, and expresses will. The child's tears fit Sartre's account of the physiological reactions characteristic of—indeed, essential to—emotion: '. . . they represent the *genuineness* of the emotion, they are the phenomena of belief . . . the behaviour without this disorder would be mere signification, empty of affect. The form we have to do with is indeed synthetic: to *believe* in magical behaviour one must be physically upset.'[47]

iii *Imagination*

I have, then, given a sketchy description of how children often behave which does seem to fit Sartre's account of emotion and its

---

[46] The example is taken from G. E. M. Anscombe, *Intention* (Oxford, 1963), sect. 10.  [47] *Sketch*, pp. 76–7.

'magical' content. I have taken it to be something like a matter of style, for instance a style of representing the world to oneself. But if it is a style, can it be contrasted with some other style? If the notion of magic is that of an affective attitude to the world, a transformation of the world through symbolic behaviour, which simplifies reality, then there is perhaps also a style of symbolic behaviour which ought not to be called magical.

Sartre writes:

... a man to whom a woman has just said that she loves him may begin to dance and sing. In doing so he turns his mind away from the prudent and difficult behaviour he will have to maintain if he is to deserve this love and increase it, to gain possession of it through countless details (smiles, little attentions etc). He turns away even from the woman herself as the living reality representative of all those delicate procedures. Those he will attend to later; he is now giving himself a rest. For the moment he is possessing the object by magic; the dance mimes his possession of it.[48]

Yet it is also possible for love and joy in the prospective possession of the beloved to enter into a life in ways which distinguish it from a mere dance of joy—to enter in the form of (in Adam's words)

> ... those graceful acts,
> Those thousand decencies that daily flow
> From all her words and actions mixed with love.[49]

For love to be expressed not in a dance of joy but in a whole pattern of life, acceptance of responsibility, marriage, children, a sense of oneself as enduring into the future through offspring—all this is for an emotion to objectify itself through being seriously lived. It is also for an emotion to become less like a passion, and more like a mode of understanding. Similarly, a child's, or anyone's, performance of grief can become the experience of real grief if it enters into 'the weave of our life'[50] over the years.

It is possible to begin with an emotion that is a passion, and struggle to set it down more precisely in words. One may find words which give a precision, and hence objectivity, to the emotion, and at the same time set it in a real world. And one may recall the past in a way that is not 'nostalgic'. An excellent description of this

---

[48] *Sketch*, p. 73.
[49] Milton, *Paradise Lost*, viii. 600–3.
[50] See Wittgenstein, *Philosophical Investigations*, p. 174.

is given by F. R. Leavis in his essay 'Reality and Sincerity'.[51] There he analyses a poem by Hardy—'After a Journey'—and wishes to show that the emotion developed in the poem, in its attachment to a clear object, its specificity, its recall of the past in a way that is not easily rhetorical, has a quality of 'reality' which is also a quality of 'sincerity'. Hardy's poem, he finds, does not talk *about* the experience—is not 'declamatory'—but presents it concretely. The precision with which Hardy constructs a scene of remembrance means that his emotion is entirely absorbed into its objective correlative. The Hardy poem is a recall of 'forty years ago' but since it is set very clearly and precisely in a particular place *now*, then the forty years ago is surely represented and felt *as* the past, a past to which one cannot return. For Leavis the distinction of 'After a Journey' lies in such achievements of objectivity, an objectivity that does not depend upon rhetorical declamation and hence eschews any easy dramatization of experience, and therefore self-dramatizing. He compares it favourably with another remarkable poem—'Cold in the Earth', by Emily Brontë—where (he suggests) the poet 'conceives a situation in order to have the satisfaction of a disciplined imaginative exercise: the satisfaction of dramatizing herself in a tragic role—an attitude, nobly impressive, of sternly controlled, passionate desolation.' For Leavis this use of a situation as a vehicle for such feelings is already a self-projection and one, in this case, 'insufficiently informed by experience'.[52]

Leavis's argument (which deserves to be read in full with the two poems—my truncated account can scarcely do it justice) is that a poem gains reality when it has a relationship to the world that is rich and complex—when through language an object is presented which justifies, limits, and at the same time develops the emotion. For the emotion to be 'realized' is at the same time for it to imply, or make allowance for, the real world. In doing this it subordinates itself to the situation presented and recalled. It is not an *excuse* for feeling, a willed indulgence. Leavis's account could be described in Spinozistic terms as a passage from immersion in an emotion to a grasp of the object of feeling which is very like the contemplation of an idea. The schematic quality disappears, and the complex presentation of the justifying object means that the emotion

[51] *The Living Principle* (London, 1975), ch. 2.
[52] Ibid., pp. 125–34.

through a full imaginative, and sensuous, development has ceased to be 'magical' and has become a means of grasping reality.

To develop, in expression, the emotion in this way is also to bring it in relation to a world of justifying objects. For the emotion to become more objective, and hence more impersonal, is for it to enter a world of objects. Hence we might think it possible through ascending a hierarchy of expression to introduce a greater coherence into our emotional life (an idea which seems implicit in what Leavis says). But since the emotion is to be seen in terms of its justifying objects, then this greater coherence in emotional life is a greater coherence in our experience of the world. To bring a greater coherence into our feelings is perhaps to bring a greater coherence and harmony into the pattern of our wishes and intentions.

One remark of Sartre's epitomizes his attitude to emotion: 'liberation can come only from a purifying reflection or from the total disappearance of the emotional situation'.[53] I have in effect suggested that the 'purifying reflection' can take the form of full and successful expression, of an imaginative development of the emotion through an imaginative development and exploration of the justifying situation. For an emotion seriously to enter into life, either as actually lived, or as grasped imaginatively, is also for it to cease to be 'magical' and, while still being a 'symbolic' dealing with the world, no longer to aim at a 'magical' transformation of the world through a 'massive' transformation of consciousness.

In imaginative expression one knows what one's feeling is in the act of setting it down. At the same time one is aware of an intention. To know 'this is the word I was looking for' is to know something in the way in which we know what we *intend*. At the same time to find an expression is to realize an intention, or, to form an intention. It is therefore possible, through an imaginative development of an experience (or of an imagined experience), to bring a greater coherence into the pattern of one's intentions, and hence into one's self-awareness.

Verbal expression also develops one's sensuous awareness of the world. The sensuous particularity that it makes possible means that one's sense of life and of the world can be enhanced. Sensuous pleasure can therefore give one an enhanced sense of reality, as can the imaginative development of an emotion. Sentimentality in

[53] *Sketch*, p. 81.

remembering goes with sensuous poverty. But equally a sensualist's excessive pleasure—for instance, a gourmand's obsession with food—is emotionally too simple. He really aims at an unreal emotional satisfaction—for instance, some childlike security which cannot in fact be attained. And indeed disordered pleasure is very much a matter of what we imagine, and of our readiness to prefer the imagined to the real good. Sir Epicure Mammon is not really a sensualist but a speaker of verse who derives an *aesthetic* pleasure in imagining luxury.

### IV *AMOUR PROPRE*

Pelagius believed that our appetites and passions are fundamentally neither good nor bad. What matters is that they should be subject to rational control. They are external forces which our better self, through reason, should combat. This is a view which is firmly based upon pagan and Stoic values.[54] Against this, orthodox Christian doctrine has held that what may be corrupt and wicked is not only our desires and appetites (when unchecked by reason), but also the human heart and imagination. Man's innate disposition to prefer the imagined over the real good, his resistance to true knowledge, his perversity and eogism—all these are sources of evil. I shall discuss them under the heading of intemperance. 'The heart is deceitful above all things, and desperately wicked.'[55] The Augustinian / Christian tradition has seen the *whole* heart of man as wicked, and not simply his uncontrolled passions and appetites. We can perhaps have some insight into what Christians have meant by this if we reflect upon the idea of *amour propre*.

La Rochefoucauld's *Maxims* is really about *amour propre*. He finds that *amour propre* enters into all human actions, feelings, aspirations, ideals. La Rochefoucauld is not simply pointing to the existence of unacknowledged human motives. When Swift paraphrases him in these lines:

> In the misfortunes of our friends
> We first consult our private ends,
> And kindly Nature, bent to ease us,
> Points out some circumstance to please us[56]

---

[54] See Peter Brown, *Augustine of Hippo* (London, 1959), p. 367 (there is also a footnote which qualifies this assertion).

[55] Jer. 17: 9.        [56] 'Verses on the Death of Dr Swift', 7–10.

he is making self-love both more rational and less interesting than it is in the *Maxims*. For La Rochefoucauld, *amour propre* is a pervasive, inescapable force, infinitely various, capable of putting on any and every disguise, even to the extent of disguising itself as its opposite. In the end, *amour propre* can sacrifice every form natural to itself so long as it can achieve its essential aim—its own existence:

It is inconstant from inconstancy, from levity, from love, from novelty, from weariness and from disgust. It is capricious, and sometimes we see it working with the utmost seriousness and with incredible energy to obtain things which are not advantageous to it, and which are even hurtful, but it pursues them because it wills to obtain them. . . . it even joins the side of those who war on itself; it enters into their plans and, what is admirable, it loathes itself with them, it plots its destruction, it even works for its own ruin; in short it cares only for its own existence, and so that it may exist, it even will become its own enemy.[57]

La Rochefoucauld is describing something that is only partly captured by the terms 'wilfulness' or 'self-love'. He is describing a force that is intrinsically perverse, and yet universal, so subtle and self-transforming, so essential to our understanding of human beings, that it is almost like life itself. (It bears a relation to the *libido* of Augustine, the *Wille* of Schopenhauer, and the *libido* of Freud.) Perhaps if we imagined a man entirely without *amour propre* we would be thinking of someone lacking all human vitality.

Two dispositions which bear upon *amour propre* are vanity and envy. I have already suggested that they are to be contrasted with pride and jealousy. The vain man desires praise even when he does not believe that he deserves it. The praise he seeks is not connected with any real self-value, any qualities which, since he values them in himself, he should correspondingly value or admire in others. Envy does not aim at a good for oneself, but rather regrets the good of another. Hence La Rochefoucauld's most famous maxim: 'Dans l'adversité de nos meilleurs amis nous trouvons quelque chose qui ne nous déplaît pas'. We can think of a self-love that is not really love of ourselves. In his discussion of friendship Aristotle says that the evil man cannot be a friend even to himself, since there is nothing in him that is lovable.[58] The man of *amour propre* does not discern something in himself that is lovable, so connecting what he

[57] *Maxims*, trans. K. Pratt (London, 1931), p. 131–3.
[58] *Ethics*, 1166^b25–30.

loves in himself and what he loves or admires in others. The man of
proper pride would admire and value in others the very qualities
which underlie his own settled self-esteem. The vain man does not
feel committed to any such reciprocity. To him other people are
rivals, espcially if they possess qualities of which he is proud in
himself. The envious man is also a rival of other people, since
their possession of a good, even of one he does not actually desire
for himself, pains him. So the *amour propre* of vanity and envy is
not much like what Butler called 'cool self-love'.[59] The self-love of
someone who is 'a friend to himself' is not impervious to the
judgement of others. It goes with an objective self-assessment, and
with conscience, with self-criticism and regret, as well as self-
approval. The man who loves himself in this sense can have peace of
mind. Aristotle says that wicked men who have no feeling of love
toward themselves 'seek for people with whom to spend their days,
and shun themselves; for they remember many a grievous deed, and
anticipate others like them, when they are by themselves, but when
they are with others they forget.'[60] The man of consuming vanity is
something like this. His love of himself is not a 'generous spirit and
self-value'[61] but only a wish that others should value, or rather
flatter, him. He substitutes the opinion of others for any true
satisfaction with himself. And the anxiety that frequently goes with
vanity, the constant demands for reassurance, suggests a man who
can live only through the opinions of others, and, in this sense
'shuns himself'.[62]

'The heart is deceitful above all things, and desperately wicked:
who can know it?' The deceitfulness of *amour propre* goes with
wilfulness in self-deceit as well as in deceiving others. (We might
recall the phrase 'the imagination of their hearts'.[63]) It also goes
with our readiness to prefer a self-will, a 'conceit' of ourselves that
does not issue in true pride but only in unbounded egoism. Our

[59] Sermons II and III 'Upon the Natural Supremacy of Conscience', *The Analogy
of Religion and Sermons*, ed. M.A. (London, 1886).
[60] *Ethics*, 1166[b]25–30.
[61] See Hume, *An Enquiry Concerning the Principles of Morals*, ed. L. A. Selby-
Bigge (Oxford, 1902), sect. viii.
[62] 'The vain man takes pleasure in *every* good opinion he hears about himself . . .
just as he suffers from every bad opinion: for he submits to both, he *feels* subject to
them from that oldest instinct of subjection which breaks out in him.' Nietzsche,
*Beyond Good and Evil*, sect. 262.
[63] Magnificat; see also Jer. 23: 17: '. . . one that walketh after the imagination of
his own heart'.

*amour propre* is, in a sense, passive in that it need not prompt us to actions which will bear out (or expose to challenge) our conceit of ourselves.

There are ways of being active rather than passive, of throwing oneself into the world (as it were), which have much in them of *amour propre* but also mark an advance upon it. For instance, there is carnality. Carnality is a higher vice than gourmandizing. Christians understand carnality in a wide sense, as including ambition and pride as well as physical lust. There is a love of degradation that is not just a surrender to physical appetite, but a way of being-in-the-world. Dostoevsky's Dmitri Karamazov is one of the most completely imagined examples of this. He throws himself into sensuality, love, greed, remorse, and murder. He is a carnal man, even spiritually. It is right that in the novel he should have a brother whose spirituality strangely resembles his own wilfully unrestrained nature. Dmitri's carnality has the character of being *chosen*—or at least it seems to express will. He is violently wilful, and this means that he sees himself as being without a fixed character. He commits himself to loving Grushenka even when he knows how degraded his love is. He hates himself, and there is no difference between his self-love and his self-contempt. His obsessive hatred of his father is little different from his obsessive love for Grushenka. But to talk of 'obsessions' obscures the sense that Dostoevsky wishes us to have that actively, and with full consent, he commits himself to his form of life.

Christians have also used the notion of carnality to cast light upon worldliness. Inordinate ambition can be seen as carnal. So it is possible to talk about the world, the flesh, and the devil as though they are aspects of the same temptation. Aristotle would presumably include excessive ambition under 'incontinence' (since the passions can be incontinent, whereas temperance is, as we have seen, concerned with the pleasures of touch). The Christian picture is of fleshliness and worldliness proceeding from the same thing, concupiscence, which includes an element of spiritual pride.

Macbeth's ambition begins as a sudden yielding to suggestion. As soon as he hears the witches' prophecy his 'seated heart' knocks at his ribs 'against the use of nature'.[64] At that very moment he realizes himself as a murderer. (Or we might rather say that the role

---

[64] Shakespeare, *Macbeth*, I. iii. 136–7.

as great letter of blood, great killer, as the king's warrior, reveals itself as having been all along essentially murderous rather than loyal.) His choice of being a murderer presents itself to him as a terrifying, yet fascinating temptation. He commits murder in a state of exaltation, fascinated by the spectacle of his own sinister intent:

> . . . and wither'd murder,
> Alarum'd by his sentinel, the wolf,
> Whose howl's his watch, thus with his stealthy pace,
> With Tarquin's ravishing strides, towards his design
> Moves like a ghost.[65]

Macbeth's terror at what he is doing goes with his dramatizing himself as a criminal and monster.

Another intermediate expression of *amour propre* is that of a man whose sense of himself does go with his idea of his place in the world and his relation to others, but is tainted with excessive subjectivity and fantasy. For instance, paranoia: a paranoid man is not a solipsist; rather his relations to others are of supreme importance to him. But it is difficult to say whether he really believes that he is being persecuted or betrayed, just because his belief seems so wilful. There is often a curious element of unseriousness, even of play. The paranoiac often behaves as though he is acting a role, a role which one could imagine him dropping if it suited his purposes. Paranoiac jealousy is like this: when Leontes suddenly jumps to the conclusion that Hermione is committing adultery with Polixenes, his absolute determination to ignore all reason is almost comical in its wilfulness.[66]

The element of play-acting that characterizes paranoia can bring into doubt the reality of the suffering a paranoid man experiences through his delusions. The anguish of jealousy at physical betrayal by a loved one is a most terrible experience. The jealousy of the lover who is just determined to be jealous seems to mimic real suffering. This is a problem that one has in understanding all 'neurotic' (or what was once called 'hysterical') suffering.

So is the suffering of wounded *amour propre* real suffering? I do not suppose this can be answered generally; sometimes it must be both intense and well founded. It may be better to take two sorts of example, first wounded vanity, and secondly wounded pride. Can we say that the suffering of wounded vanity is less real than the

---

[65] Shakespeare, *Macbeth*, II. i. 52–6.     [66] Id., *The Winter's Tale*, I. ii.

suffering of wounded pride? That wounded vanity, however it may appear to the victim, appears comic from the outside, whereas wounded pride can seem serious or tragic both to the sufferer and to the observer?

In *Twelfth Night* Malvolio suffers from wounded vanity; in *The Brothers Karamazov* Snegirov's son, Ilyusha, suffers from wounded pride:

He suddenly rushed up to me, threw his arms about my neck, and held me tight. You know, children who are silent and proud and who keep back their tears for a long time are liable to break down suddenly when in great trouble, and once they start crying, they dissolve into floods of tears. With those warm tears he suddenly wetted my face. He sobbed as though in convulsions, trembling all over and clinging close to me as I sat on the stone. 'Daddy', he kept crying out, 'Dear Daddy, how he humiliated you!'[67]

There is true suffering in Ilyusha's pain and in his 'great anger', which is a true anger, one that entirely possesses him and is greater than his childish strength. ('A great anger, sir, in a little creature like him.') To call it real suffering is to make the judgement that his love for his father is something serious and good, and goes with his deep desire that his father be shown respect—hence his furious assaults upon the other boys and his attack upon Alyosha. He is far from the passivity of the vain man who is content with words and gestures. On the contrary, Ilyusha is passionately committed, far beyond his strength, to engage with others, even physically, and make them respect his father. He has real pride and real shame. All that prevents his suffering being tragic is that he is a child, weak and desperate.

Malvolio's case is different. A modern audience may well find something painful in his being made a fool of, and tormented in noisome darkness. Yet he suffers entirely because his own malevolent (we note the etymology of his name) vanity runs up against reality (assisted by the plotters). A modern audience may pity him; but much sympathy would be misplaced. His predicament remains comic: his idea of himself as sexually attractive, his hope for future power and position—a hope based on nothing but vanity—is destroyed, and this is intensely mortifying to him. Yet we cannot really enter into his feelings. His self-deception is a mixture

[67] Trans. Magarshack (Harmondsworth, 1958), p. 240.

of the comic and the repulsive. We cannot take Malvolio's suffering seriously because we do not sympathize with its cause—his loss of an absurd picture of himself. All we can say about this picture is that it pleased Malvolio, and that a condition of his pleasure was that he expected to be exalted over his fellows and his social betters (in the slightly unlikely form of Sir Toby Belch). We cannot value Malvolio's vanity as we can Ilyusha's pride (and 'great anger'). Malvolio lacks even serious ambition. He expects to have greatness 'thrust upon him'.[68] There is no reciprocity between his self-love and any respect for equivalent qualities in others—because there is nothing in *himself* that he truly values. He cares only for being admired for quite unlikely features—such as his 'crossed garters'.[69] Therefore he cannot *claim* what he desires. To make such a claim he would have to be ready to situate himself in relation to others, to acknowledge reciprocity in self-respect and respect for others, to live in a world of pride and admiration, rather than of vanity and overweening arrogance. In fact Malvolio's world is one in which 'everything is below the level of tragedy except the passionate egoism of the sufferer.'[70]

We do commonly feel that *amour propre* is somehow barren, not sustained by any richness of relation to the real world. Perhaps that is because it does not commit people to action, but, being vanity rather than pride, allows them to indulge in dreams of grandeur which they need never openly acknowledge, and which they frequently hide from themselves, revealing it only in their fits of 'spite, pusillanimity, bitterness and despair.'[71] It is understandable that Christians have sometimes depicted Hell as a state of unredeemed egoism. If a man were truly in a state of pure egoism—were that possible—then he would not be self-conscious, just in that he would be unable to recognize or acknowledge the claims of others.

Augustine gives the classical description of the man wholly at the mercy of his *libido* (lust):

Meanwhile the reign of lust rages tyrannically and distracts the life and whole spirit of man with many conflicting storms of terror, desire, anxiety, empty and false happiness, torture because of the loss of something that he

---

[68] *Twelfth Night*, II. v. 143–5.
[69] Ibid., II. v. 157–8.
[70] George Eliot, *Middlemarch*, ch. 42.
[71] See Aquinas, *Summa*, 2a2ae, 35, 4.

used to love, eagerness to possess what he does not have, grievances for injuries received, and fires of vengeance. Wherever he turns, greed amasses, extravagance wastes, ambition entices, pride bloats, envy twists, sloth buries, obstinacy goads, submissiveness harasses, and all the innumerable things that throng and busy themselves in the kingdom of lust.[72]

## V CRUELTY

Aquinas lists cruelty as one of the sins against temperance.[73] He distinguishes it from ferocity and savagery (*saevitia* and *feritas*), which are 'bestial' vices. Cruelty is the vice of excessive severity in punishment. Its opposite virtue is clemency—the rational tempering of punishment—which Aquinas considers to be a part of temperance. These distinctions are interesting and plausible. However, I shall follow more common modern usage (e.g. in Nietzsche and Sartre) and allow cruelty to include the infliction of pain upon another purely for pleasure.

It is easy to understand the cruelty which arises from excessive anger or zeal. A punishment may be not unjust, and yet cruel because of its excessive severity. The cruelty which is hardest to understand is the sort which simply takes pleasure in inflicting pain. Aquinas calls this 'bestial', but of course that is precisely what it is not. It is specifically human behaviour.

Aquinas writes that one of the pleasures of the blessed in Heaven will be their view of the sufferings of the damned.[74] He means that what they rejoice in is the spectacle of God's justice, not the suffering of the damned for its own sake. Nevertheless, did the damned not *suffer*, it is difficult to see how God's justice could provide a spectacle to be rejoiced in. The satisfaction we may derive from a wicked man's being punished irreducibly contains satisfaction in that fact that he suffers. What stops our satisfaction being a

---

[72] *De libero*, bk. i, ch. 11.     [73] *Summa*, 2a2ae, 159, 1.

[74] This is not in the *Summa* proper, but in *Summa*, 3a, suppl., qu. 94, art. 3, completed after Aquinas's death but based on passages from his earlier writings. The passage quotes Ps. 57: 11 (Vulg.): 'The just shall rejoice when he shall see the revenge: he shall wash his hands in the blood of the sinner.' (Douai trans.) The gloss is slightly less bloodthirsty. We can rejoice in a thing either in itself, or *per accidens*. The blessed rejoice in the suffering of the damned *per accidens*, i.e. seeing in it the operation of God's justice.

cruel pleasure is that we do not wish to see the suffering exceed what we take to be a just measure. There is an analogy with anger. When I am angry I certainly wish to inflict pain, even if it is only the pain of another person's having to accept rebuke, humble his pride, purge his contempt. If, despite his having done one or other of these things, I still wished to inflict pain, then my anger would show itself to be malice or hatred. An angry parent who smacks a naughty child in the heat of the moment wishes to humble the child's wantonness through the infliction of pain. His wish to inflict pain is *per accidens*; what he is actually doing is rebuking the child.

The cruelty which Aquinas describes as bestial is a desire to hurt that is detached from justice. We can think of it as an expression of malice or hatred—but that does not tell us very much about it. The only philosopher who has written illuminatingly about this sort of cruelty—which he calls sadism—is Sarte. I would not presume to try to add to his account. I shall only suggest that his discussion of sadism does relate to wilfulness and *amour propre*.

For Sartre, the essence of sadism is that I try to appropriate the other by violence.[75] The sadist who physically tortures another person wishes, by the infliction of pain, to reduce the other to his body. The tortured person is forced, through pain, to identify himself with his flesh, he *becomes* flesh. Torture, by dispossessing the victim of his possession of his own body—a possession we understand as the body being the vehicle of his intentions and desires—removes grace from the victim. Physical grace, for Sartre, proceeds from a balance between the 'facticity' of a person's body and his ability to transcend this through intentional action. In taking away someone's physical grace through torture, the sadist renders his victim's body 'obscene'. The obscene 'belongs to the genus of the ungraceful.'[76]

Satre's discussion of sadism forms part of his account of desire. In sexual desire one sinks into one's flesh; one is 'troubled' throughout one's physical being. It is this 'being troubled' rather than (say) a man's desire to penetrate a woman that gives us the best image of sexual desire. In desiring a woman I also wish her to dissolve into her flesh, to understand herself in relation to me purely as flesh.[77]

[75] *Being and Nothingness*, pp. 379–413.
[76] Ibid., p. 400.
[77] Ibid., pp. 379–96.

Sartre thinks that both sexual love and sadism are self-defeating. When I desire someone I wish to possess her through identifying her with her flesh. But I do not want to possess only a body. For my desire to be fulfilled I need to possess her freedom as well. If she did not consent to my desire through her own desire, my love would be frustrated. Yet if she consents purely through an act of will—as a woman might consent to sleep with a man whom she admires but is not attracted to—then desire is not fulfilled. Similarly with sadism: the torturer derives his satisfaction through imprisoning a free being in his flesh. But if he fully possessed the flesh of another—say, by killing him—he could have no satisfaction. The last thing a sadist wants is to possess a corpse. Sadism, therefore, is an impossible enterprise; it is 'passion, barrenness, and tenacity'.[78]

Sarte has certainly given a plausible account of active sadism. To the man who inflicts physical suffering upon another, the imposition of his own will upon the freedom of another is necessary to his pleasure. Yet there is also what we might call passive sadism. A cruel man can take delight in the physical sufferings of others even when he is not the cause of them. Sartre's account might still be relevant: this cruel pleasure may still be directed at the victim's losing his freedom by being compelled to identify himself with his suffering flesh. One could perhaps say that the passive sadist imaginatively identifies himself with the torturer, and derives his vicarious pleasure from so doing. It is true that we can take a cruel pleasure only in the suffering of beings who are constrained, compelled, forced against their will. I doubt that someone who voluntarily accepted suffering, and never succumbed to the torment—never cried out, never lost his self-control, never identified himself with his suffering flesh—could afford much pleasure to the sadist. (Christ's silence under scourging would be an example.) The bare fact of another's suffering—say, in illness—could not support sadistic pleasure. Sadism must be directed at the *attitude* of the victim, and not simply at his sufferings. (And the sexual analogy holds. Desire is not satisfied either by enforced surrender, or by a voluntary submission without signs of reciprocal desire.)

Active cruelty involves the cruel man's interest in the will of another in relation to his own will. Even a child's cruelty to an

---

[78] Ibid., p. 399. Sartre's account is fundamentally indebted to Hegel's 'life-death struggle' and 'Lordship and Bondage'; see *Phenomenology*, sects. 178–96.

animal involves a pleasure in his own agency, in exercising his own will against the will of the creature. One's sense of one's own will is increased in one's play with and domination over animals. However, it is only in reciprocal relations with other people that one has a full sense of one's own agency. The sadist, in both relying on and wishing to annul the will of another, does not accord recognition to the other, nor receive it himself. He does not have the satisfaction of inflicting a punishment which will be recognized as merited. The lack of real satisfaction from cruelty, which Sartre describes, derives from a lack of reciprocity. Cruelty is a fantasy relation with another, in which one remains sunk in one's own egoism. To exercise one's will sadistically is to seek a relation with another in which one does not actually encounter him. Cruelty therefore has the barrenness, the lack of any rich relation to the world, that characterizes *amour propre*. We can indeed consider it a 'sin against temperance' in that it suggests a will untempered by any true engagement with the will of others, and of an egoism so helpless that it aims at annulling the selfhood of others, whilst at the same time needing the existence of other selves for its own being.

## VI THE SENSUOUS AND THE SERIOUS

The last proposition in Spinoza's *Ethics* is: 'Blessedness is not the reward of virtue but is virtue itself; nor do we delight in blessedness because we restrain our lusts, but, on the contrary, because we delight in it, therefore we restrain our lusts.'[79]

Aristotle's gourmand, praying that he might have a throat as long as a crane's, 'implying that it was the contact that he took pleasure in', can be taken as the type of passive physical pleasure. It is an amusing idea, and expresses a common view of pleasure. There is said to be a snail, the body of which largely consists of organs of generation. Some people have supposed that this snail must live a life of ecstatic physical pleasure. But our physical pleasures are probably much greater than those of snails. Human beings can attend to their sensual pleasures, be interested, absorbed, fascinated. There is a culture of physical pleasure and of luxury. There is also the sensuous imagination of physical pleasure. The range of our

[79] Pt. v, prop. 42.

physical pleasures goes with our ability voluntarily to engage in them, and to make an art, a culture, a topic of conversation out of them. We also think that people can be childish in their pleasures—thumb-sucking, for instance. We can even think, not absurdly, that someone may have infantile tastes in food. Indeed we understand the maturity of a man's pleasures as relating to the maturity of his character. An excessive interest in excretion suggests an infantile character. In other words, there is a connection between our sensual and our moral development. Freud thought that he could trace the growth to sexual maturity through a series of fixations on different parts of the body.[80] Clearly people's sexual 'tastes' obviously do go with their way of 'living' their bodies, and with their emotional and moral development. The fact that mature sexual desire is directed at another person *as* a person is central to its being as desire, and even as sensation. We can understand some sort of sexual perversion as 'truncated or incomplete versions' of the complete sexual impulse.[81] Someone who was satisfied with masturbation, and had no interest in a sexual relation with another person, would obviously be precluded from most of the emotional satisfactions enjoyed by a normal man in his sexual relations.

Our sensual nature, then, is not simply to be 'controlled'. We can develop as physical beings, and our physical pleasures will be intermingled with our moral and emotional development. Sensual pleasure, including sexual desire, can characterize one's whole being-in-the-world. In this sense our 'lusts' are not simply 're-strained', but integrated into our scheme of values and our sense of ourselves as persons. This is closer to Aristotle's understanding of 'temperance', as distinct from 'continence'.

As well as sensual pleasures, we are capable of sensuous ones. The distinction, which appears to have been introduced by Milton,[82] is a term of art. We can talk of poetry and painting as 'sensuous', meaning that it imaginatively expresses a heightened sensory awareness of the world. A sensual man might entirely lack imagination. Someone in whom there is 'a direct sensuous

---

[80] 'Three Essays on the Theory of Sexuality', *Works*, vol. vii, ed. Richards; pp. 45–169.

[81] Thomas Nagel, 'Sexual Perversion', *Mortal Questions*, pp. 39–52. See also Roger Scruton, *Sexual Desire* (London, 1986), ch. 10.

[82] When he talked of poetry as being 'simple, sensuous, and passionate': see the *Oxford English Dictionary*, s.v. Sensuous.

apprehension of thought, or a recreation of thought into feeling'[83] has imagination, and also some power of expression. In an essay on Keats, Matthew Arnold quotes Keats on the actor Kean:

'The tongue of Kean', he says in an admirable criticism of that great actor and of his enchanting elocution, 'the tongue of Kean must seem to have robbed the Hybla bees and left them honeyless. There is an indescribable *gusto* in his voice;—in *Richard*, "Be stirring with the lark to-morrow, gentle Norfolk!" comes from him as through the morning atmosphere towards which he yearns.' This magic, this 'indescribable *gusto* in the voice,' Keats himself, too, exhibits in his poetic expression.[84]

Arnold is using *gusto* to describe Keats's poetic expression. He is also using it, as Keats does of Kean, to describe a poetic voice—to describe Keats's ability to body forth the sensuous. And this is part of Arnold's endeavour to see a connection between Keats's sensuousness and his seriousness.[85] To find in a voice the quality of honey—'the tongue of Kean must seem to have robbed the Hybla bees and left them honeyless'—is an example of synaesthetic imagery, of one sense's being described in terms of another. A similar image in fact occurs in Keats's *Lamia*, when Lamia, in the form of a serpent, is speaking to Hermes:

> Her throat was serpent, but the words she spake
> Came as through bubbling honey, for Love's sake . . .[86]

A sensuous openness to the world goes, in Keats, with a desire to define one's thought and feeling as precisely as possible. His seriousness about sensation is an achievement of imagination and of self-awareness.[87]

Such sensuousness is not a 'sin against temperance'. Far from being an obstacle to objectivity, it supports it. The growth both of sensual awareness and of sensuous imagination can be a form of 'tempering', a development towards emotional and moral engagement with others.

---

[83] See T. S. Eliot, 'The Metaphysical Poets', *Selected Essays*, ed. T. S. Eliot (London, 1951), p. 286.

[84] 'John Keats', *Essays in Criticism*, 2nd ser. (London, 1938), p. 71.

[85] See F. R. Leavis, *Revaluation* (London, 1964), p. 272.

[86] I. 64–5.

[87] For a sensitive and intelligent discussion of Keats in terms of sensuousness / seriousness, see Christopher Ricks, *Keats and Embarrassment* (Oxford, 1974), ch. 1–3.

### VII POWER

Many moralists have disapproved of the desire for power. People obviously do attempt to have power over others viciously and irresponsibly. Yet there can also be a will to power that allows one to recognize the claims of others, and to have a sense of oneself as a person among persons. A man cannot achieve virtue by just abjuring power. As our sense of ourselves as persons goes with pride, so it goes with some sense of power.

Anger was discussed earlier as an example of a forceful, but rational, way of making a claim for recognition, a way which implies respect for the other person and for his autonomy. By contrast, one can reveal lack of respect for another by behaving wilfully towards him, or seeking to manipulate. Hume says that pity contains an element of contempt, mingled with a feeling of pride.[88] He contrasts it with respect, which is 'a species of affection or good-will with a mixture of humility.' It is difficult to feel respect for another whom one regards as *entirely* feeble and impotent. Respect requires that I recognize the strength, and eventually the rights, of another's will. So we might say that a desire for power can be tempered when it recognizes the power of another.

We can imagine a development from the powerful will and *amour propre* of a child into an intense ambition and lust for power in an adult. This can be an object of fear and awe. A man may have an insatiable desire for glory and honour—as did the young Julius Caesar, as represented by Plutarch. Indeed, we may see in some men of ambition the powerful presence of a childish will that has been tempered only in the sense that it has become strong, cunning, and full of a sense of how it can achieve its ends. Tolstoy's description of Napoleon in *War and Peace* is a portrait of such a man.

A will to power is central to human beings, and it would be blinkered to call it merely evil. It can certainly be a human strength, going with imagination and 'greatness of mind', and not something contemptible. It cannot be simply ruled out as a human excellence. For Nietzsche, the strong exercise of the will is in itself good, and essential to what is noble in man.

[88] *Enquiry*, sec. vii, pt. 2: '[The] sentiment of pity is nearly allied to contempt, which is a species of dislike with a mixture of pride.'

Milton calls the desire for fame 'that last infirmity of noble mind'.[89] Ambition involves strenuous activity, pride rather than vanity. You cannot just succumb to ambition in the way you succumb to sloth or lust. (It is Belial—'to Nobler deeds | Timorous and slothful'—who recommends 'ignoble ease, and peaceful sloth' in *Paradise Lost*.[90])

Plato and Aristotle thought that temperance was a political as well as a personal virtue. A state which lacked the political virtue of temperance—as in a tyranny or an ochlocracy—would be disordered. Temperance in the *Republic* means that the lower orders are willing to be obedient to the rulers.[91] A still older Greek tradition was that temperance entails a hierarchical universe in which to abandon one's place is to commit hubris. Temperance was also seen as a virtue in a ruler. Plutarch thinks it a sign of Alexander's fitness to rule that he did not take sexual possession of the women of Darius when they came into his power.[92]

The trouble with this is that it assumes too easy a fit between the private and the public virtue. What in a private individual would look like megalomania may, in a ruler, seem more like imagination and genuine greatness. (In Proust, Charlus's megalomania is partly a function of his wishing to think of himself as feudal *grand seigneur* while seated at bourgeois dinner-tables.) An absolute monarchical ruler may draw to himself what Hegel called 'the heroism of flattery'.[93]

We have come at this point to one of the great contested areas of human value. Temperance controls *amour propre*; it introduces measure, and the ability to recognize and adhere to the mean, in a man's life. It supports objectivity and a corresponding humility. But there are examples of 'intemperance'—ambition, and the love of power—which seem to war against *this* virtue of temperance. These are not contemptible or childish dispositions, even if they are dangerous and disturbing. In a public setting they may not even appear repulsive. Indeed, a pride and arrogance that in a private person would indeed seem both repulsive and mad can excite frenzied loyalty in the followers of a politician. Furthermore, such

[89] 'Lycidas'.  [90] II. 115–16, and 227.
[91] The idea is implicit in much of bk. viii, esp. negatively in the characterization of the democratic type, e.g. 555 D and 560 D–E.
[92] 'Alexander thinking it more princely for a king, as I suppose to conquer himself, than to overcome his enemies . . .' *Life of Alexander*, trans. North (London, 1899), p. 33.  [93] *Phenomenology*, sect. 511.

limitless self-esteem can be entirely rational if it goes with magnitude of achievement.

This may be an unattractive doctrine. Yet there is something deceitful in the opinion, common to moralists, that what is ugly and deformed in private life must also be unacceptable in the public sphere. Machiavelli understood this when he suggested, in effect, that the virtues will not necessarily make the man of *virtù*. Temperance manifestly is a quality which it is reasonable for everyone to cultivate. Yet if we try to extend it into areas to which some ancient thinkers thought it applicable—in particular, politics—then it can begin to look like a virtue that it is not always reasonable for everyone to cultivate. One may suggest (still more cynically) that what matters is success. An inordinate lust for power, when once the ambition has succeeded, can turn into the serene exercise of authority. One traditional view is (of course) that men of power tend to be corrupted by it. A less traditional view (which was that of Polus in the *Gorgias*) is that the belief that temperance is good for both private life and politics is, at best, a delusion.

# 4

## PRACTICAL WISDOM

KANT held that although happiness can be destroyed by fortune, moral goodness cannot. Since to be good is to have a certain disposition of will—the will to do the right for the sake of the right—moral goodness will not be vulnerable to the force of circumstance. It is clear why Kant said this. It seems intuitively right to most of us that we should not judge a person morally for what lies beyond his control. If he fails to do what is right through unavoidable ignorance, or external constraint, or because unforeseeable events produce disaster, we cannot judge him to be a bad man, or to have done wrong morally. So if a man kills a complete stranger at the crossroads who turns out to be his father whom he has never known, he cannot be blamed for his parricide. We might even go so far as to say—as Kant in effect did—that someone's possessing or lacking such desirable qualities as intelligence, benevolent feelings, or imagination cannot be relevant to the moral worth of his actions, or to his moral worth as an agent. Since morality is obligatory on all, it would be a kind of scandal, and derogation of justice, if only some were lucky enough to be capable of being morally good. Kant was not the first philosopher who sought for a human good that was not vulnerable to accident. Plato and the Stoics had done the same. But no one had gone as far as Kant in removing the contingent from the ethical life. The unchanging good which Plato offers to the philosopher could be achieved only after a rigorous intellectual ascent. Plato indeed assumed that this vision would be attainable by only a few—the Guardians—and would have to be imposed upon the rest by the institutions and laws of the State.[1] For the Stoics it was only the sage who could 'envisage circumstance all calm' and hence reach 'the top of sovereignty'.[2] Kant excludes the need of special training

[1] See Martha Nussbaum, 'Shame, Separateness, and Political Unity: Aristotle's Criticism of Plato', in Amelie Rorty (ed.), *Essays on Aristotle's Ethics* (Berkeley, 1980), pp. 395–427.   [2] Keats, *Hyperion*, ii. 204–5.

or exceptional intelligence, and makes moral goodness available to all, whatever their circumstances. If moral goodness is to be made independent of all accident, then it must be reduced to an inner act of the mind, or will, which can be thought of as entirely unconditioned. This Kant does. Anyone can aim to do the right for the sake of the right even if he can do hardly anything else at all. To aim to do the right for the sake of the right is to have a Good Will— the only thing which can possibly be conceived in the world, or even out of it, which can be called good without qualification.[3] Kant writes of the Good Will:

Even if it should happen that, by a particularly unfortunate fate or by the niggardly provision of a stepmotherly nature, this will should be wholly lacking in power to accomplish its purpose, and even if the greatest effort should not avail it to achieve anything of its end, and if there remained only the good will (not as a mere wish but as the summoning up of all the means in our power), it would sparkle like a jewel in its own right, as something that has its full worth in itself. Usefulness or fruitlessness can neither diminish nor augment this worth.[4]

Kant's determination to make moral goodness independent of 'the world', and even of man's 'empirical' nature, springs from his conviction of its supreme importance, and from a sense that it is impossible that what is obligatory on all might *in fact* be possible for only a few.

The doctrine that the true good for man is within his own power, because it can be gained by an act of his will, is one way of making human goodness invulnerable to circumstance. It is an egalitarian doctrine which insists that in regard to the most important thing in life, we all start off as equals. No doctrine has loomed larger in our moral, spiritual, and indeed political tradition. Among its consequences will be that a stupid man is as capable of being good as a clever one, since to have a good will does not depend upon special gifts or skills.

It is not surprising that many philosophers have considered that prudence—or, as I shall usually call it, practical wisdom—is not a virtue at all. As Kant himself put it: 'There are rules of skill, counsels of prudence, but *commands* of morality.'[5] And philosophers here reflect common opinion: to call a judgement 'prudential' is taken by many people as meaning that it is not 'moral'.

---

[3] *Fundamental Principles*, sect. i.      [4] Ibid., para. 3.
[5] Ibid., sect. ii.

Nothing could be more opposed to this in spirit than Aristotle's understanding of *phronesis*, practical wisdom. Intelligence is necessary to this virtue—which Aristotle indeed defines as an intellectual one—and *phronesis* is central to the good life. Aristotle's idea of *phronesis* is of a unity in man of reason and desire—*orexis dianoetike* or *orektikos nous* ('rational desire' or 'desiring reason'). Practical wisdom is 'a reasoned and true state of capacity to act with regard to human goods.'[6] It is neither a science, nor an art or skill. It involves deliberation not with regard to specialized goods (as the banker deliberates with regard to money) but about 'what sorts of thing conduce to the good life in general'.[7] Furthermore *phronesis* provides for Aristotle a principle of the unity of the virtues, in that all the other virtues imply, and employ, practical wisdom.[8]

It is clear then . . . that it is not possible to be good in the strict sense without practical wisdom, nor practically wise without moral virtue. But in this way we may also refute the dialectical argument whereby it might be contended that the virtues exist in separation from each other . . . This is possible in respect of those in respect of which a man is called without qualification good; for with the presence of the one quality, practical wisdom, will be given all the virtues.[9]

Aristotle also says that political and practical wisdom are the same state of mind, but their essence is not the same.[10]

Practical wisdom is not just the unproblematic applying of rules to a situation. It is an ability to 'see' what is at stake where the application of rules may not be at all obvious, and to know how to respond. It can go beyond knowing how to act. We can think of the man of practical wisdom as having moral imagination. The ability to imagine, to think outside received moral categories, which we find in many of Christ's parables, can be related to this virtue. The parable of the Prodigal Son brings into question any simple idea of desert for good deeds. Practical wisdom is also an ability to see when and how certain responses are called for, and being able to make them. It is an ability to know what moral (or prudential) principle to act by, and when; not to recognize it as the only one, but as decisive, or decisive in combination with other principles. And as I shall suggest later, practical wisdom can include boldness

---

[6] *Ethics*, 1140$^b$20–5.          [7] *Ethics*, 1140$^a$25–30.
[8] *Ethics*, 1144$^b$10–20.          [9] *Ethics*, 1144$^b$30–1145$^a$5.
[10] *Ethics*, 1141$^b$20–5.

and daring in bringing about the right outcome in a situation of difficulty or danger.

We all have the idea of a sensible man—the man of good judgement, who seems to get all sorts of things right, and not just things of which he has already had experience, or of which he has specialized knowledge. We are not surprised at the range of such a man's practical understanding. It will be revealed in his principles of conduct, and in his moral assessment of particular situations. It can be shown in financial dealings, in qualities of 'leadership', in appreciation of public affairs, in assessment of character. Such a man may also have various practical skills. Indeed, one would be surprised if a person of practical intelligence in large matters showed himself to be helpless in smaller ones. And the intelligence and good sense he shows seems to be the same sort of thing in all these different areas; it strikes us as just the sort of practical intelligence *he* would have. One can only appeal to common experience that such people do exist. If they do, they are men of practical wisdom. This is an idea which has been more or less lost to modern moral thought. How far can we go in reviving it?

## I ARTS AND SKILLS

Actions can express knowledge. I know how to tie up my shoe-laces, how to play the piano, how to ride a bicycle. My knowing how is expressed in action, and, in some cases, uniquely in action. My knowing how to ride a bicycle could perhaps not be expressed in words. And certainly my being unable to express my knowing how in language would not show that I did not truly know. Much practical knowledge is uniquely expressed in the particular action. I can show that I know how to play the 'Hammerklavier' only by playing it. It would not be possible to express the same practical knowledge by some other sort of action—like painting a landscape, or playing a violin sonata.

Some sorts of practical knowledge are skills—playing a musical instrument, or riding a bicycle, for example. Others are arts—medicine or seamanship. I shall go on to suggest that practical wisdom, being a virtue, is neither an art nor a skill. There is no art or skill of being prudent, any more than there is an art or skill of being brave. Nevertheless, it is useful to think of practical wisdom—unlike other virtues—in relation to both arts and skills.

One reason for thinking of practical wisdom as a virtue rather than an art or skill (or science) would be if it involved deliberation (as Aristotle says) not with regard to specialized goods, but about what sorts of thing conduce to the good life in general. But is the distinction quite so clear as this seems to suggest? Can we approach the idea of practical wisdom through arts and skills, and their contribution to a very general human good?

## i *Skills*

People are capable of taking pride in just about any skill. Men (i.e. males) are characteristically proud of being skilled with their hands; of knowing how machines work; of being knowledgeable about business and public affairs. Many men—perhaps the vast majority—would feel their masculinity called into question if they were useless at all these things. These skills are not thought of as just knacks, but as somehow revealing a masculine way of being-in-the-world. Men think that their practical skills, and their knowledge of the world, give them grounds for not having to denigrate themselves. A motor-mechanic, for instance, might feel that his is a masculine skill and occupation. In feeling this he does not have to believe that women are incapable of doing what he does, but only that he finds that his work somehow expresses and affirms his sense of his maleness. Traditionally, skills have been divided between the sexes. Women have taken—and the great majority still do take—an equivalent pride in their domestic skills, and have felt that they support their self-respect as women. But for both sexes, what seems the true basis for pride is that they are taken to make possible what is an undoubted human good: work.

A craftsman takes pride in his work. He takes pleasure in a thing well done; and others respect him for his skill. But how do we understand this pride and respect? Can we understand a man's pride in his work unless we can see that his work has meaning? Kant says this about *occupation*:

It is by his activities and not by enjoyment that man feels that he is alive. The busier we are the more we feel that we live and the more conscious we are of life. In idleness we not only feel that life is fleeting, but we also feel lifeless. Activity is part of life's substance . . . Life is the faculty of spontaneous activity, the awareness of all our human powers.

Kant also says that if life has been filled with play, 'memory will find it empty', and that 'time can be filled up only by action.'[11]

Although what Kant says has the ring of truth, it does not make plain how we should distinguish mere frenetic 'activity' (which can go with a life filled with play) and what he calls 'occupation'. We undoubtedly do feel that work (occupation) is of its nature humanly significant, and that some activities, however laborious, lack this significance. The definitive picture of insignificant labour is in the myth of Sysiphus. But what distinction are we making?

It will be generally agreed that the work of a craftsman is satisfying and has meaning for him. The work of a stonemason, a cabinet-maker, a dressmaker, a chef, obviously engages human energy and practical intelligence in a satisfying way. Perhaps we can say that a craftsman puts himself into his work and finds in the finished product an expression of his own activity. Hegel writes, in his *Aesthetics*, that man has the impulse to produce himself in external objects, and therein to recognize himself:

This aim he achieves by altering external things whereon he impresses the seal of his own inner being and in which he now finds again his own characteristics. Man does this in order, as a free subject, to strip the external world of its stubborn foreignness and to enjoy in the shape of things only an external realisation of himself. Even a child's first impulse involves this practical alteration of external things; a boy throws stones into the river and now marvels at the circles drawn in the water as an effect in which he gains an intuition of something that is his own doing.[12]

This reflects Hegel's expressivist theory of the human subject,[13] who achieves self-consciousness through theoretical and practical activity. For Hegel one of the highest modes of self-recognition is in the creation and appreciation of works of art. And we can see how this is a persuasive model of activity that obviously has intrinsic meaning. Indeed, many people would say that the satisfaction an artist has in his work is the paradigm of intrinsically meaningful human activity. The artist's self-expression has a peculiar whole-ness; it exhibits a remarkable fullness of human powers.

With this may go the conviction that forms of practical expression akin to the artist's, but less 'whole', may be less intrinsically meaningful. (And this idea that the work of art is the

---

[11] *Lectures on Ethics*, trans. Infield (New York, 1963), p. 160.
[12] *Aesthetics*, Introd., p. 31.　　　[13] See Taylor, *Hegel*, ch. 3.

paradigm of meaningful activity underlies the belief of the young Marx that some kinds of repetitive, mechanical work are dehumanizing and alienating.[14]) So in the case of a craftsman—for instance, a cabinet-maker—we might say that although the exercise of his skill engages and satisfies him, this does not guarantee that it is humanly satisfying when judged by some purportedly more objective criterion. If he is compelled by customer demand always to make furniture in execrable taste, or furniture that will soon fall to pieces, then there may be some doubt about how satisfying his work is, or should be. A tradition of thought, stemming from Hegel and early Marx, would hold that someone's pleasure in his work cannot be entirely detached from the actual human significance of what he does. He may take pleasure in a job well done, but this does not guarantee that he (unlike the artist) is not engaging in skilled, but useless labour.

Of course there are many other sorts of activity which seem intrinsically meaningful as well as useful. Man can celebrate and take pleasure in hunting, and represent it in painting, not simply as necessary for survival, but also as a way of life. Men have frequently thought of themselves simply *as* hunters. Hunting is strenuous and graceful, and sets the hunter against a fierce, or cunning, or fleet animal. Tribes of hunters can think of what they do as both laborious and as something to be celebrated in works of art.

The value of a skill is related to its social setting. A skilled man may make a very small but complex part of a very large machine. For reasons of security (let us imagine) he might have no idea of the significance of the part he makes to the machine as a whole, nor of the relation of his own work to the work of others employed on the project. His work is not mechanical, but on the contrary very intelligent and skilful. Yet his relation to the end-product is remote. If he is always and only employed in this sort of work, there could be some doubt about what sort of satisfaction he gets from it.

A watchmaker is (or used to be) responsible for the production of a complete watch from start to finish. His work is the expression of skill and intelligence, and he has truly put himself into his work. His immediate satisfaction in what he has done is comparable to that of the artist. When a worker knows how the whole machine

---

[14] See 'Estranged Labour', *Economic and Philosophic Manuscripts of 1844*, trans. Milligan (Moscow, 1959), p. 69.

functions, rather than how to make one cog in it, then he obviously has a higher sort of knowledge. There is a 'natural' hierarchy, in which the architectonic arts come higher than sheer skills. And the man who knows the whole machine knows what it is for—what social needs or demands it answers. He is in a position to have a fuller, more 'political' understanding of the significance of the work he does than has the man of one simple skill.[15]

## ii *Arts*

The same is true of arts (nearly all of which include what I have been calling 'skills'). It is characteristic of an art—and part of what we mean by the term—that one cannot possess or master it just by applying rules. Medicine, for instance, is an art. It is true that many people now think of medicine as purely a science. And it sometimes seems as though scientific methods—exhaustive testing of a patient's condition by machines, for instance—will replace the traditional physician's art of diagnosis. Yet although the art of diagnosis can be greatly assisted by science and technology, it seems that it still distinguishes a good from a mediocre doctor. The lack of the diagnostic art—and the lack of confidence that there can be such a thing—often leads to exhaustive tests being carried out unnecessarily, in order to eliminate possibilities that a good diagnostician might discount. The good or great physician will possess all the scientific and medical knowledge that is necessary, but beyond that he will have a gift, a quality of insight, an art which cannot be captured by a set of rules, and cannot be taught except by personal influence. (The physician Sir Luke Strett in James's *The Wings of the Dove*, who tries to persuade the sick Milly Theale to 'live', is an example.[16]) No one could learn to be a good physician

---

[15] I leave out, as beyond the scope of this book, the important question of the rewards of the craftsman. Suppose every watch is taken away from the watchmaker by his employer and sold for a great price, while he himself receives only a pittance. His work has still been the expression of skill and intelligence. He is, however, unable to enjoy the fruits of his labour. It might be argued that his subjective sense of the meaning and value of his work is an illusion. The expressivist theory of the subject, which runs from Hegel through to early Marx, might lead to the conclusion that the true description of the worker's situation is to be found not his subjective state of mind, but in such objective conditions as the nature of the work itself and the rewards it attracts. It might hold that in the light of the objective conditions, the satisfaction felt by the worker is a less than fully human satisfaction.

[16] Book Fifth, ch. 3.

from a book, but only by being the disciple of a good physician. The same applies—perhaps still more obviously—to becoming a great musician, rather than simply a skilful one. Everybody knows that the art a great teacher passes on to his pupils cannot be captured by a set of written precepts, but is much more like— indeed, is—the passing on of a tradition, a practice.

Arts are higher than skills, for an art presupposes and includes any number of skills. The art of being a cricket captain presupposes particular cricketing skills (i.e. no one could master the art of captaincy who could neither hit nor throw a ball). But the captain also has to judge tactics, to organize his field, know which bowlers to bring on and when, when to declare, how to judge a pitch. In this sense the art of captaincy embraces the skills of cricket. There is also a 'political' element in being a captain. He has to inspire confidence and respect, to have qualities of 'leadership', to be a judge of men. He cannot learn to be a good captain by studying and slavishly copying the tactics of past games. The art of captaincy cannot be reduced to a closed set of precepts, since new conditions are always arising. This is true of other arts which have a 'political' component. There are arts of leadership in war and in peace, which everyone can recognize, but which cannot be reduced to rules. One of the absurdities of Proust's Saint-Loup is that he constantly studies the art of war under the impression that it is a science, and as though modern generals can win battles by imitating the tactics of their predecessors. To attempt to express the art of war as though it were an exact science, rather than a set of precepts and *exempla*, from which only a talented general can learn, is to encourage commanders to lead their men to disaster. The most telling image is the art of politics. It has usually been thought that there is an art of statesmanship, an art which may distinguish the statesman from the mere 'politician'. But it is an art which can only be learned retrospectively. Those Bolsheviks who tried to decide whether Trotsky was Napoleon, and wondered who were going to be the Thermidorians of the Bolshevik Revolution, were taken grievously by surprise by the quite unforeseen, and new, phenom- enon of Stalin. Marxists have, of course, committed themselves to the view that a 'scientific' politics is possible. As is well known, the predictive power of the 'science' has been *nil*.

In the *Politics* Aristotle discusses the arts of household manage- ment, and of the acquisition and use of property. He explicitly uses political analogies to describe the relations between husband and wife, and parents and children. The husband in relation to his wife is like a statesman who, for the time being, rules over his fellow citizens. The father's rule over his children is like that of a king over his subjects.[17] These are not merely analogies: Aristotle really does seem to understand authority within the family in political terms. The art of household management (which he regards as a moral art) is an art of rule and of economics (or acquisition—'chrematistic'). Within such a household it would be easy to mark out a specific role for the wife. She will, for instance, have a particular role in educating and bringing up the children, one substantially independent of the father. Her role in chrematistic might be as far-reaching as it is in Proverbs:

> She seeketh wool, and flax, and worketh willingly with her hands . . .
> She considereth a field, and buyeth it: with the fruit of her hands she planteth a vineyard . . .
> She perceiveth that her merchandise is good: her candle goeth not out by night.
> She layeth her hands to the spindle, and her hands hold the distaff . . .[18]

In all this she too will exercise an art, and one which cannot be codified. (Proverbs does not codify what the virtuous wife does; rather it gives examples, each one of which illuminates a wifely virtue.) In the *Oeconomicus* Xenophon has Socrates lay out in some detail exactly how the wife rules over the household economy, exercising a wifely chrematistic which is equal to the husband's in importance.[19] To argue whether or not any such distinction between the sexes, in the exercise of arts, is right is to miss the point. What is important is that the arts of private life can have a 'political' component. (Clearly this is easier to assert if one believes, as Aristotle did, that the household can be described in directly political terms. This can include organizing the different spheres of human life—in the family, for instance—where sexual roles will seem natural.)

We have been reflecting on the arts appropriate to (*a*) an individual, (*b*) a family, and (*c*) the State. There is a hierarchy from skills to arts, which include skills, and one within arts themselves.

---

[17] *Politics*, 1458$^a$40–1259$^b$10. Aristotle says that the husband is permanently in the position that the statesman temporarily is.  [18] 31: 13, 16, 18–19.
[19] Bks. vii–viii.

All these arts reveal and depend upon an application of practical wisdom. In all cases what the man of practical wisdom would do is the best guide. We cannot lay down a rule how to behave which would be a substitute for 'what the man of practical wisdom would do'. The wisdom that the Book of Proverbs recommends throughout is to be attained by those who 'listen', 'hear', 'receive the instruction', and who are not 'fools'. To acquire it one has to have a certain character.

The possible hierarchy among arts is a tentative suggestion. It depends upon our assenting to some sort of primacy for the political realm, and upon there being an art of politics. It cannot be assumed that there will be general agreement on both these points.

So although it is right to say that practical wisdom is not a skill, in the sense that being able to tie up one's shoe-laces is a skill, it *is* like an art. It is especially akin to those arts which we can think of as, in one way or another, both expressing character, and exercising those various capacities which I have summed up with the word 'political'.

## II INTELLIGENT GOODNESS

### i *Knowing and Not Knowing*

We sometimes seem to lose our practical knowledge; and sometimes it seems to fail us. This applies to both arts and skills. A politician, after a successful career controlling, or at least riding, events may suddenly find he is overwhelmed by trivial misfortunes. (This happened to Harold Macmillan in 1963–4.) Or a tennis player may find that he has lost his old ability to foresee where his opponent will return his serve. We can also lose our skills by not exercising them. There are some sorts of 'knowing how' which are not simply skills (like playing tennis), but include propositional knowledge—being able to speak one's native language, for instance. People do sometimes forget their native language when they have not spoken it for many years. But it is next to impossible to imagine how someone could forget how to *speak*. All sorts of circumstances may prevent our bringing to mind what we in fact know. Sheer fright may make an examination candidate unable to set down on paper what he knew perfectly well before he went into the examination room, and will know equally well when he comes out.

Stage fright may make an actor forget his lines; a nervous pianist may simply forget how a piece goes on. Being a pianist, as a practical skill, involves being able to remember (quasi-propositionally) the details of a piece. Therefore a failure in propositional knowledge (forgetting what comes next) is akin to forgetting how to act. But these momentary lapses do not mean that the actor has lost the skill of acting, or the pianist the skill of playing the piano.

These lapses in knowing how are, then, different from each other. But we can say of all of them that they do not necessarily indicate something about a man's character, except, perhaps, that some people are less self-possessed than others. (This is not to deny that some people show heroic self-possession, and that this can reveal character. A pianist who forgot his piece because a pistol was let off just behind his head would not lack self-possession. But if he remained calm and did not forget his piece, we might think him remarkably self-possessed, and perhaps brave.)

Are there cases where failure in practical knowledge does reveal something about someone's character? Suppose someone has received a great benefit from another, and is extremely pleased at what has been done for him, but fails to express gratitude, and fails to feel grateful. What would we say about him? Let us assume that he knows about gratitude, and has, in general, a good grasp of when it is appropriate to show it. Let us suppose also that in this case we could, by going through the facts, easily convince him that he does owe a debt of gratitude. He simply did not think of it.

Some people fail to express, or to feel, gratitude simply because they are ill-bred. There is no doubt but that to express and feel gratitude is connected with good manners. And heartfelt gratefulness shades over into purely conventional expressions of thanks. (Similarly true remorse shades over into quite easy expressions of apology. The upper classes perhaps find graceful apology easier than do the lower classes. This does not mean that they are more sincere.) There can, in other words, be a skill in being grateful, being sorry, feeling sorry for others. Indeed, a truly civilized code of manners will to a considerable extent replace, or at least massively supplement, rough and spontaneous sincerity.

Nevertheless, someone who simply fails to realize that he should be grateful, or sorry, to whom gratitude or apology (or remorse) has genuinely not occurred, may in this reveal something of his character. He may be so selfishly occupied with the good he has received, that he can think of nothing else. Or he may be so accustomed to receiving benefits—as is a spoiled child—that he has no practical understanding of the sacrifices others make to confer them. Or (in the case of apology) he may be so habituated to thinking well of himself, that it genuinely does not occur to him to consider that he may be wrong. This can even go so far as to prevent his acknowledging even to himself that he has committed a crime. Many criminals habitually lie, to the point at which they seem to have convinced themselves of their own innocence. We may say of a man that he cannot admit to himself what he has done. Indeed the confirmed liar is most likely to be someone who lies unconsciously. In a sense he does not know when he is lying.

The person who fails to realize that he should be grateful may not, then, simply lack a skill. His failure to think and to feel, when he is in a position to know what he should think and feel, seems like a defect of character. The man who regularly feels the appropriate gratitude is not someone with a special skill, but a grateful man. He has a keen sense of what has been done for him, of what it may have cost others, of the benevolence that has been shown him, of how unselfishly kind people sometimes are. To think these things on appropriate occasions is to feel grateful: they are the thoughts of a grateful person. The ungrateful man does not think like this. Gratitude is not a skill, and cannot be taught in the way a skill can be taught. Although one may learn the social grace of gracefully thanking those who have, say, provided one with a very good dinner, one cannot learn to be grateful without acquiring certain dispositions of thought and feeling. Gratitude is directed not simply at the actions, but at the attitudes of those to whom one is grateful. A good deed done me unintentionally would not earn my gratitude. But only a certain sort of person habitually brings to mind the good intentions and unselfishness of others. He is a man with some benevolence, with some sense that others besides himself have claims, and with a sense of justice. What he thinks is conditioned by how he feels; and what he feels is explained by how he thinks.

The man who owes an obligation of gratitude and who, through inadvertence, or egoism, or levity, is genuinely unaware of his obligation, behaves (one might say) ignorantly. Yet he is in a position to know. And in a sense he does know, because he knows all the facts that the grateful man knows. Aristotle distinguishes between the man who acts *from* ignorance, and the man who acts *in* ignorance.[20] Oedipus, who could not possibly know that the man he was about to kill was his father, and the woman he was about to marry was his mother, acted from ignorance. But a man who acts in such a passion that what he knows is driven from his head acts in ignorance. Aristotle considers that actions from ignorance are excusable, whereas actions in ignorance are not. The distinction may be less clear in practice than it sounds in principle. Othello murders Desdemona in the erroneous belief that she is an adulteress. He has been presented by Iago with evidence that seems to him conclusive. Yet is he (as some critics have argued) only too ready to believe Iago, because he is only too ready to be jealous? It could be that the evidence convinces Othello only because there is something corrupt or too self-regarding in his attitude to her. If he really loved her, would he not silence Iago rather than immediately insist on hearing all his 'suspicions'?

Obviously the ungrateful man does not act from ignorance if he knows all the facts which should lead him to be grateful. Can we say that he acts in ignorance? We can do so in cases where his unawareness of what he owes springs from his selfishness, his unwillingness to acknowledge his dependence on others, his lack of interest in the attitudes of those who do good to him. If he simply lacks moral imagination, this could be because his habits of mind are selfish. Even had he been brought up to assume that others should make the world a comfortable place for him—as a spoiled child assumes—I am not sure that we could say he acts from ignorance. His character has developed in such a way that he has a false and egoistic view of the world. He may not be able to help himself thinking like this, but he nevertheless has a vicious character. There is no difference here from a character that might have been formed by years of vicious living. There is a characteristic forgetting, or inadvertence, or negligence where a man acts, or fails to act without bringing to mind what he knows, and where such 'ignorance' does not excuse.

In discussing gratitude I have been treating practical wisdom as (one might say) a virtue which informs other virtues. It could well be argued[21] that gratitude is a 'part' of justice, rather than an example of practical wisdom. Nevertheless, being disposed to be grateful how and when one should, and seeing that justice requires

---

[20] *Ethics*, 1110$^b$15–1111$^b$5.

[21] As it is by Aquinas, *Summa*, 2a2ae, 106, 1.

it in just these circumstances, is to manifest practical wisdom. This goes with Aristotle's remark that practical wisdom enters into all the moral virtues.[22]

Someone who through instinctive or habitual egoism fails to feel gratitude acts in ignorance. We can make a comparison with negligence. I am negligent if I fail to attend to what I am doing, so that some harm occurs. It may be that because I was day-dreaming, or bored, I genuinely did not have in mind what I ought to be doing. Hence I acted inadvertently. But although that means that I cannot be accused of (for instance) malice, I cannot be wholly excused. I was in a position to attend to what I was doing, and I failed to do what I could and should have done because I allowed my thoughts to wander. A surgeon who habitually operates without negligence is not just a man with certain skills—although he certainly is that. He is also someone who concentrates upon what he is doing, rather than let his thoughts wander on to what he hopes to do when he goes off duty; he subjects himself to habitual discipline, which might well go against his natural inclinations. Perhaps he cares about his patients, and regards what he is doing as not just a job but a vocation. This surgeon's always knowing what he is about—his successful application of his practical knowledge in the form of skills—is the outcome of virtuous dispositions—dedication to duty, strength of purpose, resistance to various pleasures which would distract him, and also (one hopes) an habitual benevolence towards those who fall under his care.

We can, then, fail to bring to mind what we know, when we are under the influence of various temptations and pleasures. We act inadvertently, negligently, recklessly, absent-mindedly, thoughtlessly, insensitively; and also callously, basely, crudely, and unjustly. Can we say what sort of knowledge can be lost in this way? Can pleasures and other temptations deprive us of knowledge of fact? Certainly they sometimes can. If I am tempted to drink one glass of wine too many, I may fail to bring to mind what I certainly know—that excessive wine gives me a hangover. More importantly, perhaps, I may fail to bring to mind my serious conviction that sobriety is good. Aristotle—attempting to explain, in opposition to Socrates, how *akrasia* is possible—suggests that I act in ignorance when, overcome by pleasure, I fail to bring the universal principle

---

[22] *Ethics*, 1144$^b$30–1145$^a$5.

'Sobriety is good' to bear upon my particular case. So practically speaking, I act *in* ignorance.[23] As Donald Davidson sugests,[24] Aquinas gives a more plausible description of such action in ignorance than does Aristotle. He says, in effect, that when I am tempted to drink too much, it is not that I fail to bring my action under a universal principle—'Sobriety is good'—but that I bring it under a universal principle that allows me to drink in good conscience: e.g. 'Sociability is good'. I fail to allow what I know to enter into my deliberations. But it is only when I should be deliberating that I can be induced in this way by pleasure (among other things) to fail to bring to mind what I really know. And a thoroughly corrupt person will go so far as to adopt wrong moral principles which fit his desires. Again, someone who has a strong wish to consider himself (say) intellectually superior to another may habitually turn his attention away from all the evidence that would contradict his conceit of himself.

There are many examples of practical knowledge which it is difficult to imagine going out of one's mind because one is overcome by pleasure: e.g. knowing which shutter-speed to choose when taking a photograph. But there is much practical knowledge that *is* vulnerable. There are, for instance, all those cases where my seeing what should be done goes with my attitudes—with my being considerate, benevolent, unselfish, imaginative. Cases where I realize that I should be grateful, or that I should apologize, or that I should recognize someone else's claims as well as my own; or that this is the honourable, but difficult thing to do; or that this is the brave, but fearful thing to do—all these would be examples.

We can surely imagine someone whose emotions and appetites are well ordered, whose egoism is under control, whose *amour propre* and wilfulness are tempered, and who, as a result, does not act 'in ignorance'. This might be a man of practical wisdom. In describing him we are not describing someone with special skills, but someone whose ability to deliberate correctly, to bring what he knows to bear on what he has to decide, is part of his moral character. Some knowing depends upon character and well-ordered passions; it is (in Aristotle's words) 'preserved by temperance'.[25] *Phronesis* refers to a state of knowing that can be dimmed by

---

[23] *Ethics*, $1110^b1–1111^a5$.
[24] How is Weakness of Will Possible?', in Joel Feinberg (ed.), *Moral Concepts* (Oxford, 1969), pp. 93–113.  [25] *Ethics*, $1140^b10–15$.

egoism and wilfulness, and (as Aristotle says) by pleasures and pains: 'For it is not any and every judgement that pleasant and painful objects destroy and pervert, e.g. the judgement that the triangle has or has not its angles equal to two right angles, but only judgements about what is to be done.'[26] So that sort of practical knowledge which we could call practical *wisdom* is preserved by temperance. Aristotle writes: 'This is why we call temperance [*sophrosyne*] by this name; we imply that it preserves one's practical wisdom [*sozousa ten phronesin*].'[27]

However, I shall later go on to suggest that although practical wisdom is best thought of as supervenient on virtuous dispositions, it would really be too restrictive to say (as Aristotle seems to say) that temperance is the only virtue which sustains it. That would make practical wisdom into a timid, cautious virtue, which it may not be. As we shall see, it can also spring from boldness, and even excess.

## ii *Intelligent Goodness*

There is reason to think that intelligence may be relevant to moral goodness, and may even sometimes be a moral quality. I shall explore this idea further by reflecting on a writer to whose moral outlook a virtue very like *phronesis* is important: Jane Austen.[28] If we sketch the ethic implied in Jane Austen's novels, we find something like the following: moral goodness requires the disciplining of our imagination by objective truth. It implies judgement and analytical skill. An appropriate choice of husband or wife is a central sign of the coming together of private and public. Practical wisdom, which is a necessary condition of moral goodness, is undermined and rendered nugatory by selfishness, insincerity, dishonesty, and pride. To understand is not necessarily to pardon.

If these are indeed features central to Jane Austen's ethic then she is what Marilyn Butler calls her—a conservative writer.[29] Jane Austen rejects beliefs central to such Sentimentalist writers as Hume and Adam Smith, who assume an innate goodness in man, and place weight exclusively upon benevolent sentiments as the

---

[26] *Ethics*, $1140^b10{-}20$.    [27] Ibid.

[28] What I say will be influenced by Marilyn Butler's stimulating book, *Jane Austen and the War of Ideas* (Oxford, 1974). See also my review of this: 'Practical Wisdom', *Essays in Criticism*, 27 (Oct. 1977), 348–54.

[29] Butler, *Jane Austen*, p. 165.

basis of moral goodness. The Sentimentalist tradition prizes passive states of feeling above the cultivation of active habits, and underplays the need to cultivate a realistic view of the world. Let us briefly test these ideas in relation to *Mansfield Park* and *Emma*. *Mansfield Park* maintains a balance between subjective and objective, 'really good feelings'[30] and moral judgement. After Fanny Price has been attacked by Mrs Norris for refusing to join in the theatricals '. . . very ungrateful indeed, considering who and what she is'), Mary Crawford immediately moves to comfort her, and 'the really good feelings by which she was almost purely governed, were rapidly restoring to her all the little she had lost in Edmund's favour.'[31] The 'really good feelings' which govern Mary Crawford can go at the same time with self-will and cynicism. Principle is one of the things which the novel sets against 'really good feelings'. Principle is what Edmund finally appeals to in upholding the position of the clergy, at Sotherton:

I cannot call that situation nothing, which has the charge of all that is of the first importance to mankind, individually or collectively considered, temporally and eternally—which has the guardianship of religion and morals, and consequently of the manners that result from their influence . . . The manners I speak of, might rather be called conduct, perhaps, the result of good principles . . .[32]

Towards the end of *Mansfield Park*, when Henry Crawford sincerely wishes to marry Fanny, he reflects upon her 'charms'—her 'beauty of face and figure', her 'gentleness, modesty, and sweetness of character, her understanding and manners'. But then:

Nor was that all. Henry Crawford had too much sense not to feel the worth of good principles in a wife, though he was too little accustomed to serious reflection to know them by their proper name; but when he talked of her having such a steadiness and regularity of conduct, such a high notion of honour, and such an observance of decorum as might warrant any man in the fullest dependence on her faith and integrity, he expressed what was inspired by the knowledge of her being well principled and religious.[33]

Marilyn Butler describes this by saying that in Jane Austen 'the moral human being wages war with the natural human being'.[34] The natural human being is man as a creature of passive sensation delineated by Hume, and by the Sentimentalist writers. There is no

---

doubt but that *Mansfield Park* dramatizes, amongst other things, a conflict which can illuminatingly be described, as Marilyn Butler describes it, in terms of a clash between an ethic of sentiment, which prizes 'really good feelings', and an ethic of active effort that lays stress on one's ability to analyse a situation correctly, and to arrive at the right conclusions for action. In the theatricals episode, only Fanny reads the play through in such a way as to have a clear sense of it as a whole,[35] and to realize that it is quite unsuitable to be performed. Mary Crawford is blind to the effect her words have upon others, and to what others can see. Speaking of her acquaintance with admirals, she says to Edmund: 'Of *Rears* and *Vices*, I saw enough. Now do not be suspecting me of a pun, I entreat.' Edmund again felt grave, and only replied, 'It is a noble profession.'[36]

Mary has struck the wrong note. At Sotherton Mary is pertinacious in failing to detect Edmund's feelings, and is therefore quite unaware of the impression she is making on him—which is quite the opposite of what she would wish.

Can one say anything in general about what makes it possible for one to be honest with oneself? It is not a matter of intelligence alone. We must also strive to see ourselves objectively, rather than simply to prefer our own valuation of ourselves. Self-knowledge has to include some sensitivity to others, some acknowledgement that they too have claims. Correspondingly, self-deception also attempts to deceive others. Johnson expressed this well in writing of self-love:

Self-love is often rather arrogant than blind; it does not hide our faults, but persuades us that they escape the notice of others, and disposes us to resent censures lest we should confess them to be just. We are secretly conscious of defects and vices which we hope to conceal from the public eye, and please ourselves with innumerable impostures, by which, in reality, no body is deceived.[37]

Lack of self-knowledge is not simply a passive state, but reflects one's attitudes towards others. One of Emma's most important moments of self-awareness comes when she is rebuked by Mr Knightley for her rudeness to Miss Bates. In rebuking her he appeals to her generous feelings, but as informed by her awareness of social facts:

[35] *Jane Austen*, p. 230.  [36] *Mansfield Park*, ch. 6.
[37] *The Rambler*, No. 155.

'How could you be so unfeeling to Miss Bates? How could you be so insolent in your wit to a woman of her character, age, and situation? . . . Were she your equal in situation—but, Emma, consider how far this is from being the case. She is poor; she has sunk from the comforts she was born to; and, if she live to old age, must probably sink more. Her situation should secure your compassion.'[38]

Emma's response is not only shame, but also active anger towards herself.[39] The coming together of subjective and objective is shown most clearly in her choice of a husband. Her active, self-accusing acceptance of Mr Knightley's rebuke sets in train the line of thought and feeling which (assisted by Harriet Smith's attachment to Mr Knightley) issues in the conviction that 'darted through her with the speed of an arrow that Mr Knightley must marry no one but herself!'[40] Emma's love for Mr Knightley has something to do with her sense of his moral rightness and authority.

Moral goodness in Jane Austen is not something independent of active intelligence. Emma's desire for truth is frequently in danger of being undermined by egoism, just as it is supported by qualities such as sincerity, honesty, and directness. It is precisely this vision of the combination of knowledge and feeling as essential to moral goodness that makes sense of Jane Austen's valuing of the active and analytical as against passive feeling.

In *Emma* the perception of truth is shown to depend upon moral qualities, and can be presented in terms of character. And the capacity of a character to be objective is shown through dialogue. Language enacts the difference between the false and the true. For all her faults, Emma is essentially sincere, and honest with herself, and this comes out in how she speaks. As Butler puts it:

Her behaviour to her father is consistently selfless, and she seems quite unaware of it. But the fact that it is characteristic for her to think unselfishly and outwardly is best conveyed in the rhythms of her speech, its frankness and decisiveness, its quality of being immediately directed at the other person present. The comic characters are monologuists, whereas Emma, like Mr Knightley, is supreme in dialogue:

'Whom are you going to dance with?' asked Mr Knightley.
She hesitated a moment, and then replied, 'With you, if you will ask me.'[41]

Emma's inner speech is also usually direct, enacting truth and

---

[38] *Emma*, ch. 43.    [39] Ibid.
[40] Ch. 47.    [41] *Jane Austen*, p. 272, quoting *Emma*, ch. 38.

sincerity. When she is dishonest this also shows itself in her inner speech. Emma's frequent inability to see clearly, to grasp the truth, is therefore a matter of will, intention, and moral failure. In Jane Austen 'it is a moral virtue to be able to receive external evidence.'[42] I have already suggested that if *phronesis* is indeed necessary for morality, then a fool may not be morally good. Stupid characters are not truly good in Jane Austen, since goodness (as Marilyn Butler writes) is 'an active, analytical process, not at all the same thing as passive good nature.'[43] The sign of such analytical ability may well be linguistic. Comic characters like Miss Bates do not communicate; rather they 'surround themselves with a web of words which convey their own selfhood, their own individuality, and make little or no impact upon the consciousness of others.'[44] This leads us back to Emma's real moral goodness: she *can* speak directly—as she does at the ball to Mr Knightley—and her habitual frankness is a sign of her readiness to expose herself to reality.

It is essential to self-knowledge that one be able to take an active attitude to oneself. One has to be capable of frankness with oneself, angry with oneself, ashamed and proud of oneself. Emma weeps with chagrin after Mr Knightley has rebuked her. Her ability to be remorseful and angry with herself is the condition of her seeing the truth in what he has said. To be angry with oneself is to adopt something like an impersonal point of view. This objectivity is shown in the frankness of one's inner dialogue, which is the shadow of one's frankness with others in one's spoken dialogue. The language of self-accusation is also the language of apology.

I should at this point acknowledge that in invoking two novels of Jane Austen as examples, I have grievously simplified them. For Jane Austen is not simply a moralist of principle, strenuous self-knowledge, and active habits of reflection. She is also a novelist who is exceptionally able to portray states of 'passive feeling'. Emma, throughout all the time when she lacks self-knowledge, all the time when she misinterprets one situation after another, is extremely likeable and attractive. It would be wrong to suggest that we can understand Emma as a moral being whilst discounting all that makes her attractive. And Fanny, for all her rightness of principle, and all her ability to understand how the theatricals are wrong, is not very attractive. And where Fanny *is* attractive, this has much to do with those states of 'passive feeling'—for instance,

---

[42] Butler, *Jane Austen*, p. 271.          [43] Ibid.          [44] Ibid.

her shyness, her weakness, her being so often a victim, even her jealousy of Mary Crawford's interest in Edmund—which soften the impression of her excruciating rightness. But this surely reminds us that although it is right to think of virtues in the abstract, our actual experience of them will never have the simplicity of textbook examples. Perhaps one reason why *Emma* is incomparably the greatest of Jane Austen's novels is that the narrative structure of concealment, misapprehension, and revelation shows self-knowledge and objectivity as they actually emerge into consciousness.[45]

Can one adopt the external point of view simply through a canny knowledge of what others are likely to think and feel, even though one has no respect whatsoever for their attitudes? Suppose I believe that I feel moral disapproval of a sexually licentious friend, when really I am consumed with envy at his success. Could I become aware of my jealousy simply by realizing that other people believe that I am jealous? Perhaps not. It is more likely that we only deceive ourselves when we are ashamed of the feeling we hide from ourselves, and that in deceiving ourselves we actually adopt the *values* of the disinterested observer, as well as his viewpoint, and that we wish also to deceive him. Johnson suggests that self-deception always does involve a resentful but ashamed awareness of the judgement of others. He writes of advice:

Advice is offensive, not because it lays us open to unsuspected regrets, or convicts us of any fault which had escaped our notice, but because it shows us that we are known to others as well as to ourselves; and the officious monitor is persecuted with hatred, not because his accusation is false, but because he assumes that superiority which we are not willing to grant him, and has dared to detect what we desired to conceal.[46]

One might say that honesty with oneself entails setting limits to one's *amour propre*, and hence curbing one's innate tendency to weight judgements in favour of oneself. Self-deception, like self-will, involves setting oneself against others, and not simply being attached to one's own view of things. Self-knowledge and self-deception have a social context, and imply what is right and wrong in one's relations with others. The man with self-knowledge is frank and honest towards others, shows due respect, does not always make special allowances for himself, takes others seriously

---

[45] I owe this to Colin Burrow.    [46] *The Rambler*, No. 155.

as persons. This means both that self-knowledge issues from certain qualities of character, and also that it is practical—it grows out of one's social life. The man who knows himself is not one who contemplates himself steadily, but one whose character disposes him to certain relations with others.

Self-knowledge is perhaps a necessary condition of intelligent goodness. Unacknowledged self-love, envy, or malice may prevent one from entering imaginatively into the feelings of others, or understanding their claims. Beyond that, it may well be that there are qualities of sheer intelligence and imagination which are necessary if one is to treat others well, but which an ordinary good man, bound, perhaps, by the traditions of his upbringing, will simply be unable to command. The parable of the Good Samaritan is, precisely, addressed to such ordinary good men, and aims to persuade them radically to re-examine their understanding of their moral duties. Ordinary intelligent goodness would not enable a man to think in the terms of such a parable. It would certainly not inspire him to invent it.

### III DOCILITAS

Aquinas includes *docilitas*, or 'teachability', as a part of prudence.[47] He quotes Aristotle's opinion that 'the unproved assertions and opinions of experienced, old, and sagacious people deserve as much attention as those they support by proofs, for they grasp principles through experience.'[48] In other words, 'opinions' are part of the 'phenomena' which Aristotle wishes to save.[49] Aquinas also says that although nature makes us apt to be taught, the fullest *docilitas* calls for much effort, that of a man 'who carefully, frequently, and respectfully attends to the teaching of men of weight [*majorum*—perhaps, also, "elders"] and neither neglects them out of laziness nor despises them out of pride.'[50] Furthermore, 'by prudence a man commands not only others but also himself.'[51]

It would be easy to interpret this as meaning that the man of *docilitas* is traditional, conservative, respectful of authority, and—

[47] *Summa*, 2a2ae, 49, 3.　　　　　　　　　　[48] *Ethics*, 1143$^b$10–15.
[49] See Martha Nussbaum, *The Fragility of Goodness* (Cambridge, 1986), pp. 240 ff.　　　　　　　　　　[50] *Summa*, 2a2ae, 49, 3.
[51] Ibid. and 2a2ae, 47, 12.

well—*docile*. But we do not have to understand teachability in this way. Indeed, docility and ductility may actually war against the true virtue of *docilitas*.

We notice that Aristotle says that the reason why the unproved assertions of old and sagacious people deserve attention is that 'they grasp principles through experience.' Grasping principles through experience is essential to those arts and skills which form a context in which we understand practical wisdom. A teacher is needed who, through his personal influence and example, passes on a tradition of practice. What can be described in textbooks is only an abbreviation of what is learned in experience from the teacher. Tradition, or something like it, is essential to passing on and acquiring arts and skills.

As we saw, Aristotle says that political and practical wisdom are the same state of mind, but their essence is not the same.[52] Politics is essentially a practice. An understanding of politics which makes it, in effect, 'the same state of mind' as *phronesis* is that of Michael Oakeshott in his celebrated lecture 'Political Education'.[53] Oakeshott defines politics as 'the activity of attending to the general arrangements of a set of people whom chance or choice have brought together,' and particularly of 'hereditary, co-operative groups, many of them of ancient lineage . . . which we call "states".' For Oakeshott, this 'attending to' arrangements is something quite different from *inventing* arrangements, from founding politics upon some abstract theory, such as 'democracy' or 'the rights of man' or 'scientific materialism'. There cannot be political beliefs outside an actual political tradition, any more than there could be a scientific theory outside a tradition of experimental science, or cookery books without an actual practice of cuisine. One cannot found one's politics upon such principles as 'freedom', or 'democracy', or 'social justice' because these ideas themselves have meaning only as an 'abbreviation' of the practices and attitudes of an actual (perhaps 'hereditary') tradition. It does not follow from what Oakeshott says that one cannot reasonably use such words at all. When English statesmen have talked of freedom, for instance, they have not been invoking a purely theoretical idea, but invoking specific traditions, traditions which

---

[52] *Ethics*, 1141$^b$20–5.
[53] In *Rationalism in Politics* (London, 1962), pp. 111–36.

are involved in English history and enshrined in the English common law.

So the virtue of *docilitas* in political education will not (on a view such as Oakeshott's) be an ability to grasp principles 'scientifically'. Attempts to define political principles are anyway really abstracts of already existing traditions of practice. (It is only within an already existing tradition of practice that attempts can be made to theorize the practice.) Political education is practical rather than theoretical, and is, not accidentally but necessarily, a matter of engaging with a tradition.

This does not mean that the tradition cannot be criticized. To engage with a tradition may be radically to reassess it. But the tradition has to exist as the condition (at the very least) of 'directed negation'.[54] The idea of a tradition here is not that of an object of reverence, but as the precondition for any structured understanding.

There is, perhaps, a continuum in the possibilities of criticism of and innovation in a tradition from (say) the law at one end to the arts at the other. Judges in the past were more creative than they are today, within the common law tradition. But they always interpreted the law in the light of and with an eye to precedent. To cease to do that would be to cease to occupy the role of judge. Newman argued for something similar, but weaker, in the case of development of doctrine. He sought to discover the marks which distinguished a true doctrinal development from innovation (and heresy).[55] Catholic traditionalists can argue today over whether some modern theologians have departed so far from tradition as to be inventing new doctrines rather than developing old ones. But again, no one could suggest that it is possible to be a Christian theologian *de novo*, outside of any canons of theological interpretation.

One might point to the arts for a different emphasis. Lutyens was a classicist in architecture. But he radically recast the 'language' of the classical orders into something quite unexpected and (at first sight) scarcely classical at all. But admirers of Lutyens will argue that his buildings breathe more of the classical spirit than do those of some more superficially 'correct' contemporary classicists. Finally, Wagner, in *Parsifal*, gives an essentially sexual interpretation to Christian renunciation of the self. Because of this, many have

---

[54] See F. R. Leavis, 'Swift', *The Common Pursuit* (Harmondsworth, 1962), p. 75.

[55] *An Essay on the Development of Christian Doctrine* (New York, 1968), pp. 169–206.

never accepted that he produced an interpretation of Christian experience. Those who find the opera fully successful may well argue that it is precisely what shocks in *Parsifal* that makes it a genuinely modern version of a Christian theme, rather than a piece of historical reconstruction. 'Sensibility alters from generation to generation in everybody, whether we will or no; but expression is only altered by a man of genius.'[56] One of the happiest representations of this idea in art is the prize-song in *Die Meistersinger*. At first it is anarchic and rejected, then, still new and strange, but engaging with the tradition, it wins hearts.

A respectful attending to the words of our elders can also be a critical responsiveness to their words. To revolt against the elders, to find them not to live up to their own highest principles, to accuse them and rebuke them, can still be to manifest *docilitas*. This is not to cast them from one's memory. The idea of tradition can itself be radically reinterpreted to allow for the most radical reinterpretation. This is what T. S. Eliot did in suggesting that tradition has to be re-invented in every age, in accord with the expressive needs of each age.

We can also distinguish between an inert 'traditionalism' and 'tradition' by invoking Newman's distinction between 'notional' and 'real' comprehension and assent. The difference between real and notional comprehension is that the former is accompanied with emotion, or vitality. It engages our emotions and not only our abstract intellect. Similarly with real as distinct from notional assent. A child's faith in the veracity of its mother is real assent:

... though the child assents to his mother's veracity, without perhaps being conscious of his own act, nevertheless that particular assent of his has a force and life in it which the other assents have not, in so much as he apprehends the proposition, which is the subject of it, with greater keenness and energy than belongs to his apprehension of the others. Her veracity and authority is to him no abstract truth or item of general knowledge, but is bound up with that image and love of her person which is part of himself, and makes direct claim on him for his summary assent to her general teaching.[57]

Again, a man might have an antiquarian or Romantic interest in an aristocratic ethic of honour (as Don Quixote did). He may argue

[56] T. S. Eliot, Introduction to Samuel Johnson, 'London: A Poem' and 'The Vanity of Human Wishes' (London, 1930), pp. 9–17.
[57] John Henry Newman, *A Grammar of Assent*, ed. Ker (Oxford, 1985), p. 18.

for it, entertain its precepts in his writings. But *real* assent to an ethic of honour would require some imaginative recreation, or finding it possible to live such an ethic without becoming a solipsist like Don Quixote. Alternatively, it can take the form of an ironic half-attachment, as it often does in Conrad.

Real assent tests our actual, living engagement in a tradition. And it tests the tradition against our need to find in it something alive. A sign of real assent could indeed be extreme impatience with what are taken to be fossilizations, or trivializations, or perversions of the tradition.

The man of practical wisdom cannot be imagined to exist outside of a tradition. He may be radical, but then he criticizes the tradition. Or in criticizing the tradition he may be 'traditionalist'— i.e. he may call for the tradition to be revivified. He may do what is unexpected; but he will not do what is random. When valves were added to trumpets, the capability of the instrument was increased, but the art of trumpet playing remained essentially the same. A cricket captain may start using spin bowlers much more freely than previously. But this innovation presupposes, and does not dispense with, the already existing arts of bowling and captaincy. The practice is still understood in relation to the arts of one's predecessors. And the respect for the experience of older people, which both Aristotle and Aquinas see as part of *phronesis*, is an analogous relation to one's 'predecessors'. Learning which principle of conduct applies in *this* situation, and its relative weight in relation to other principles; even knowing when what has seemed morally obvious is actually of little authority—all this is an exercise of wisdom which is not unlike the exercise of an art. Intelligent goodness does not spring fully disarmed from nowhere, but requires the support of a tradition of human life.

IV CONCLUSION: BOLD PRUDENCE

I suggested earlier that practical wisdom informs, and is the outcome of, other virtues. Following Aristotle I suggested that it is especially connected with temperance. This emphasis on temperance, combined with the fact that practical wisdom cannot be imagined as existing outside a tradition of practice, may make *phronesis* look like a timid, or inertly conservative, virtue. Is that right?

There is no reason to think of practical wisdom as a cautious virtue. Fabius's tactics of delay are not the only possible image of *phronesis*. The man of practical wisdom will, in some circumstances, be someone who knows how to take great risks. De Gaulle in 1940 was such a man. A statesman may act out of passionate conviction, rather than cautiously, and thereby do what turns out to have been wisest. Pericles was such a statesman. Another example would be someone who by background and experience would seem obviously not equipped for a task, yet who discovers extraordinary resources to carry the task through. For instance, Mrs Thatcher and the Anglo-Argentinian War. In other words, practical wisdom may often be the outcome of courage or ambition (Mrs Thatcher knew that if she did not prosecute the war, her administration would fall) more than of temperance. Machiavelli's *Discourses* is full of examples of men who by exceptional boldness (and cunning) rescue situations which on any conventional view would be hopeless. Indeed, Machiavelli makes a 'theory' out of all this in *The Prince*—that Fortune is female, and is most likely to fall in love with brave men.[58] Again, one may do the wisest thing from liberality or friendship. I do not refer just to cases where liberality is unexpectedly rewarded (e.g. Baucis and Philemon, sharing their humble fare with gods in disguise, are given divine rewards),[59] but also to those where motives of liberality and friendship help one to see what is to be done, what ought to be done. It is part of practical wisdom to know what is the correct moral principle to bring to bear upon a situation. Courage, generosity, and friendship may be as necessary for this as not being overcome by pleasure. Furthermore, an intellectual boldness or imaginativeness may be what is required to see and do the right thing.

Practical wisdom cannot, then, be understood just as a matter of following rules—which is how Kant would have us understand the moral life. Indeed, we cannot say that the man of practical wisdom is a good man just because he does what we can say in advance is good. For we also understand the good as being the sort of thing that the man of practical wisdom would choose. This is a way of saying what Mill says—that 'morality is not a science but an art',[60] and what Aristotle says—that practical wisdom is a virtue, and *not* an art.

[58] *The Prince*, ch. 25.     [59] Ovid, *Metamorphoses*, viii. 631 ff.
[60] *A System of Logic* (New York, 1950), bk. v, ch. 9.

# 5

## JUSTICE

### I DISPOSITIONS FOR JUSTICE

WE can think of certain virtues as overcoming particular weaknesses, and ordering particular appetites and emotions. The temperate man does not surrender to short-term satisfactions; he is not a slave to sensual pleasure; he is not overcome with sloth; he is not inordinately wilful. The brave man overcomes his fear of pain and death; he sees what would be the honourable or intelligent thing to do in the face of danger, and does it; he is capable of large loyalties. Practical wisdom is different. The practically wise man does not resist particular weaknesses; but his being practically wise depends upon his having various good dispositions, including temperance. But we can think of the *phronimos* as a particular sort of man.

Justice seems different. Not only does the just man not seem to be a particular sort of person; there does not seem to be any particular weakness that he overcomes, or any particular emotions and desires that his justice regulates. Rather justice seems to be the outcome of some very general harmony in a man's personality, and to denote the most general sort of moral goodness. Indeed, 'just' has often been a synonym for 'good': the centurion at the foot of the cross says: 'This was indeed a just man.'[1] Aristotle says that in one sense of 'justice' it may be taken as not a part of virtue, but as 'virtue entire'; and that in one sense of 'injustice' it may be taken as not a part of vice, but as 'vice entire'.[2]

Yet we can say something about how a just man will characteristically behave. He will not be overweeningly egoistic, instinctively subordinating the interests of others to his own. He will be capable of yielding, if there are good grounds for doing so. He will not pursue any and every gratification, regardless of the effect on

---

[1] Luke 23: 47 (Douai trans.). The AV has 'righteous'. The Greek is *dikaios*, and the Latin *justus*.  [2] *Ethics*, 1130$^a$5–10.

others. Equally he will not go in for unnecessary self-abasement, submission, endless humility, a yielding to any and every demand, unable to claim what is due to himself or to another. The just man will be capable of being stern, properly angry, and indignant. He will be interested in appropriate punishment. (Torquatus condemned his own son to death for treason.[3]) His justice may need to be tempered by mercy. He will judge equal cases equally.

Aristotle also says that justice, alone among the virtues, is thought to be 'another's good', because it is related to our neighbour. The best man is 'not he who exercises his virtue towards himself but he who exercises it towards another; for this is a difficult task.'[4] And this is why, for Aristotle, justice can be seen as virtue entire.

In discussing anger[5] I suggested that the angry man claims what is due to him, and that anger is indeed concerned with justice. In the words of Aquinas, 'anger and justice have the same object.'[6] A man may be justified in making a claim on his own behalf, as well as on behalf of another. It is true that we would not normally call someone who failed to claim what was his due 'unjust'. We think of the disposition to justice as being a readiness to acknowledge the claims of others, rather than a promptness on one's own behalf. It is this that is 'a difficult task'. Yet a man *should* know what are his own just claims. If moralists do not much talk of the vice of failing to do so, this is perhaps because it is uncommon.[7] Injustice is frequently a genuine failure to recognize the claims of others, a failure that results from a (frequently unconscious) preference for one's own interests. Attached as he may be to his own interests or passions, the unjust man may well act 'in ignorance'. Lear undoubtedly believes himself justified when he disinherits Cordelia, but this is because he is in a passionately egoistic rage. A failure to be just can, then, be very like a failure of practical wisdom. And as practical wisdom may require temperance, so may justice. Although anger may go with and support our sense of justice, it is also one of the passions most likely to darken it.

Let us begin with a simple example of a disposition to justice: gratitude. I have already discussed gratitude in connection with

---

[3] See Livy, bk. viii. 7.      [4] *Ethics*, 1130ᵃ5–10.
[5] See ch. 1, pp. 10–15 above.      [6] *Summa*, 1a2ae, 46, 7.
[7] Aristotle regards it as the vice of poor-spiritedness, or undue humility: *Ethics*, 1107ᵇ20–5.

practical wisdom. I suggested that a failure to feel gratitude may often be related to defects of character. Can something analogous be said about gratitude in relation to justice?

Gratitude is something which is justly owed, and which can be claimed. Someone entirely without a sense of justice (if he could be imagined) could neither feel grateful nor claim gratitude from others. This would be a profound deficiency. Gratitude is not simply the faithful fulfilment of a contract. Someone with no sense of justice could still understand his contractual obligations, and could have good reasons—for instance, of a utilitarian sort—for honouring the contract. Gratitude, like anger, is essentially directed at the attitudes of others, and not simply at their deeds. It is certainly a response to benefits received, but is not simply a pleasure in these benefits. If someone proposed to do something very wicked in order to benefit me—as Menas does in *Antony and Cleopatra*, when he offers to set a boat containing the triumvirs adrift in order to make young Pompey the master of the world— then even were I to be pleased at the results of his action, I might well not be grateful to him for it. I might see that what he has done is evil, and hence (if I am a righteous man) disapprove of his act, and at the same time feel grateful for the loyalty or benevolence it shows. A truly good man—a surpassingly good one, perhaps— would consider that the wickedness of the deed outweighed the love and loyalty it showed, and would not feel grateful at all. (In the face of Menas' offer, young Pompey shows himself to be a man of only modest rectitude: 'Ah, this thou shouldst have done, | And not have spoken on't! In me 'tis villainy, | In thee, 't had been good service.'[8]) Gratitude goes with approval of the benefactor's action, as well as pleasure in the benefit, so that where the act is wicked there ought at least to be a conflict in one's attitude. The conflict can arise also if one believes the benefactor to be unworthy of oneself. In *Great Expectations* Pip is horrified when he discovers that his benefactor is a convict.[9] Spinoza makes the connection between gratitude and personal response when he says that, whilst ingratitude is not itself an emotion, 'it is nevertheless base because it generally shows that a man is too much affected by hatred, anger, pride or avarice.'[10] Spinoza says that a stupid man who, because of his stupidity, does not know how to return a gift, is not ungrateful. But ingratitude is

---

[8] II. vii. 74–6.     [9] Ch. 39.     [10] *Ethics*, pt. IV, prop. 71.

characteristically related to the vices he mentions. If gratitude were simply a matter of knowing when it is expedient to honour a contract, then ingratitude would not arise from *these* defects of character. Hatred, anger, pride (although not, perhaps, avarice) make us unwilling to feel grateful to the person who has conferred the benefit; they would not prevent our rejoicing in the benefit itself, or in realizing that we should offer thanks publicly. Genuine gratitude requires that we approve of the act, and that we respond benevolently to the benevolence of the person conferring the benefit.

Our capacity for gratitude is, then, bound up with our capacity for benevolence. A primitive example of this is the baby's pleasure in being suckled. The child's characteristic smile of beatific contentment, which so much resembles an adult's expression of sexual contentment, is not just a sign of physical pleasure, but can be thought of as an expression also of gratitude. Byron describes several sorts of pleasure as though they are part of the same phenomenon:

> An infant when it gazes on the light,
>   A child the moment when it drains the breast,
> A devotee when soars the host in sight,
>   An Arab with a stranger for a guest,
> A sailor when the prize is struck in fight,
>   A miser filling his most hoarded chest
> Feel rapture; but not such true joy are reaping
> As they who watch o'er what they love while sleeping.[11]

Adopting an Hegelian emphasis on *telos* rather than *arche*, on (that is) the most developed rather than the most primitive description of this 'rapture', we can say that the most adequate description of what the child feels is not a description of what *children* feel. We can look on the child's expression of pleasure as being in a line of development to what, fully realized, involves personal recognition of the mother. Indeed, for the child to fail, as he grows older, to make the transition from something that most resembles physical contentment to something that is best described as love and gratitude, is for him to remain deeply unassuaged. (This description in terms of final causes is, of course, the opposite of the one which would be given by psychoanalysis, the assumption of

---

[11] *Don Juan*, Canto II, st. 196.

which is that the description of the feelings and activities of the young child is the royal road to understanding the behaviour and feelings of adults.) In using the word 'rapture' to describe such different feelings, Byron—with some irony, to be sure—exemplifies the point.

Spinoza says something about gratitude that leads on to our next topic: 'If we confer a favour . . . upon any one because of our love towards him, we do it with a desire by which we are possessed that we may be loved in return, that is to say . . . from the hope of self-exaltation . . .'.[12] Spinoza bases this idea of 'self-exaltation' upon his peculiar doctrine that joy goes with an enhancement of our powers. Yet perhaps we could be allowed to detach his remark from its metaphysical underpinning, and ask in what circumstances one characteristically looks for or demands gratitude when one has conferred a benefit upon another. Given the relation of gratitude to love and benevolence, can we say that when one confers a benefit out of love or benevolence, one looks for a return? Or that love itself seeks a return? Or should we say instead that the highest sort of love and benevolence is that which is purely disinterested, seeking no return whatsoever?

## II LOVE AND BENEVOLENCE

I earlier suggested that we can usefully distinguish between those emotions and attitudes which imply a claim upon (or recognition of a claim by) others, and those which do not. Those which do include anger, indignation, pride, shame, embarrassment, remorse, guilt, jealousy, and gratitude. Those which do not include hatred, envy, fear, hope, despair, covetousness, lust, grief, dejection, and pity. It may well seem that my discussion of moral psychology has tended to concentrate upon the darker side of human nature. Certainly I have as yet said nothing about an emotion that can scarcely be ignored in any account of human goodness, and the inclusion of which may lighten the picture slightly: love.

The empiricist tradition in philosophy has not been particularly eloquent about love. Descartes says that love is what we feel to what seems good or convenable to us, and hatred is what we feel to

---

[12] *Ethics*, pt. III, prop. 42.

its opposite.[13] Hobbes says that love is the same thing as desire, which he has already defined as 'endeavour'.[14] For Hume, love and hatred produce simple impressions, so that no definition of these passions can be given.[15] Love and hatred are traditionally taken together as complementary opposites; and I have already classed hatred among those emotions that do not imply a claim on others. So do we want to include love among those emotions and attitudes which we simply feel, and which do not imply a claim on others (or of others on ourselves) which we think justified? Or does love look for, and claim, a return?

Many people would undoubtedly say that a love which sought no return would be noble and unselfish, perhaps the highest love of all. The love of parent for child is one of the highest examples of selfless devotion. Spinoza also regarded disinterested, selfless love as the highest form of love, for it is necessary to *amor intellectualis dei*, which is itself the highest state to which man can aspire. Spinoza says that in loving God I cannot hope that He will love me in return.[16] Can we take Spinoza's account of man's disinterested love of God as an ideal of human love? Can we imagine a love or benevolence towards other people which is entirely disinterested, and seeks no return whatsoever?

What would a love be like which genuinely desired and expected no return? It would, presumably, mean that the person who loved desired no recognition. He would wish, perhaps, to do deeds of benevolence towards those whom he loves, but would have no wish to be known as the benefactor. Such an unselfish love undoubtedly bears a resemblance to the Christian ideal of charity. Charity 'seeketh not her own':[17] perhaps that entails that charity does not claim gratitude from those whom it benefits. How easy is it to understand love such as this? It is interesting that when he comes to discuss charity, Aquinas defines it as friendship.[18] He quotes Aristotle as saying that friendship is not without love reciprocated.[19] Good will is not sufficient for friendship. However, when we love a friend we may love for his sake all who belong to him—children, servants, 'or anyone connected with him at all, even if they hurt or hate us, so much do we love him.'[20] Now our love of God is a sort

---

[13] *The Passions of the Soul*, pt. II.   [14] *Leviathan*, pt. I, ch. 6.
[15] *Treatise*, bk. II, pt. ii, sect. I. Hume does, however, go on to develop an elaborate psychology of love.   [16] *Ethics*, pt. V, prop. 19.
[17] I Cor. 13: 5.   [18] *Summa*, 2a2ae, 23, I.
[19] *Ethics*, 1155ᵇ30–5.   [20] *Summa*, 2a2ae, 23, I.

of friendship, in that we share with God because God shares his happiness with us. Therefore 'the friendship of charity extends even to our enemies, for we love them for the sake of God'.[21]

Charity (as Aquinas understands it) is not, then, simply unselfish benevolence. That he produces this rather elaborate argument to prove that it is a form of friendship points to the difficulty there may be in comprehending a love which seeks no return. Indeed, it is essential to love, including erotic love, that it be directed at what can love in return. It is not possible to love animals or inanimate objects.[22] (Of course many people do believe that they love animals; they seem also to believe that animals love them in return.) If a beloved person goes mad, then it is certainly possible that those who loved him will continue to do so. (But one could not even pretend to love a mad dog.) Love can, indeed, outlive every circumstance that made it 'reasonable':

'No, I believe you capable of everything great and good in your married lives. I believe you equal to every important exertion, and every domestic forbearance, so long as—if I may be allowed the expression, so long as you have an object. I mean, while the woman you love lives, and lives for you. All the privilege I claim for my own sex (it is not a very enviable one, you need not covet it) is that of loving longest, when existence or when hope is gone.'[23]

It is not possible to fall in love with a hopelessly insane person. Again, although one may look with love upon the corpse of someone one loved in life, one could not begin by loving a corpse, or by falling in love with it. There are, of course, stories of people falling in love with artefacts. Pygmalion falls in love with a statue he has made, and Tamino falls in love with Pamina's picture. However, it is Pamina whom Tamino loves *through* her picture; and the sign of the reality of Pygmalion's love is that he wishes to bring the statue to life.

A love which sought no return, no recognition whatsoever, would obviously not be erotic love; and nor would it be the love of friendship. Let us call it the love of benevolence. If I am benevolent towards someone, and express my love by conferring benefits upon him, but care nothing about the attitude he has towards me, then is not this a very attenuated sort of love? Is there a great difference

---

[21] *Summa*, 2a2ae, 23, 1.　　　　[22] Ibid.

[23] Jane Austen, *Persuasion*, ch. 11.

between this love and an intense interest—the interest an engineer might take in the performance of a machine he has created? If we imagined a powerful, invisible being doing good to his creatures by stealth, so that those who benefited from his acts had no knowledge either of him or of what he did, then he would seem to be treating them like toys or pets. We could regard his interest in them, in its profound disinterestedness, as aesthetic, or functional, or curious: it is not clear why we should call it 'love'. Spinoza says that in loving God we cannot wish that He should love us in return.[24] This expresses his doctrine that *amor intellectualis dei* is a sort of calm contemplation of the laws of the universe. It is not a 'passion', and hence we are free when we love God. And Spinoza's pantheism has had its influence upon Hegel, upon Romanticism and all doctrines about man's ability to identify himself with the natural order. But if what Spinoza is talking about is love, then it is a love which transcends not only passion, but also good will. Spinoza's free man is not *well disposed* towards the universe—rather he calmly contemplates it. If it were possible to love an individual person in such a calm and free way, then I doubt that one could even wish to confer benefits—that would be a sort of interference in the order of things. But even if one could have a calm interest in what would benefit him, this would presumably be something like the interest an engineer takes in the good functioning of a mechanism. If he failed to do what was best for himself, one could be perhaps grievously disappointed. That would not show that one loved him, since one could equally well be disappointed in the failure of an experiment. The God of Genesis, who drowns the whole world because of the abominations of men who do not return His love, since they disobey His laws, is certainly the God of Abraham, Isaac, and Jacob, rather than of philosophers, Schoolmen, and Spinoza.

What might look like benevolence towards others could actually proceed from a scientific interest, an aesthetic attitude, or sheer curiosity. A dog-breeder may have great solicitude for his pups; but he has an end in view—the breeding of valuable dogs for sale. Or he may simply be interested in dogs, with all the affection, connoisseurship, and enthusiasm that characterizes dog-fanciers. But it would not be right to call an enthusiasm for champion dogs 'benevolence'. Early twentieth-century enthusiasts for eugenics were genuinely

[24] *Ethics*, pt. v, prop. 19.

interested in improving the human 'stock'. This was not benevolence, and contained all the possibilities of treating people as less
than human—possibilities which became actualities later in the
century. When God sends the Flood to destroy mankind, He is not
represented as deciding that an experiment has failed, and that He
should go back to the drawing-board. Rather 'God saw that the
wickedness of man was great in the earth . . . And it repented the
Lord that he had made man on the earth, and it grieved him at his
heart.'[25] Being grieved at man's wickedness, and wishing to punish
or even destroy him could indeed be a sign of love. Dante captures
the apparent paradox, with the inscription over hell's gate:

> Giustiza mosse il mio alto Fattore;
> fecemi la divina Potestate,
> la somma Sapienza e il primo Amore.[26]

I suggest earlier that when we are angry with others we care about
their attitudes, and look for apology. In hating I need care nothing
for the other's remorse, apology, or repentance. Yet I can hate
someone just because I know that he is incapable of repentance—
say, because he is frozen in self-righteousness. Perhaps the God of
Genesis is angry with men; perhaps He hates them because they are
incapable of repentance. Either way, He cares about their attitudes
to His laws and (presumably) to the benefits He has conferred. I
suggest that this is a condition of our thinking of God as loving His
creatures. The orthodox Christian (and Augustinian) doctrine is
that God left His creatures free to obey or not to obey, so that what
counted was their inward dispositions. He would not have been
satisfied with putting the spiritual equivalent of fluoride in their
drinking-water so that they obeyed all His laws by compulsion. A
creator whose 'benevolence' was satisfied by the fact that his wishes
were obeyed, regardless of whether those who obeyed them did so
out of reverence or love of him, could not be said *ipso facto* to love
his creatures. For to love them as persons must entail caring about
their attitudes. But how could you care about their attitudes if you
did not seek some recognition, and some return? If the person you
love hates you, and you are entirely unaffected by this, then it is not
true that what you feel for him is some admirably disinterested

---

[25] Gen. 6: 5–6.
[26] *Inferno*, iii. 4–6: 'Justice moved my High Maker; Divine Power made me,
Wisdom Supreme, and Primal Love.'

love. It is not love at all. Or, if anyone insists on calling it love, it is
not necessary to argue about the *word*; one can simply ask what the
value and the point of such love is. And (to repeat) this would not
be the equivalent of Christian charity, for it is essential to that that
it be mediated through a love of God.

The truth is that for the lover to care deeply about his beloved's
attitude to him is the most obvious sign of love. The withdrawal of
affection, even momentarily, is regarded by the lover as the greatest
of evils. This was noted by St Augustine: 'A girl may say to her
lover, "Don't wear that sort of cloak"; he won't. If she tells him in
winter: "I like you best in your short tunic", he would rather shiver
than offend her. Surely she has no power to inflict punishment? . . .
No, there is only one thing he fears: "I shall never look at you
again."'[27] Again, lovers wish to agree on many things; they wish to
be 'at one'. Dispute and anger are evils for them. A love which was
not grieved by strife and contention, and which had no interest in
being 'at one', either erotically or in the way of friendship, would be
a mysterious, and perhaps slightly sinister, attitude.

This is not to deny that we can love those who are prevented
from recognizing or returning our love. We can love severely
retarded children, and hopelessly senile adults. Yet we are still
loving those in whom we see the possibility of recognition. A
retarded child does show signs of affection, and of needing love. We
have the sense that something has been baffled—not that it could
not exist at all. It is true that some people devote their lives to
caring for those who are so severely mentally damaged that they
seem to have no response to other people at all. It is here that we
might want to talk about charity. Their love is not, perhaps, an
emotion, or a spontaneous attitude. Rather it is more like what
Aquinas describes when he analyses charity as a form of friendship.
Or it is like Kant's 'practical love'. It is a practical benevolence
which we can think of as a duty laid upon us to have and to
exercise, rather than a feeling, the capacity for which we may or
may not be born with. One can set oneself to 'see Christ in others'.

Can I treat someone's loving me simply as a fact about him; or
am I also aware, as it were, of a question to be answered, a decision
to be made? If the person loved feels an enormous disparity
between himself and the lover, he may not feel that there is any

---

[27] Sermon 161, sect. 10.

question to be answered. So a grown man for whom a child develops an infatuation does not feel that he has to respond, except, perhaps, with a kindly humour. A firm womanizer, approached by a homosexual, might simply feel incredulous distaste. And a very beautiful woman, wooed by an ugly and insignificant man, might respond with frigid tranquillity. Nevertheless, love, where there is any sort of equality, is experienced by the person loved as making a claim. Where there is no great disproportion, one experiences the erotic love of another, where it is not returned, as embarrassing, or pitiable, or perhaps annoying. This need not be because the lover is importunate. It is the love itself which makes a claim, and which therefore troubles. I suggested earlier[28] that anger directed at someone far more powerful than oneself is more like melancholy than true anger. Erotic love directed at someone whom one can never meet and does not know is, analogously, not quite like love. It is not quite *unlike* love, either, for at the centre of love is appreciation, delight, and sheer desire, as well as a wish for recognition and return. With anger the wish for an exchange, in the way of rebuke and apology, is as important as a desire to hurt. The love of friendship also implies a claim, and equally can give rise to embarrassment when it is not reciprocated. Indeed, one has a certain sense that one deserves the friendship of the person to whom one is attracted. It does not, at any rate, seem the miracle that the return of erotic love does.

Everyone knows that love—both erotic love and the love of friendship—frequently (perhaps usually) arises just in response to being loved. Spinoza expresses this fact as a necessary truth: 'If we imagine that we are loved by a person without having given any cause . . . we shall love him in return.'[29] Spinoza explains this in terms of gratitude, which is a response to a good conferred upon us. Both Aristotle and Aquinas suggest that the benefactor loves the person whom he has benefited more than he is loved in return.[30] The arguments they give for this are, perhaps, interesting rather than persuasive. However, it is significant that they both take love either to include, or to be, a conferring of a benefit, to which love of the person loved and benefited is an appropriate return. Aristotle

---

[28] See chaper 1, p. 12 above.
[29] *Ethics*, pt. III, prop. 41.
[30] Aristotle, *Ethics*, 1167$^b$15–20; Aquinas, *Summa*, 2a2ae, 26, 12.

says the most sensible thing about a purely disinterested benevolence:

> Goodwill is a friendly sort of relation, but it is not *identical* with
> friendship; for one may have goodwill both towards people one does not
> know, and without their knowing it, but not friendship . . . friendly feeling
> implies intimacy while goodwill may arise of a sudden, as it does towards
> competitors in a contest . . . we feel goodwill suddenly and love them only
> superficially . . . Goodwill seems, then, to be a beginning of friendship, as
> the pleasure of the eye is the beginning of love.[31]

A benevolence which we could not think of as the beginning of
friendship, and in that sense seeking a return, would have about it
something not easy to understand. This is another way of saying
that love is an emotion that makes a claim, and hence aims at an
actual relation with another.

### III FRIENDSHIP

Modern writers on ethics do not usually consider the philosophy of
friendship an essential part of their subject. And many people
would be surprised to find reflections on friendship in the middle of
a discussion of justice. Aristotle does discuss friendship in the
*Ethics*, and he also sees it as relevant to politics. I shall suggest that
it is because we can indeed see friendship as a moral relationship,
and in a political context, that we can also understand it as relevant
to justice.

Most of us would agree that a capacity for friendship is a
distinctive human characteristic. We would probably agree also
that the love of a friend involves something disinterested, but also a
desire for his company. Perhaps we would also recognize different
sorts of friendship. People are often simply thrown together by
chance and form an habitual intimacy. Or they may have tastes and
pleasures in common, and for that reason enjoy each other's
company. Again, people may be united in a common enterprise,
and a friendship may grow up which is a sort of *esprit de corps*, or
the trust and reliance upon each other which is necessary if the
enterprise is to be successful. (They might call themselves 'com-
rades'.) But few would see the differences between these various

---

[31] *Ethics*, 1166$^b$30–1167$^a$5.

examples of friendship as having a special significance. Aristotle, however, not only distinguishes systematically among the different sorts of friendship; he also thinks that one sort is the best, or most like the truest friendship. He says that there are three objects of love: the good, the pleasant, and the useful.[32] Analogously, there are three sorts of friendship. Those who love each other for their utility 'do not love each other for themselves but in virtue of some good they get from each other.' So too with those who love for the sake of pleasure: 'It is not for their character that men love ready-witted people, but because they find them pleasant.' Therefore 'those who love for the sake of utility love for the sake of what is good for *themselves*, and those who love for the sake of pleasure do so for the sake of what is pleasant to *themselves*, and not in so far as the other is the person loved but in so far as he is useful or pleasant.'[33] And Aristotle concludes that such friendships are only 'incidental', for 'it is not as being the man he is that the loved person is loved, but as providing some good or pleasure. Such friendships, then, are easily dissolved, if the parties do not remain like themselves; for if the one party is no longer pleasant or useful the other ceases to love him.'[34] For Aristotle 'perfect friendship is the friendship of men who are good and alike in virtue; for these wish well to each other *qua* good, and they are good in themselves.' Good men love other good men 'by reason of their own nature, and not incidentally; therefore their friendship lasts as long as they are good—and goodness is an enduring thing.'[35]

The confidence with which Aristotle distinguishes between sorts of friendship, and values one sort most highly, may not answer to the experience of the modern reader. Nor will he necessarily be persuaded by the argument about the possible objects of love. How far can we go in taking such a picture of friendship seriously?

Let us go back to the assumption that a capacity for friendship is a distinctively human characteristic. One thing this might mean is that friendship is a relation of which only human beings are capable, and that it is to be understood in the context of other relations which are distinctively human. If human beings were related to each other only by a more or less blind instinct—like members of a herd or a hive—then they could not form friendships. If, again, they were members of a tribe in which the tribal life

---

[32] *Ethics*, 1155[b]15–20.      [33] *Ethics*, 1145[a]5–20.
[34] *Ethics*, 1156[a]15–25.      [35] *Ethics*, 1156[b]5–15.

was all, and the individual life nothing, then it is unlikely there would be any place for friendship. In such circumstances friendship would be a sort of treason, a withdrawal of part of the total loyalty demanded by the tribe. (Family life would be equally subversive.) In religious communities, where there is a demand for total obedience, 'special' (i.e. particular) friendships are frowned on, as derogating from the life of the community.

A benevolence that sought no recognition from or community with those whom it benefited would evidently be very unlike friendship. Aquinas says that the lover always has thoughts of his beloved, and that 'union' (*unio*) is an effect of love, as is 'mutual indwelling' (*mutua inhaesio*).[36] The person loved is said to dwell in the person who loves in the sense that he is constantly present in the lover's thoughts.[37] The constant presence of which Aquinas speaks is not a matter of the lover constantly calculating what will benefit the beloved. He takes pleasure in the sheer thought of him. The delight in the thought of him goes beyond a deliberation about what will benefit him. Love is a way of being interested in someone, of attending to him, as well as a desire to benefit him. (Indeed, one seldom has to consider the well-being of friends, unless they are ill or distressed, because 'benefiting' them is involved in simply being with them. The interests of friends coincide, so that to do what I want is to do what he wants.) It is not to be bored, to find ever new grounds of interest.

This is a description of a love which issues in friendship. It is not desire, since what is sought is the good not of oneself, but of the person loved. Yet neither is it a purely solitary benevolence that seeks no return or recognition. It involves a disinterested appreciation of the person loved, a delight in him, which leads to his being 'constantly present' in the thoughts of the lover. Yet what goes most naturally with a 'constant presence' in thought is a constant presence in actuality. Aristotle indeed says that 'there is nothing so characteristic of friends as living together' and enjoying the same things.[38] As Martha Nussbaum points out, Aristotle seems to envisage friends literally 'spending their days together', and 'going through time together'.[39]

---

[36] *Summa*, 1a2ae, 28, 1–2.  [37] *Summa*, 1a2ae, 28, 2.
[38] *Ethics*, 1157$^b$15–25.
[39] *The Fragility of Goodness*, p. 348, citing *Ethics*, 1158$^a$5–10, 1171$^a$5, and 1157$^b$20–5.

This is an ideal of friendship, then, that includes an element of disinterested appreciation of the friend. It is this which distinguishes the best sort of friendship from relations based upon utility or upon pleasure. It would also distinguish it from associations which people do not freely choose. So although friendship can exist within the family, between husband and wife, and parents and children, this is something that is achieved. It is not guaranteed by the fact that the members of a family love one another.

Can anything be said to commend this picture of friendship? It is not, after all, inevitable that human life should include such a relationship. Is it, therefore, merely the expression of one particular ethical or cultural ideal? What would be lacking if we tried to imagine human beings who lacked any capacity for friendship so understood?

The answer must surely be that, first, friendship, as understood by Aristotle and Aquinas is not an inevitable part of any recognizably human life. It *is* an ethical and cultural ideal. But secondly, it has a very good claim to be considered part of the good life for man.

If friendship is not a relation of utility, or the pursuit of pleasure, and if it is not purely instinctive, or tribal, or familial, or erotic, what is it? I have suggested that it includes some element of disinterested appreciation of the friend. But this idea—redolent of Kant's account of the disinterestedness of aesthetic experience perhaps—does not take us very far. For unlike aesthetic experience, the disinterested appreciation of one's friend depends upon a certain state of character. It is not difficult to think of the vices which damage friendship: envy, wrath, incapacity for proper anger, vanity, lack of proper pride, cowardice, disloyalty, lack of affection. Envy destroys friendship because it makes one incapable of taking the good of the friend as one's own good, or of prizing the good of the friend as good in itself. Envy destroys affection for the friend. Lack of generosity, both material and spiritual, makes a friend contemptible. Excessive pride makes us see slights where none were intended, and to refuse to yield where yielding is called for—to refuse, for instance, to apologize. Lack of proper anger may prevent one from showing that love of a friend that is sensitive to his honour, and issues in correction. It may also lead one to harbour subterraneous resentments rather than openly to rebuke. Cowardice would obviously prevent one from being a good and reliable friend. Lack of self-respect may prevent any true equilibrium in the friendship. One's friend may be tempted always to have his own way. Indeed a healthy friendship may require something more than equilibrium—perhaps a polarity or tension.[40]

The virtues which support friendship, and the vices which undermine it, seem general rather than specialized. If we are taking part in a particular enterprise—such as an expedition to find the Golden Fleece—then certain particular virtues and skills would be called for: cunning, good navigation, boldness, hardiness. But the virtues which support friendship seem to be the virtues that would assist any successful personal relationship. Or we might say, one way of understanding what we might mean by the modern phrase 'personal relationship' is to think about the virtues that assist friendship, and the vices that war against it. If defects like envy, wrath, and ungenerosity make friendship difficult or impossible, then this means that evil men find it difficult or impossible to be friends. If loyalty, generosity, affection, candour, benevolence make friendship possible, this means that friendship is something that good men find possible. Friendship seems to be not a skill, or a contract, or an instinctive relationship, but more like a virtue, or something supervenient upon other virtues.

Those dispositions which destroy friendship also reduce one's sense of the other person as an end. To attach due weight to his desires and needs, to respect his feelings simply because they are his feelings, to care about his attitudes, to wish to be at one with him, to delight in him, are all ways of treating him as an end, rather than as a means to pleasure or utility. Egoism, envy, wrath, and other vices all darken one's sense of the other as an autonomous agent to whom reasons for action can be offered. There is an analogy with practical wisdom which depends upon an ordering of one's passions and appetites, and is a very general sort of human goodness, or the whole of human goodness under a certain aspect. Similarly, the dispositions which make friendship possible suggest that it is not a specialized good, one which we could imagine human beings doing without and yet still leading good lives, but a very general sort of good, or the whole of the human good under a certain aspect.

---

[40] See Nietzsche: 'The capacity for and the duty of protracted gratitude and protracted revenge . . . a certain need to have enemies . . . fundamentally so as to be able to be a good *friend* . . . all these are typical marks of noble morality . . .'. *Beyond Good and Evil*, sect. 260.

We can therefore have an idea of friendship as a relation between good men, who value each other as ends. This sort of friendship will be freely chosen, and answerable to rational considerations. We value in a friend qualities which we should also value in others. But friendship is particular. We do not want to be friends with all who have the qualities that we find in our friends. So although a friendship is not just a taste—I do not prefer one person as a friend over another in the way I might prefer a particular blend of tea—it is nevertheless inescapably particular, although looking for good qualities of character in the friend which would be good qualities of character in anybody at all.

Aristotle understands friendship as an expression of human virtue, and necessarily part of the good life for man. It looks for qualities which are enduring—good qualities of character—rather than on the useful and the pleasurable which can pass away. Friendship, then, expresses human virtues which are in some sense invulnerable to the accidents of the world. Yet at the same time Aristotle treats friendship as particular, as limited to a small number of people, perhaps only to one person, and as in some ways dependent upon particular circumstances.

For Aristotle friendship is an ethical relationship, rather than one which depends upon shared particular purposes, or common pleasures, or two people being simply thrown together. However, Martha Nussbaum writes persuasively in *The Fragility of Goodness* of 'the elements of Aristotelian *philia* that make it real personal *love*, something more vulnerable, more rooted in time and change, than a Kantian "practical love".'[41] We remember that Aquinas had said that *amor amicitiae* involves the constant presence of the beloved in his friend's thoughts,[42] and that Aristotle says that friends would wish actually to live together.[43] Clearly this sort of friendship relies upon circumstances which are difficult to establish, and which might easily change. Nussbaum also points out that Aristotle's *philia*—unlike Kant's practical love—'requires taking pleasure in the other person's physical presence'.[44] Friendship does not entirely escape circumstance, for absence can damage and even destroy it. There are, Aristotle says, necessary absences, which, at first, 'dissolve not the love *simpliciter*, but its activity'.[45] Further-

---

[41] p. 370.                           [42] *Summa*, 1a2ae, 28, 2.
[43] *Ethics*, 1157$^b$10–15, 1171$^a$5.        [44] *The Fragility of Goodness*, p. 369.
[45] *Ethics*, 1157$^b$10–15, quoted by Nussbaum, *The Fragility of Goodness*, p. 360.

more, 'if the absence is of long duration, it appears to bring about forgetfulness of the love itself.'[46] Martha Nussbaum also says that Aristotle thinks that people who are physically ugly will find it difficult to find 'the most fulfilling loves' since these occur 'between two people of similar character and aspirations who also find each other physically, socially and morally attractive . . .'.[47] If this is so, then friendship is influenced by a number of contingencies. Nevertheless, at the centre of friendship is a compatibility between two people who are of good character. This is, as it were, the enabling condition of friendship, and we could perhaps imagine friendship surviving, if not exactly flourishing, without quite the degree of daily closeness that Aristotle desiderates, and quite without the physical attractions. But we could not imagine friendship between two thoroughly wicked people.

So Aristotle's account of friendship is of a relationship which we have to describe in ethical terms—as existing between two good men, each of whom loves the good character of the other. It is a relationship that answers to rational considerations. To this extent it is like Kantian practical love, and very unlike erotic or passionate love. At the same time it depends, as well as upon moral compatibility, on various contingencies. But if such things as living together and good looks contribute to friendship, or the long list of qualities that we find in the *Rhetoric*,[48] they do so by actualizing what is central to friendship. Living together may sustain and develop friendship, but not, say, living in London rather than in Rome. Good looks may also help, but not the friend's being fair rather than dark. And it could not be that only Englishmen, and not Frenchmen, could be capable of friendship, just because of their nationality.

## IV FRIENDSHIP AND THE CIVIL CONDITION

Friendship is not, then, like a purely disinterested benevolence that seeks no return or recognition. On the contrary, friends wish to be

---

[46] *Ethics*, 1157$^b$10–15, trans. Nussbaum, *The Fragility of Goodness*, p. 360.

[47] *The Fragility of Goodness*, p. 359. She refers to the *Ethics*, 1099$^b$3–4, and the *Rhetoric*, 1381$^b$1.

[48] 1380$^b$34–1381$^b$35. Aristotle says that we are disposed to be friends with those who have treated us well, those who are enemies to our enemies, those who are willing to treat us well where money or our personal safety is concerned ('and

with each other, to be at one with each other, mutually to recognize each as bearing good will to the other,[49] and for each to see in the friend another self.[50] Friendship, understood in this way, does not achieve an external good—as do friendships of utility, or of pleasure. Friendship is itself the good. Aristotle asks whether the supremely happy and self-sufficient man will need friends. His answer is in the nature of an assertion: 'Surely it is strange . . . to make the supremely happy man a solitary; for no one would choose the whole world on condition of being alone, since man is a political creature and one whose nature is to live with others.'[51] Aristotle clearly believes that a man deprived of a political existence would lack something intrinsic to the good life.[52] But what is significant is that he alludes to this belief when discussing the significance of friendship. For he thinks of the *polis* itself as an association, enjoying a common life, and possessing the quality of friendship. Indeed, we have to understand different states, and different political associations, in terms of the sorts and quality of friendship which they exhibit.[53] 'All the communities . . . seem to be parts of the political community; and the particular kinds of friendship will correspond to the particular kinds of community.'[54] He also says that the political relationship of men is like friendship, but 'friendship of association or compact'.[55] Although we must understand states as essentially held together by the virtue of justice, Aristotle seems to think that this public relationship of justice is rooted in civic friendship:[56]

Friendship seems too to hold states together, and lawgivers to care more for it than for justice; for unanimity seems to be something like friendship, and this they aim at most of all, and expel faction as their worst enemy; and when men are friends they have no need of justice, while when they are

therefore we value those who are liberal, brave, or just'), temperate men, those with whom it is pleasant to live and spend our days, those who mind their own business, those who praise such good qualities as we possess, if we are not quite sure that we do possess them, etc. There is nothing very surprising in the list.

[49] Aristotle, *Ethics*, 1156ᵃ1–5.　　　　　　　　　　[50] *Ethics*, 1166ᵃ30–5.
[51] *Ethics*, 1169ᵇ15–20. He also says that friends 'are thought the greatest of external goods', and that the noble man needs to confer benefits, and on whom better can he confer them than friends?, etc.
[52] For a persuasive account of the considerations underlying Aristotle's belief, see Nussbaum, *The Fragility of Goodness*, pp. 345–53.
[53] See Barker's app. III, *Politics*, p. 373.
[54] *Ethics*, 1160ᵃ25–30.　　　　　　　　　　　　[55] *Ethics*, 1161ᵇ10–15.
[56] See Jacques Maritain, *The Rights of Man and Natural Law* (London, 1944), pp. 22–3; quoted by Barker, *Politics*, app. III, p. 373, n. 1.

just they need friendship as well, and the truest form of justice is thought to be a friendly quality.[57]

Aristotle thinks of the political association as having self-completeness (*autarkeia*) and as not having any 'extrinsic substantive purpose'.[58]

We can see that this picture of political association—or of what, following Michael Oakeshott, I shall call the 'civil condition'—answers to the Aristotelian view of friendship. Friendship does not achieve a good extrinsic to itself. Analogously, we can think of the civil condition not as achieving a good for man that can be independently specified, but as fulfilling man's nature. The 'end' of the *polis* is the same as that of human conduct in general—the good life, or human excellence.[59] But this end cannot be understood apart from the activities which characterize it. The good to be achieved is the good of man *qua* 'political animal'.

To attempt to deal with the extremely contentious issues in political philosophy raised by what I have just said would be beyond the scope of this book. But I will sketch them extremely briefly. There could be an association of people which existed entirely for the exchange of commodities. We might imagine a city founded purely as a trading-post. The laws of the city will reflect its original purpose, and have to be understood in relation to this purpose. Contracts will be vigorously enforced however unreasonable or unjust, because it is of the highest importance to retain the confidence of those with whom the city trades. Indeed, the notion of a contract's being 'unjust' will have no meaning. All education will be subordinated to the need to produce an 'enterprise culture', and no subject will be studied as an end in itself. The rulers of the city will regard themselves essentially as managers of the enterprise. Their tasks will be to maximize wealth and promote trade. The most important thing to understand is that the city has a 'purpose', and the rulers, or managers, will do their best to promote that purpose. (In *Nostromo* Conrad depicts a state—Costaguana—which is subordinated by 'material interests' to just such a purpose.) Many people would say that this is not the picture of a rather unusual sort of city, or state, but an accurate (if primitive) description of the civil condition. Any city or state, they might say,

[57] *Ethics*, 1155ᵃ20–30.
[58] See Michael Oakeshott, *On Human Conduct* (Oxford, 1975), p. 110.
[59] See Oakeshott, *On Human Conduct*, p. 118.

exists to achieve certain purposes. These might include public peace, the protection of property, the enforcement of contracts, and protection from foreign invasion. Many would now add to the list the development of economic resources, the promotion of a welfare state, social justice. Others would desiderate the rule of Christ, or the Prophet, on earth.

Michael Oakeshott has described a state, so understood, as an 'enterprise association', and he opposes it to what he calls the 'civil condition'. For him the civil condition does not exist in order to obtain what everyone has reason to want, but which could not be obtained otherwise. The civil condition has finally to be understood morally. The laws governing a civil association are of a certain kind: '. . . the terms of relationship are exclusively rules of a practice which may concern any and every transaction between agents and is indifferent to the outcome of any such transaction: the practice of being 'just' to one another.'[60] The essence of civil association is that people are related through their 'common recognition of the authority of a practice of just conduct defined by law.'[61] Oakeshott argues that people cannot want 'happiness', but only specific satisfactions. A man is happy when his projects tend to be fulfilled, and he is not regularly disappointed. The pursuit of happiness is a 'formal' description of human conduct, and does not attribute to men the desire for a 'substantive' end. Analogously, civil association does not aim at such substantive ends as prosperity, 'social justice', or the kingdom of Christ upon earth, even though some of these ends may in fact help to make possible and preserve the association. (Similarly, for Aristotle, a degree of material prosperity may be necessary for happiness, but is not part of happiness.[62]) Oakeshott traces his picture of the civil condition to Aristotle, and finds it, in another form, in Hegel's *Philosophy of Right*.[63] He suggests that in those states where people are disposed to cultivate the freedom inherent in human agency, the understanding of the state will be that of the 'civil association' which he has described.[64] States which set themselves substantive purposes

---

[60] *On Human Conduct*, p. 128.

[61] See J. E. J. Altham, review of Oakeshott, *On Human Conduct*, *The Cambridge Review*, 97 (Oct. 1975), 24.

[62] *Ethics*, 1099$^a$30–1099$^b$10; in the *Rhetoric* (1360$^b$20–30), Aristotle includes wealth among the 'constituent parts' of happiness, but calls it 'external'.

[63] *On Human Conduct*, pp. 257–63.

[64] See ibid., pp. 236–42, and Altham, review, p. 25.

('The Soviets *plus* electrification equals Communism') fall away from the condition of civil association into that of 'enterprise associations'. The modern state engaged in war is perhaps the prime example of an enterprise association.[65] Oakeshott does not suppose that his picture of the civil condition will be universally persuasive. But he suggests that in the modern, polarized, European political consciousness, the oscillations between civil and enterprise associations *are* the poles of political debate 'and that all other tensions (such as those indicated in the words "right" or "left" or in the alignments of political parties) are insignificant compared with this.'[66]

One might say of an ideal of friendship that does not achieve certain goods external to friendship itself—the useful or the pleasant (to use Aristotle's categories)—but is a relationship between two good men who love each other for their good characters, that there is something empty about it. Even if we surround it with an account of what helps it actually to exist— living together, for instance—it still has a quality of extreme abstraction. Friends do not pursue specific goods, such as money or power; they are not lovers, nor even, *qua* friends, husband and wife.[67] If friendship does depend upon certain states of character, and can be damaged by such vices as vanity, envy, and disloyalty, then the best way to describe friendship is as a moral relationship. If we are to look for the category that best fits the virtues that underly friendship, can we do better than call it justice? Friends treat each other justly. The moral relationship between them is, as it were, an informal version of the justice, in the form of law, that holds states together. And the justice, in the form of law, that holds states together, requires as its basis a 'civic friendship' between citizens. If we can envisage a relationship between individuals which has no further purpose than to achieve the good which is inherent in virtuous mutual love, then we can also envisage an analogous relation amongst men in the public sphere. We might call this 'civil association'. To envisage such a mode of association in the public sphere adds something to our understanding of friendship under- stood as a private relationship. Aristotle's vision of friendship is of

---

[65] See *On Human Conduct*, pp. 272–4.

[66] Ibid., p. 320.

[67] But Aristotle does say that between husband and wife friendship seems to exist by nature (*Ethics*, 1162[a]14–20).

a proto-political relationship, of something which bridges the divide (so much deeper in our world than in his) between private and public life. To call it a 'proto-political relationship' may seem less chilling if we can relate it to his understanding of political association itself in terms of 'friendship'.

My suggestion is, then, that something like Aristotle's account of friendship, which is a moral relationship, is also an account of justice in action. The virtues which sustain friendship, and the vices which destroy it, are virtues of justice and vices of injustice. Friendship is a distinctively human capacity, just because it is a relationship of justice. It is also a distinctively human capacity because it is part of, or prefigures, or is an image of, that other distinctively human capacity—political association. And political association, if it is not membership of an enterprise, or of a race, or of a religion which seeks to impose its character on a state, nor of any other of the multifarious, excluding human activities which require special loyalties, special skills, accidental endowments, is best understood, on the analogy of friendship, as a relationship of justice.

### V  *PIETAS*

Aquinas discusses the virtues, or parts of justice. The first of these is *pietas*.[68] To have the virtue of *pietas* is to render due homage (*cultus*) to those to whom we owe it, and specifically to parents, blood-relations, and country. (Homage to God is demanded by religion, which is a step above piety.[69]) *Pietas* can be called a form of respect; but it is a richer, more concrete notion than a Kantian 'respect for persons'. It involves manifesting in one's behaviour the debt (*debitum*) one owes—for instance, to one's parents and country—and manifesting one's love to them, and thus repaying the debt. There is a great advantage in analysing the 'parts' or 'virtues' of justice. For it is very difficult to imagine what someone could be like who entirely lacked the sense of justice. Indeed to try to imagine him would be like playing an intellectual game. But if we resolve justice into its 'parts' as Aquinas does (following Cicero and many other writers), then we can raise that sort of question more

---

[68] *Summa*, 2a2ae, 101.
[69] *Summa*, 2a2ae, 101, 1.

intelligibly and in more detail. What would a man be like who lacked some or all of those feelings and dispositions which come under the heading of *pietas*? Among the virtues which Aquinas relates to *pietas* are respect and obedience. Although he treats them as distinct, we might as well bring them under the heading of *pietas* since the differences are not great. And since in the ancient world *pietas* (in Greek, *eusebeia*, as Aquinas duly notes) drew to itself a very wide range of virtuous behaviour, we can feel free to treat it less restrictively than Aquinas does.

So what would someone who largely lacked *pietas* be like? I hope the following is less random than it might at first seem: he would fail to show respect to the dead, either to dead bodies, or to the memory of the dead. Perhaps he would show an inappropriate levity. Or, he would have no sense of the majesty of death which ends quarrels and jealousies, and in which 'even Mrs Gradgrind . . . took upon her the dread solemnity of the sages and patriarchs.'[70] He would not see the ceremonies of grief as demanding a certain sort of sober, respectful behaviour. He would not understand how behaviour which harms no one might still be wrong. He might see no especial outrage in an insult offered to a father in front of his children ('"Daddy, how they humiliated you!"').[71] Indeed, all those feelings which go with honouring parents (and which the Greeks marked emphatically by having gods whose peculiar function it was to avenge outrage offered to parents) would be lacking in him. The *pietas* owed to parents is not simply a matter of 'moral' respect, but has also a sacred character. 'Respect' is a secular, individualist (dare we say, bourgeois?) substitute for *pietas*. The piety that is expressed by patriotism, for instance, cannot be captured by the notion of respect for persons.

*Macbeth* provides an interesting contrast between someone who has—or at least understands—*pietas* and someone who entirely lacks it. Macbeth's great soliloquies before the murder of Duncan do not simply express qualms of conscience. He feels awe and terror in the face of what he is to do, for he is breaking a bond which is at once a bond of hospitality and kinship, and one of nature. And once the bond is broken, his horror also ceases to exist. He becomes simply a criminal, a horror to others rather than to himself. The impious man lives in a world emptied of significance.

[70] Dickens, *Hard Times*, bk. ii, ch. 9.
[71] See ch. 3, p. 133 above.

By contrast, Lady Macbeth never experiences the dread of breaking the bond. Instead she is possessed of a shallow bravado ('Had he not resembled | My father as he slept, I had done't.').[72] She understands only personal loyalties, and personal courage and cowardice ('Was the hope drunk | Wherein you dress'd yourself? Hath it slept since? . . . From this time | Such I account thy love').[73] Her sleep-walking scene reveals only that she is oppressed with a guilty secret, a private horror at a private crime. She never consciously thinks of Duncan as king, but only as 'the old man' who had so much blood in him. Dr Johnson rightly says, in his notes to the play, that Lady Macbeth 'is merely detested', whereas 'the courage of Macbeth preserves some esteem'.[74]

*Pietas*, then, includes the love, loyalty, and respect that good men feel and actively show to what transcends and sustains them, to parents, blood-relations, benefactors, and country. (And for Aquinas, *religio*, which binds us to God, is a higher form of *pietas*.[75]) As a rendering of due homage, it will express itself in reverence, loving admiration, allegiance; respect for old age, for those to whom one owes the debt of life, for those to who one owes the security of one's country. The man of *pietas* is a serious man, who knows how to feel, who has a sense of 'whatsoever is grave and constant in human suffering'. Someone without this virtue would not know, in the widest sense, how to feel and behave. He would not fully understand what constituted insult; he would not see old age as venerable; he would lack attachment to forms, traditions, language, liturgy. He would lack any sense of a hallowed place, any feeling for the *genius loci*. This means that he would lack the deepest sense of community, of being born into a human tradition, of life being not his unique possession, but common to all. He would not know how to speak of the dead.

*Pietas* is, no doubt, a fluid concept, and cannot be defined in a simple formula. It can be expressed in all the ways in which men attach themselves to the realm of what Hegel called 'objective spirit'—the world of institutions, custom, culture. The feelings and dispositions which reveal it—homage, respect, awe, veneration, fear, a sense of belonging—are all appropriate, or owed. It is the

---

[72] II. ii. 12–13.  [73] I. vii. 35–9.
[74] *Johnson on Shakespeare*, in *Works*, ed. A. Sherbo, vol. viii (Yale, 1968), p. 795, discussing *Macbeth*, v. i. 38–9.
[75] Aquinas seems to be saying this in the *Summa*, 2a2ae, 101, 3.

operation of the virtue of justice in our relations to others not simply *qua* individuals, on whom we might justly make claims, and whose just claims we should acknowledge, but to others *qua* parents, benefactors, teachers, superiors, kings; and also to institutions, language, the country into which we were born. *Pietas* is what Mary Crawford lacks in the chapel at Sotherton, and Mr Rushworth when he cuts down his avenue of trees.[76]

One reason why *pietas* is not a particularly fashionable virtue is precisely that it is not directed at people simply *qua* individuals. At the beginning of his discussion of justice[77] Aquinas argues that the rights of a father and a master should be especially distinguished. Many people feel uncomfortable with the idea that our duties to others can so clearly be defined by their social role. Everybody agrees that love and respect is indeed owed to parents, but many would think that this is to be explained entirely by what the parents have done, and what they feel. Aquinas, like Aristotle, sees the right of parents over their children as to be understood on the model of political rule. Aquinas understands *pietas* as including our duties towards our rulers.[78] *Pietas* does not seem to be directed at people simply as rational agents, but also in their capacity as parents, benefactors, etc.

It is interesting that most people now use 'just' to refer only to states of affairs, rather than to dispositions. The primary question is often taken to be what would constitute just political, economic, or social arrangements. The just man will then simply be the man who is disposed to bring about whatever arrangements are deemed to be just. This must indeed be part of what we mean by justice. Aristotle defines justice as 'that kind of state of character which makes people disposed to do what is just and makes them act justly and wish for what is just'.[79] But if people had grotesquely misconceived ideas of what actually constituted just states of affairs, then we might be puzzled whether or not to call them just, whatever their good intentions. Justice is a very large subject, and my exclusive emphasis on those dispositions that make up the virtue of justice can fairly be criticized as ignoring all the questions about just states of affairs, and 'justice as fairness', that have

[76] See Jane Austen, *Mansfield Park*, ch. 6.
[77] *Summa*, 2a2ae, 57, 4.
[78] *Summa*, 2a2ae, 101, 1. That is, if one can understand 'indebtedness' to one's country as including obedience to its civil rulers.     [79] *Ethics*, 1129$^a$5-10.

interested modern theorists. However, I believe that this latter emphasis has led to the *virtue* of justice being more or less forgotten. It is true that we all, on occasion, refer to someone as a just man. But this is almost like referring to a specialized trait of character (for instance, he can appreciate the good qualities of his professional rivals), rather than to what is necessary for a good man. The advantage of breaking down the virtue of justice into its parts is that it helps us to see that the disposition to be just is not specialized, but has to be seen as part of a set of dispositions which are crucial to moral goodness. I very much doubt that we could derive these dispositions from the idea of the man who is disposed to bring about just states of affairs. My suggestion is that the full picture of the parts of justice that we find in Aquinas does in fact illuminate what is to have 'the lasting and constant will of rendering to each one his right'.[80] We can ask ourselves whether we could have any clear idea of a man disposed to bring about just states of affairs, unless this followed from a picture of someone who had the virtues, or parts, of justice. In other words, to what extent do we have to think about just states of affairs as being those states of affairs which a just man would want to bring about? To think in this way would make the notion of the virtue of justice prior to the notion of just states of affairs. (The analogy would be the idea that the truly good human pleasures are those which the man of practical wisdom would choose.)

As parts of justice Aquinas also discusses *dulia*, or 'respectful service', obedience, gratitude, vengeance, truth-telling, boasting, friendship, liberality, and equity. By the time he has reached the end of his discussion he has given us a sense of justice as covering a vast range of human conduct and human relationships. It will be evident from this list that the virtue of justice, as he understand it, will elude certain influential modern accounts of it. For instance 'justice as fairness': some justice clearly *is* fairness, but the virtues to be discerned in liberality, or friendship, or *pietas*, or truth-telling, whatever they are, cannot be identified with the disposition to be fair. Indeed, I very much doubt that we can, in the end, reconcile the modern exclusive emphasis on just states of affairs with any account of justice as a virtue.

[80] *Summa*, 2a2ae, 58, 1.

# 6

## PAGAN VIRTUES?

AUGUSTINE holds that there are' three chief sources of sin: *superbia, curiositas,* and *lascivia*—the 'pride of life', the 'lust of the eye', and the 'lust of the flesh'. These were, he says, the three temptations which Christ overcame in the wilderness. They are above all sins of pride, choice of the lesser good—oneself—over the greater good, which is God.[1] Pride is, for Augustine, the *radix omnium malorum* ('root of every evil'), the sin of Satan himself. Pride is that 'perverse self-exaltation' by which a man seeks 'to become and to be a principle to himself, abandoning the one true principle to which the soul should cleave . . . The proud therefore is not Israel.' And the triple answer to the triple source of sin is 'first humility, second humility, third humility'. Without humility 'all the good of our joy in any right action is wrested from us by pride.'[2] It is not surprising that for Christians pride is one of the seven deadly sins.

Perhaps the most notorious passage in Aristotle's *Ethics* is where he describes the *megalopsychos,* or great-souled, or magnanimous man—sometimes translated as 'the proud man'.[3] These are some of the things that Aristotle says about him: the magnanimous man thinks himself worthy of great things and *is* worthy of them. The greatest thing is honour and it is therefore with this that the magnanimous man is most concerned. Magnanimity is a sort of

---

[1] Augustine, *De vera religione*, pp. 69 ff; *Enarratio in Psalmos*, bk. viii, ch. 13; *De trinitate*, bk. xii, ch. 14; *Confessions*, bk. x, chs. 41 ff. See John Burnaby, *Amor Dei* (London, 1938), p. 185.

[2] Augustine, *Ep.* 118, s. 22, and Burnaby, *Amor Dei*, p. 71.

[3] This is Ross's translation in the Oxford text. It is a translation favourable, perhaps, to the themes of this book. However, I am unhappy with what is closer to an interpretation than a translation. 'Great-souled' is too clumsy for regular use. 'Magnanimous' and 'magninimity' have the advantage of literalness, and are a little more distant from common usage than 'proud' and 'pride'. With some hesitation, therefore, I have decided in this chapter to continue (usually) using Ross's translation, but to take the liberty of substituting 'magnanimity' for 'pride'. Nevertheless, 'pride' has much to be said for it as an interpretation of *megalopsychia*.

crown of the virtues (and the magnanimous man is great in each of the virtues); therefore it is hard to be truly magnanimous. The magnanimous man does not run into trifling dangers, nor is he fond of danger, because he honours few things; but he will face great dangers, and when he is in danger he is unsparing of his life, knowing that there are conditions on which life is not worth having. And he is the sort of man to confer benefits, but he is ashamed of receiving them; for the one is a mark of a superior, the other of an inferior. He is open in his hate and in his love; he does not flatter. He does not make his life revolve around anyone, unless it be a friend; for this is slavish, and for this reason all flatterers are servile and people lacking in self-respect are flatterers. He is one to possess beautiful and profitless things rather than profitable and useful ones; for this is proper to a character that suffices to itself. Further, a slow step is thought appropriate to the magnanimous man, a deep voice and a level utterance; for the man who takes few things seriously is not likely to be hurried, nor the man who thinks nothing great to be excited, while a shrill voice and a rapid gait are the results of hurry and excitement.[4]

The magnanimous (or 'proud') man has not proved to be the most durably popular of Aristotle's ethical portraits. It goes without saying that he is directly opposed to Christian humility. But modern dislike of him extends far beyond the ranks of believing Christians. He offends that spirit of equality—partly rooted, of course, in Christianity—which few of us can escape even if we try. The kindest thing that now seems to be said about the *megalopsychos* is that he is a crystallization of an aristocratic ethic prevalent in Aristotle's time, which Aristotle is not able to transcend.

Aristotle, however, seems to regard the magnanimous, or proud man, if not as an ideal, then at least as a crux, some sort of summation of his account of the virtues. The portrait of him certainly does not read like an intrusion of unexamined prejudice. It is probably better to assume that he is integral to Aristotle's picture of the good life, and to ask what sense we can make of the portrait.

Aristotle says that in so far as the magnanimous man deserves most, he must be good in the highest degree; for the better man always deserves more, and the best man most. Therefore the truly

---

[4] *Ethics*, 1123$^a$30–1124$^a$20.

magnanimous man must be good. Indeed, greatness in every virtue would seem to be characteristic of the magnanimous man.[5] I take it that by 'greatness in every virtue' Aristotle does not mean simply greatness of effort to possess each of the virtues, but actual and outstanding success. Aristotle discusses *megalopsychia* immediately after *megaloprepeia*, or magnificence. Magnificence is necessarily on a grand scale. It resembles liberality (*eleutheristes*) except that it is concerned only with spending money and not with getting it.[6] But it surpasses liberality in that it implies expenditure on a grand scale.[7] Aristotle says that excellence in achievement involves greatness.[8] So a liberal man may simply not have the chance to be a magnificent man. Whatever his inward dispositions, or his potential to be magnificent were he given the chance, *megaloprepeia* is a virtue which he simply cannot possess if he is a man of modest means. Yet since magnificence is a greater virtue than liberality, it seems that Aristotle would consider a magnificent man a better man than a simply liberal one. And presumably he would consider that he 'deserves more' in the way of honour and recognition. It does indeed seem that Aristotle thinks that the greatness of the magnanimous man is judged objectively by actual achievement, and is not simply a quality of a man's intentions, for he says, 'magnanimity implies greatness, as beauty implies a good-sized body, and little people may be neat and well-proportioned but cannot be beautiful.'[9]

Many people find Aristotle's portrait of the magnanimous man odious. How can we think that such a coldly self-sufficient, self-regarding, calculating man can be morally good, let alone some sort of ethical ideal? The dislike goes perhaps deeper than disapproval of qualities which Aristotle seems to admire. For even if the *megalopsychos* were thoroughly admirable, even likeable, he would still, surely, be a notable example of moral luck.[10] It is only because he, like the magnificent man, has the good fortune to be able to act on a grand scale that he can be 'worthy . . . of the greatest things'.[11] And his good fortune does not seem to be simply a matter of his having been born with a great soul (since a slave could be born with

[5] *Ethics*, 1123[b]24–35.  [6] *Ethics*, 1122[a]15–25.  [7] Ibid.
[8] *Ethics*, 1122[b]15–20 (Rackham's trans.).  [9] *Ethics*, 1123[b]5–10.
[10] For the term 'moral luck', see Bernard Williams, 'Moral Luck', *Moral Luck* (Cambridge, 1981), pp. 20–40; and Thomas Nagel, 'Moral Luck', *Mortal Questions*, pp. 24–38.  [11] *Ethics*, 1123[a]15–20.

that—although Aristotle, with his doctrine of 'slaves by nature',[12] would presumably not agree), but also of his having great opportunities in a worldly sense. Admittedly, Aristotle does not make that as plain as he does in his discussion of magnificence, where he says that a man without great means who tried to be magnificent would be just 'a fool'.[13] But he does say that 'the goods of fortune are also thought to contribute towards magnanimity. For men who are well-born are thought worthy of honour, and so are those who enjoy power or wealth; for they are in a superior position, and everything that has superiority in something good is held in greater honour.'[14] Aristotle adds, somewhat equivocally: 'But in reality only the good man ought to be honoured, although he that has both virtue and fortune is esteemed still more worthy of honour.'[15] Aristotle nowhere seems to suggest that sheer goodness can in some circumstances constitute greatness. The magnanimous man's interest in only great things, his desire for beautiful but useless possessions, his use of irony (*eironeia*—i.e. self-depreciation) in talking to simple folk, and his wish to pursue high honour and achievement can only make sense, taken together, in a man favoured with a distinguished position in the world. (And Aristotle's analogy with the handsome man seems to allow no other interpretation.)

As I have already suggested,[16] the notion that what is obligatory on all—moral goodness—might be possible only for people favoured by fortune, or much easier for them, will strike many of us as a sort of scandal. If moral goodness is our supreme obligation, then to be morally good must be in the power of everyone, and not only, or especially, of those with special skills, or kindly feelings, or exceptional intelligence, or luck in other ways. Kant's doctrine of the Good Will—the firm intention of doing the right for the sake of the right—is the most rigorous attempt by a philosopher to make moral goodness independent of contingency. Nothing could more directly oppose the Kantian vision than the idea that greatness of achievement—a greatness of achievement that seems to be a *criterion* of magnanimity, or greatness of soul—is part of a man's essential goodness, or worth, or desert.

Plutarch represents Julius Caesar as a man of remarkable gifts

---

[12] *Politics*, 1254ª10–15.              [13] *Ethics*, 1122ᵇ25–30.
[14] *Ethics*, 1124ª20–5.                  [15] *Ethics*, 1124ª25–30.
[16] See ch. 4, p. 144 above.

and personal qualities. He is eloquent, has a courteous manner which makes people 'love him marvellously'. He is outstandingly brave, and inspires exceptional courage in his soldiers, and conspicuous devotion to himself. Although of delicate constitution—'lean, white and soft-skinned, and often subject to the falling sickness [i.e. epilepsy]'—Caesar trained himself to hardness: '. . . [he] yielded not to the disease of his body, to make it a cloak to cherish him withal, but contrarily, took the pains of war as a medicine to cure his sick body, fighting always with his disease, travelling continually, living soberly, and commonly lying abroad in the field.'[17] Caesar is, of course, gigantically ambitious, and has political and military genius. He is capable of terrible ruthlessness (and what we would now undoubtedly call war crimes). He is also capable of outstanding magnanimity towards his enemies.

Plutarch's Julius Caesar clearly displays certain virtues—courage, temperance, practical wisdom, magnificence, and magnanimity (in the common, rather than specifically Aristotelian, sense of the term). Unlike most men, he is in a position to manifest these virtues on a grand scale. He surrounds himself with many former enemies, whom he trusts, and by certain of whom (e.g. Brutus) he is betrayed. This trust and magnanimity is essentially connected with his worldly greatness. The condition of Caesar's clemency is conquest; his most famous virtue depends on moral luck in that its enabling condition is power.

To Plutarch it seems natural that Caesar should be loved and honoured both for what he was and for what he did. And he could be loved and honoured for his good fortune.[18] Plutarch's frequent use of the term 'noble' to describe Caesar's character and life, and the character and lives of other 'noble Greeks and Romans', seems readily to embrace much that proceeds from *fortuna* as well as much that flows from a jewel-like intention.[19] There is little doubt that many people would indeed honour such a man were they to have the fortune of meeting him, and that they would show in their behaviour much the same admiration for his qualities and

[17] Plutarch, *Life of Julius Caesar*, trans. North (London, 1899), p. 141.
[18] 'As Caesar loved me, I weep for him; as he was fortunate, I rejoice at it; as he was valient, I honour him; but, as he was ambitious, I slew him.' Brutus, in Shakespeare, *Julius Caesar*, III. ii. 25–7.
[19] My quotations are from North's trans. of Plutarch. North followed Amyot in regularly adding the adjective 'noble' to nouns which, in the original Greek, are not qualified by an adjective.

achievements that Plutarch does. Nevertheless they might at the same time worry whether their attitude was justified. Their worry might amount to their wondering whether the honour they pay, the admiration they feel, comes to the same thing as moral approval. Do they regard this man as *morally meritorious*, whether or not he is an impressive example of human powers, or of *Romanitas*?

One way of understanding people who admire, love, and honour someone, not only for his jewel-like will, but also for his greatness of soul, his achievements, his imagination, his genius, is to say that in so far as they admire such things they are not judging him morally. Perhaps their appreciation should be called 'aesthetic'. If they have no idea of another, higher, decisively more authoritative judgement, based entirely on a sense of the purity of a man's intentions, and leaving out of account how far his intentions are realized, and leaving out of account also how 'great' his achievements are, then they seem to lack the category of the moral.

Yet that is not the only way to understand them. We could instead say that if a philosopher analyses the idea of the moral so that it excludes a priori many of those qualities and achievements in people that call forth admiration, love, and honour, then he is not really giving us the criteria for 'the moral point of view', but rather propounding a particular *morality*. Or, if it be true that in a particular tradition the idea of the moral is indeed understood in the way this philosopher analyses it, then it is still quite possible for those outside this tradition to choose to guide their lives by criteria or rules that might be other than 'moral'. We might call them 'ethical' just to mark a different set of serious rules. In this alternative tradition the notion of 'moral merit' might have a different, and perhaps lesser role. But as soon as we mark this difference between the two traditions, or forms of life, we see that there is no very good reason for calling them different analyses of the idea of the moral, rather than two different systems of values. This was essentially Nietzsche's criticism of Kant, that in attempting to elicit the criteria of any genuine morality, he produced a particular morality of selfless obedience.[20]

There is, however, another reason for thinking that the admiration one may feel for one of Plutarch's noble Greeks and Romans is 'aesthetic' rather than 'moral'. If it is true that an element of the contingent—special talents, opportunity, *fortuna*—might be part of

[20] See *Beyond Good and Evil*, sect. 187.

what we admire, or rejoice in on his behalf, then it follows that not everyone is in a position to imitate or emulate him, and that therefore not everyone is obliged to do so. Greatness of achievement is something we might enjoy as a spectacle, or a story, without feeling any obligation that we should try to do likewise. Aristotle clearly does not think that everyone has an obligation to try to be a great-souled, or a magnificent man, or that people should feel guilty or ashamed if they are neither. In other words, it can be argued that this ethic lacks the feature of *normativity* which very many philosophers, influenced by Kant, have taken to be a requirement of any judgement which expresses a genuinely moral attitude. In adopting a moral principle I implicitly will it as a law for all mankind.[21]

Thomas More clearly dissented from the Royal Supremacy, and was probably anti-Erastian throughout his life. It would have been contrary to his deepest convictions, and a failure of personal authenticity, for him to have taken the Oath. In this sense we can say that it was, for him, a matter of conscience. That he was willing to suffer death for his principle supports the use of that word. But he never spoke or wrote as though he thought that others had the same obligation of conscience. He had to be true to himself, to show a coherence in his own life. This conviction seems to have been independent of what others might do, or ought to do. That he seems to have felt no indignation that others accepted the Supremacy, that he manifested no desire that all men should refuse the Oath, might show that he fundamentally misunderstood the nature of moral judgement. Then again, it might not. To be ready to suffer death for one's beliefs does seem to suggest that one takes them seriously, even if one does not seem to will them as a law for all mankind. More's objection to the Oath does not seem to be like a distaste for oysters—a mere preference or whim. Rather it seems to proceed from and express a way of life.

Those philosophers, influenced by Kant, who wish to draw a sharp dividing line between those attitudes and principles that express the 'moral point of view' and those which do not, will be inclined to doubt that More's refusal to take the Oath sprang from a genuinely moral conviction. But suppose we bring to mind the variety of ways in which men can be serious about their values—

---

[21] See Kant, *Fundamental Principles*, sect. i, par. 22: 'I am never to act otherwise than so that I could also will that my maxim should become a universal law.'

even to the point of dying for them. If all such forms of seriousness, failing as they may of the requirement of normativity, are excluded from the category of the moral, then we would seem to be arguing about a word. We can understand what it is for people to admire, love, and honour the qualities and achievements of others; to reverence certain ideals which are captured in the concepts of greatness of mind and magnificence; to shrink with shame and disgust from ignoble, or bestial, or just cowardly actions. If we open our eyes or imaginations to the phenomenology of a form of life which encourages and illuminates such attitudes, then we will surely not find ourselves thinking of them simply as 'tastes'. We can find seriousness even in the proud refusal of some men even to want others to live up to *their* ideals.[22]

Kant's picture of the good man is of someone to whom we feel constrained to bow inwardly even if—perhaps because of his humble circumstances—we do not bow outwardly. Aristotle's great-souled man would seem to be someone to whom we would also bow outwardly. The honour he claims implies public respect. Aquinas is interesting on the outward respect which is owed to virtue. As part of his account of justice he considers *dulia*, or the virtue of respectful service.[23] He suggests that the honour we owe to someone's excellence is appropriately shown in outward signs of respect. The result of showing these outward signs is 'glory' which makes a person's excellence clearly known to many. Aristotle's *megalopsychos* looks for honour, and this will include outward respect. The *megalopsychos* would not show his great soul by amassing riches (that would be the vice of *pleonexia*), or even power. It would seem that he looks for honour as a citizen, who would run into danger and be unsparing of his life above all in the public good. Or, if he is willing to let his life revolve around a friend, this is because friendship is a disinterested relationship, so that love of a friend would not be flattery or self-seeking. We might recall Hegel's assertion that 'peoples of antiquity' had their honour

---

[22] Nietzsche: 'Signs of nobility: never to think of degrading our duties into duties for everyone . . .'. *Beyond Good and Evil*, sect. 272.

[23] *Summa*, 2a2ae, 103, 1, 3. 'Respectful service' is the translation in the Blackfriars edition of the *Summa* (edited by T. Gilby). The Greek word *douleia* originally means slavery or bondage. In Catholic tradition, *dulia* is the honour or worship properly paid to angels and saints; *hyperdulia* is what is owed to Our Lady; and *latria*—the state of hired service or slavery—is the worship owed to God.

'only in their substantial unity with that ethical relationship which is the State.'[24]

In his book *Arabian Sands* Wilfrid Thesiger tells several stories of the extraordinary generosity of extremely poor bedouin. One of his companions, Bin Kabina, a boy almost destitute, gives away first his loincloth, and then his shirt, simply because a man even poorer than himself had asked for them:

> 'God, why did you do that when you have only a rag to wear?'
> 'He asked me for it.'
> 'Damn the man. I gave him a handsome present. Really you are a fool.'
> 'Would you have me refuse him when he asked for it?'[25]

In the same book there is an account of a once-rich bedouin who had ruined himself through excessive generosity. Far from being thought 'a fool', he is intensely admired by the other bedouin. It seems that for the bedouin, purity of intention is what is good and noble. This is obviously not a worldly ethic, and is much closer to the Christian prizing of inner states than it is to Aristotle. Is Bin Kabina 'magnificent'? In one way he is as magnificent as anyone could be, since he shows a generosity of spirit that could not be greater. Do we want to call this a spiritual equivalent of *megaloprepeia*? It would not obviously be wrong, and would obviously not be absurd to do so. But we might equally say that the bedouin system of values is profoundly different from one in which Aristotle's virtue of magnificence could find a place. This is also true of a passage in the New Testament where rich men have been casting money into the Temple treasury, and a poor widow casts in 'two mites which make a farthing'. Jesus says 'this poor widow hath cast more in, than all they which have cast into the treasury: for all they did cast in of their abundance; but she of her want did cast in all she had, even all her living.'[26]

The Aristotelian virtues of magnificence and magnanimity seem to entail that the greatest virtues depend upon circumstance and opportunity for their full actualizing. It would presumably follow that Pericles, in constructing the buildings of the Acropolis, is more to be admired than the poor widow. This is a conclusion which to

---

[24] *The Philosophy of Mind*, sect. 432, *Zusatz*. Hegel adds, talking of the modern State, that the citizen 'derives his honour from the post he fills, from the trade he follows, and from any other kind of working activity.'

[25] Harmondsworth, 1964, p. 315.     [26] Mark 12: 42–3.

the Greeks would have seemed obvious, but which to Christians would be not 'foolishness' but deeply shocking.[27] That even those who are not believing Christians would probably also be disturbed by such worldliness might show that we have all become inured to the Christian paradox. Christ's saying that the widow 'hath cast more in' is indeed a paradox, and one which can be understood only against a normal usage in which to cast more in is literally to cast in more. To bless the 'poor in spirit' ('for theirs is the kingdom of heaven') and 'the meek' ('for they shall inherit the earth')[28] is to introduce a way of thinking that entirely rejects the worldiness implicit in an ethic of the virtues. The meek do not *merit* the kingdom of heaven, nor the poor-spirited that they inherit the earth. Rather ideas of merit and desert are rejected. Meek and poor-spirited people do not believe that they have a right to these things—otherwise they would not be meek and poor-spirited.

Pride, a desire for worldly glory, a sense that one can be 'a principle unto oneself', a lack of any apprehension that there might be some order of values in comparison with which those of the world are as nothing—all these are included in what Christianity has called 'paganism'. And 'paganism' has always seen the good life as being to a significant extent under the sway of fortune. That there should be a good for man independent of circumstance is asserted again and again in the Christian texts:

For I am sure that neither death nor life, nor angels, nor principalities, nor powers, nor things to come, nor might, nor height, nor depth, nor any other creature, shall be able to separate us from the love of God which is in Christ Jesus our Lord.[29]

'Lay not up for yourselves treasures upon earth, where moth and rust doth corrupt, and where thieves break through and steal: but lay up for yourselves treasures in heaven, where neither moth nor rust doth corrupt, and where thieves do not break through and steal: for where your treasure is, there will your heart be also.'[30]

The virtues delineated in Aristotle neither surrender completely to contingency, nor suggest that the good for man can completely escape it. Although a man's virtue is fully realized in activity in the world, Aristotle allows that the possession of virtue seems

---

[27] 'But we preach Christ crucified, unto the Jews a stumbling block, and unto the Greeks foolishness.' 1 Cor. 1: 23.
[28] Matt. 5: 3, 5.  [29] Rom. 8: 38–9.  [30] Matt. 6: 19–21.

compatible with being asleep, or with lifelong inactivity (and, further, 'with the greatest sufferings and misfortunes').[31] Martha Nussbaum has put it well:

> The central excellences of character reside, so to speak, *in* the person; they are states *of* the person. Activity in the world is their perfection or completion; but if activity is cut off there is still something stably there, an underlying core of good character whose natural expression is in the excellent activity. The core is not invulnerable; but it is relatively stable, even in the absence of activity.[32]

This would allow us to think that a particular person would, if he had the opportunity, be liberal; and that a particular liberal man would, in the right circumstances, be magnificent. At the same time, it allows us to think of the 'perfection or completion' of these states of character as being action in the world. If the natural expression is in the excellent activity, then we could not systematically substitute, for the natural activity, pure intention.[33] We can think of certain activities as the natural expression of states of character only if we have some reason for thinking that the state of character exists; and good intentions alone would not give us sufficient grounds for thinking this. Someone whose whole life had shown that he was brave and resourceful might become, through illness, incapable of any sort of action. Yet we should still think of him as brave and resourceful—not as someone who used to be brave. (Some sorts of mental illness might make us think differently.) Another man who throughout his life was always forming good intentions, but then abandoning them out of fearfulness, levity, or weakness of will, might also fall ill, and we could not think of him as having a core of good character which unfortunately could no longer be realized in action. Aristotle's man of lifelong inactivity is presumably judged to be virtuous on grounds solider than his often expressing beautiful sentiments.

Although the virtues in Aristotle enable people to achieve the good life, they are not simply means to an end. The goods which the virtues make possible include those which are internal to the practice of the virtue. If friendship is made possible by the virtue of

---

[31] *Ethics*, 1095$^b$30–1096$^a$1.
[32] *The Fragility of Goodness*, p. 343.
[33] In the sense of pure willing—which would be like pure wishing. I do not suggest that we could coherently imagine this.

justice, this does not mean that justice is merely one way of achieving the good of friendship, a good which we could understand and perhaps gain without justice. It is only in being just that we are capable of friendship; but in its turn friendship is justice in action, one of the chief ways in which that particular element of an 'underlying core of good character' can find its natural expression in excellent activity. Accidents of fortune may help one to exercise a virtue to the fullest extent. These may include being born into a high culture, or a free polity; having a good moral education; being healthy, clever, and beautiful. In that sense an ethic of the virtues does not assume that everyone, in seeking to be good and to lead the good life, starts from a position of absolute equality with everyone else.

If my account of the virtues is at all persuasive, then it points to dispositions which in general people have reason for cultivating. It is difficult to imagine how the good life could be lived without courage, temperance, practical wisdom, and justice. The courageous man does not simply pursue an end which he desires, with intelligence and determination, despite the pains and terrors. Rather his virtue, connected as it is with pride and shame, implies from the beginning an understanding of himself as a person amongst persons, with values and loyalties which go with that understanding. Courage enables him to transcend his purely selfish or limited concerns, and to desire and pursue what is noble in life. Temperance implies an ordering not only of passions and appetites, but also of the will, a tempering of egoism and *amour propre*. It is a virtue of civilization, enabling people to attach due weight to the wishes and claims of others, and not simply to their own. Indeed, it is only through such tempering that we can properly understand our own claims. Practical wisdom seems necessary to many arts and skills, including the art of politics. It is also necessary to moral goodness, in relation to which it is not purely an art or skill, but a capacity for intelligent goodness which is itself the outcome of virtuous dispositions. Like practical wisdom, justice issues from good dispositions, and can be understood through benevolence, love, and friendship.

It is extremely difficult to imagine how a good life could be lived without these virtues. Indeed all of them seem necessary for every individual. Yet to exercise them requires the co-operation of Fortune.

# 7

## POSTSCRIPT: HOMER, SHAKESPEARE, AND THE CONFLICT OF VALUES

H AV E I been attempting to excavate and commend 'pagan' values? Certainly the thrust of the book has been towards eliciting sympathy for ways of thinking about the virtues that owe very little to Christian tradition. Excavation, however, is an antiquarian pursuit, and rarely leads to the revival of a tradition of architecture. My suggestion has implicitly been that we do in practice think about human excellences much of the time in ways which could be described (or censured) as 'pagan'. We do value greatness of achievement as well as pure intentions; we respect proper pride in others, and need to have it in ourselves; we do understand the virtues as somehow fulfilled in a public sphere; we admire and love people more for the active virtues of courage and practical wisdom than for what Hume called the 'monkish virtues' of humility and self-denial.[1] Yet at the same time it would be absurd to deny that we are all inescapably influenced by another tradition, one which teaches that he who would save his life must lose it; that the poor in spirit shall inherit the earth; that unless we become as little children we shall not enter the kingdom of heaven. (We are also influenced by such Stoic ideas as that the wise and good man can be happy even if he is enslaved; and by Kant's doctrine that the only absolutely good thing in the world is the Good Will.) On the face of it, these different traditions cannot be reconciled. It is true that Aquinas made an heroic attempt to reconcile the ethics of Aristotle with the teachings of Christ, and the many men of the Renaissance were quite unembarrassed by the conflict—just as they were happy to mingle Christian and pagan mythology in their art and literature. (And that remarkable work of the seventeenth century— the *Oracle* of the Jesuit Gracian—after two hundred and ninety-nine

---

[1] Cf. *Enquiry*, sect. ix, pt. i.

paragraphs containing purely worldly wisdom, can begin the three-hundredth—and last—with the surprising remark: 'In a word, be a saint.') Are we in the happy position of any of these? One may reasonably doubt that we are. The history (let alone the genealogy) of morals is, however, beyond the ambitions of this book. I content myself with suggesting that Nietzsche's insistence that there is an irreconcilable conflict within our moral inheritance seems close to accurately describing the modern predicament. One can understand Nietzsche not as attempting to reintroduce Homeric ethics into the modern world, but as trying to make us sharply aware that the conflict between different ways of valuing human character has never been stilled.

As no more than a footnote to Nietzsche, and as evidence that the conflict may still be alive, I end by pointing to two different ways of understanding tragedy.

One of the themes of this book—which may have been found particularly eccentric—has been the significance of anger in active virtue. If there is any general way of distinguishing Christian from 'pagan' values it may broadly coincide with a different valuing of the 'irascible' and the 'concupiscential'.[2] I understand the irascible as going with pride and shame, a sense of the noble, a certain valuing of courage and ambition. The concupiscential goes with sympathy and pity, and finds its highest value in love. One might indeed say that a 'pagan' system of values will consider honour to be a higher value than love. T. S. Eliot writes that the key word in Virgil is *fatum*, destiny: 'Aeneas is a man guided by the deepest conviction of destiny . . .'. Aeneas' destiny—to found the *imperium romanum*—is the 'one far off divine event' to which the whole poem moves. Eliot adds that there is a term which one justifiably regrets the lack of in Virgil, and that is *amor*: 'There is tenderness and pathos enough in the *Aeneid*. But Love is never given, to my mind, the same significance that *pietas* is given; and it is not love that causes *fatum*, or moves the sun and the stars.'[3]

One way in which we can sharpen our sense of the difference between an ethic in which ideas such as *pietas*, *fatum*, and honour are central, and one which finds its highest expression in love, pity,

---

[2] I take the terms from Aquinas, although I shall not use them in exactly the way he does. I owe the idea to Colin Burrow.

[3] 'Virgil and the Christian World', *On Poetry and Poets* (London, 1957), pp. 121–31.

and sympathy, is by meditating on differences between ancient and modern tragedy. I shall take two texts: the scene in the *Iliad* when Priam comes to Achilles to beg the body of Hector for burial;[4] and *King Lear*.

Priam does not utter a simple appeal for pity. He certainly does not look for the sort of pity that makes Dante faint after hearing the story of Paolo and Francesca:

> ... che di pietade
> io venni men cosi com' io morisse;
> e caddi, come corpo morto cade.

So that I fainted with pity, as if I had been dying; and fell, as a dead body falls.[5]

What does Priam do? The first thing he does is to make the ritual gesture of submission and appeal for mercy: 'Unseen of these great Priam entered in, and coming close to Achilles, clasped in his hands his knees, and kissed his hands, the terrible man-slaying hands that had slain his many sons.'[6] In order to prevent Achilles' wrath (and advised by the god to do so) he *immediately* bids Achilles think of his own father, whose age is as grievous as his own, and who might even now, without his son to protect him, be suffering from the unjust treatment of those living around him. He ends the speech: 'Nay, have thou awe of the gods, Achilles, and take pity on me, remembering thine own father. Lo, I am more piteous far than he, and have endured what no other mortal on the face of the earth hath yet endured, to reach forth my hand to the face of him that hath slain my sons.'[7] (The words Priam uses are *eleeson* and *eleeinoteros*, which connote mercy and wretchedness as well as pity.) Achilles weeps for his own father, and for his beloved friend Patroclus, whom Hector had slain. Having wept he wonders how Priam had dared to come to him in disguise: 'How hadst thou the heart to come alone to the ships of the Achaeans, to meet the eyes of me that have slain thy sons many and valiant? Of iron verily is thy heart.'[8] He then reminds Priam that all men are subject to Fate, and that his own fate is to die young, never to be a comfort to his father's old age. Priam adjures him to return the body; and Achilles 'with an angry glance' tells him not to provoke him, since he was

---

[4] Homer, *Iliad*, xxiv. 468–677.     [5] *Inferno*, v. 140–2.
[6] *Iliad*, xxiv. 477–9.     [7] *Iliad*, xxiv. 503–6.
[8] *Iliad*, xxiv. 519–21.

going to give Hector back anyway, because he believes that this is what the gods command. Priam is silent, seized with fear, while Achilles 'like a lion' springs forth from the house to give his orders about the body of Hector. Achilles commands that the body be washed, lest the sight of it, disfigured, arouse Priam to anger, which would in turn arouse Achilles' wrath, so that he slay Priam. Achilles certainly does pity Priam. It would be better to say, perhaps, that he takes pity upon him, in a way that is like deciding to have mercy (*kyrie eleison*). It is not like the almost amorous sympathy that Dante feels for Paolo and Francesca. Between Achilles and Priam there is potential antagonism and anger, aggression and distance, a sort of wondering respect. It is a sense of being subject to a common fate, a fellow feeling, a recognition of the common human lot, of the vulnerability of human life. Achilles' pity for Priam is mediated through this sense of the human lot. It is not self-pity, but a sort of lament over man's fate, a general fate which includes his father, Patroclus, and himself. It is not unimportant that Priam has brought a large ransom—indeed, that is the main justification Achilles offers, in his invocation of the dead Patroclus, for agreeing to return the body. Priam has not only been asking for pity; he has also been negotiating. He has been using every resource to bring about something of the highest importance, which is also an inescapable obligation for him—proper funeral rites for Hector. Had Achilles not wondered at his strength of mind and courage, as well as pitying him, he would not have succeeded. Nor is Achilles' pity enough: there must also be a material compensation to appease the spirit of Patroclus.

If we want to choose the most important idea in the passage, it would be not love, but fate. The tragic note is the recognition of the inevitability of suffering and death by men who retain their pride, wrath, and strength.[9] This comes out in lines which Matthew Arnold was moved to include among his 'touchstones' of a style of high seriousness:

καὶ τέ γέρον, τὸ πρὶν ἀκούομεν ὄλβιον εἶναι

('Nay, and thou too old man, in former days wast, as we hear, happy.')[10]

There is no play of Shakespeare that has precisely *this* tragic note, but *King Lear* most insistently brings it to mind, even as it negates

---

[9] See MacIntyre, *After Virtue*, p. 117.  [10] *Iliad*, xxiv. 543.

it. The history of *Lear* criticism makes an interesting subject. During most of its theatrical history the play was not particularly popular. In the eighteenth century it was always performed in Tate's version, with its heightened 'love interest' (Edgar loves Cordelia) and notorious happy ending. Even Johnson condoned Tate's version on the grounds that Shakespeare's ending is intolerably painful and outrages our sense of justice. It was not until the early nineteenth century that Kean and Macready finally reintroduced to the stage the play as Shakespeare had written it. But although all modern critics (it goes without saying) prefer the authentic text, and although *King Lear* has come to be regarded as Shakespeare's greatest achievement—whether or not it is his best play[11]—attempts by critics to demonstrate an ethical coherence in it have mostly succeeded in confronting us with tensions, and perhaps contradictions, within the morality we inherit. I suspect that the moral objections to the play which were expressed by readers and critics of the eighteenth century have behind them a more coherent ethic than is implicit in many modern attempts to understand *Lear*.

Lear is represented by Shakespeare as not so much a proud man, than as a man who may once have been proud, but whose pride has, with age and flattery, degenerated into childish vanity and irascibility. A. C. Bradley characterizes Lear's behaviour to both Cordelia and Goneril as hubris. He thinks that there is an extraordinary disproportion between Lear's rage and what occasions it. Bradley attributes this to 'a presumptuous self-will'.[12] It is not only Lear's disinheritance of Cordelia which shows hubris, but the words which announce it:

> The barbarous Scythian,
> Or he that makes his generation messes
> To gorge his appetite, shall to my bosom
> Be as well neighbour'd, pitied and relieved,
> As thou my sometime daughter.[13]

A similar violence is shown in his cursing of Goneril. Bradley writes that 'up to the moment of its utterance Goneril has done no more than to require him "a little to disquantity" and reform his train of

---

[11] A distinction lucidly drawn by A. C. Bradley, *Shakespearian Tragedy* (London, 1926), pp. 244 ff.  [12] Ibid., p. 282.

[13] *King Lear*, I. i. 115–19.

knights.' Certainly her manner and spirit in making this demand
are hateful . . . But surely the famous words which form Lear's
immediate reply were meant to be nothing short of frightful:

> Hear, nature, hear; dear goddess hear!
> Suspend thy purpose, if thou didst intend
> To make this creature fruitful!
> Into her womb convey sterility!
> Dry up in her the organs of increase;
> And from her derogate body never spring
> A babe to honour her![14]

Bradley's description of Lear's behaviour as hubris is too simple.
For instance, Lear's speech to Cordelia contains dramatic irony.[15]
Does not Lear unconsciously characterize himself when he talks of
the Scythian who gorges himself on his own children? His vanity
seeks to gorge itself on his daughters. Then there is his strangely
elaborate imagining of the same Scythian needing his 'bosom' to be
'neighbour'd, pitied and relieved'. It is Lear who had looked to set
his rest on Cordelia's 'kind nursery'—with its suggestions of both
sustaining care and second childhood. He feels exiled from
Cordelia's bosom. His 'hubris', that is to say, has about it a
vulnerable quality. Indeed from the beginning of the play we have
an impression of Lear's helplessness. This makes his description of
himself as a 'dragon' absurd, even as he shows his power in
banishing Kent.[16] And his cursing of Goneril is too obviously
impotent to be terrible. Furthermore, Goneril, in requiring him 'a
little to disquantity' his train of knights, had used words which
Bradley does not quote:

> . . . be then desir'd
> *By her, that else will take the thing she begs,*
> A little to disquantity your train . . .[17]

Goneril has, as clearly and insolently as possible, asserted her
superior power, and her contempt for the agreement which Lear
had made with his two daughters. Lear's rage is less hubristic than
impotent.

For Bradley, Lear's hubris is broken by what happens to him,

<hr/>

[14] I. iv. 272–9.
[15] Noticed by S. L. Goldberg, to whom I am indebted, in *An Essay on King Lear*
(Cambridge, 1974), p. 25.
[16] I. i. 122.     [17] I. iv. 255–7 (my italic).

and it is in this breaking of his pride that his redemption is found. The breaking of Lear is often described by critics as a redemption. Bradley goes so far as to suggest that the play ought to be called *The Redemption of King Lear*. It would not be too much of a simplification to say that Lear's 'redemption' is found to be based on two things: first, his discovery of humility, and secondly, his rediscovery of his love for Cordelia. Lear comes to see himself as 'old and foolish' and 'not in my perfect mind'.[18] He is ready to drink poison to satisfy what he believes to be Cordelia's just desire for revenge.[19] As to his discovery of love, Bradley writes forthrightly that Lear is brought by his suffering to see 'how power and place and all things in the world are vanity except love.' He adds that 'there is nothing more noble and beautiful in literature than Shakespeare's exposition of the effect of suffering in reviving the greatness and eliciting the sweetness of Lear's nature.'[20]

Now Lear had asked the gods for something other than redemption through humility and love:

> ... touch me with noble anger,
> And let not women's weapons, water-drops,
> Stain my man's cheeks![21]

Bradley says that the business of 'the gods' with him 'was neither to torment him, nor to teach him a "noble anger", but to lead him to attain through apparently hopeless failure the very end and aim of life.' And the very end and aim of life is indeed that 'all things in the world are vanity except love.'[22]

It is interesting that the pagan gods of Lear's world should enforce something resembling the Christian message. It is interesting also that Bradley does not feel that it is necessary to say anything in support of the idea that the only thing in life which is not vanity is love. This sound like a secularized version of the famous passage at the beginning of the *Imitation of Christ*, which in turn alludes to the opening of Ecclesiastes: '*Vanity*, saith the Preacher, *all is vanity*, save, loving God and serving Him alone.'[23]

It is true that Lear, and the spectator, '[see] some meaning

[18] IV. vii. 84, 63.
[19] IV. vii. 71–5.
[20] *Shakespearian Tragedy*, pp. 284–5.
[21] II. iv. 274–6.
[22] *Shakespearian Tragedy*, pp. 284–5.
[23] Thomas à Kempis, *Imitation of Christ*, bk. i, ch. 1.

embodied in the immediate living fact' of Cordelia.[24] Bradley is
right in finding in Lear's love for Cordelia a profound significance
in the play. But can we not also find ourselves disturbed by this
love, by its pathos, by the element of despair or fantasy in it? When
Lear and Cordelia are taken, after the battle has been lost, Cordelia
says:

> Shall we not see these daughters and these sisters?[25]

It seems that even now Cordelia would confront Goneril and Regan
with their crimes. Bradley says of these 'strange last words' of
Cordelia: 'Their tone is unmistakable. I doubt if she could have
brought herself to plead with her sisters for her father's life; and if
she had attempted the task, she would have performed it but ill.'[26]
Cordelia's love for Lear includes her wish to uphold his 'right'.[27]
Lear replies to Cordelia:

> No, no, no, no! Come, let's away to prison;
> We two alone will sing like birds i' the cage:
> When thou dost ask me blessing, I'll kneel down,
> And ask of thee forgiveness: so we'll live,
> And pray, and sing, and tell old tales, and laugh
> At gilded butterflies, and hear poor rogues
> Talk of court news: and we'll talk with them too,
> Who loses and who wins; who's in, who's out;
> And take upon's the mystery of things,
> As if we were God's spies . . .[28]

Bradley calls this speech 'that great renunciation of the world with
its power and glory and resentments and revenges', a renunciation
that 'would never have been offered but for the knowledge that
came to Lear in his madness'.[29] Lear's words in fact show a desire
for a life with Cordelia hidden from the rest of the world. The love
with which he is now possessed is blended with egoism. Unlike
Cordelia, he excludes knowledge of the mortal danger they are in. It
is not just that he cannot think that anything worse can happen to
them than prison. He is not thinking about such things at all. We
cannot read his words as a great renunciation of the world. They

---

[24] Goldberg, *King Lear*, p. 169.
[25] v. iii. 7.
[26] *Shakespearian Tragedy*, p. 322.
[27] '. . . love, dear love, and our ag'd father's right.' IV. iv. 28.
[28] v. iii. 8–17.
[29] *Shakespearian Tragedy*, pp. 289–90.

express the dream of a broken man. The language is a childlike version of a traditional language of renunciation, bordering upon delusion. Lear's original error and wrongdoing were produced by a baffled love, a blameable voracity for love mixed up with vanity. After his madness Lear is never fully restored to mental strength. His love for Cordelia from Act IV Scene vii until the end of the play has an intolerable pathos. She is, after all, all he has left. Lear's pride is indeed broken; he is never touched with noble anger, and loses all desire to be. But the condition of all this is that he is a broken man.

My suggestion is that Lear's love for Cordelia becomes a matter of intolerable pathos, something we can hardly bear to witness. It is not the love of a whole man. Why do not people find this—and not simply Lear's entry with Cordelia dead in his arms—painful? One answer might be that certain ideas about gaining one's life through losing it, a Christian tradition of renunciation, tend to blind us to what is pitiable in *this* 'renunciation'. Indeed, one could even see Lear's exclusive concentration upon Cordelia and his love for her as a disturbing parody of the traditional Christian theme of renunciation. Perhaps critics have found the idea that Lear renounces the world, its resentments and revenges, extremely attractive because it imposes a consoling pattern on what otherwise might look—as it did to the eighteenth century—like simply unbearable suffering, even adventitious cruelty.

In a famous essay, G. Wilson Knight drew attention to what he called 'the comedy of the grotesque' in Lear.[30] He showed how the play repeatedly strikes down pride in ways that are close to the absurd. When Lear's daughters betray his expectations, his range frequently borders on the comical:

> But yet thou art my flesh, my blood, my daughter;
> Or rather a disease that's in my flesh,
> Which I must needs call mine: thou art a boil,
> A plague-sore, an embossed carbuncle,
> In my corrupted blood. But I'll not chide thee . . .[31]

There are many such examples of 'the comedy of the grotesque' in the play. And (as Knight also suggests) the whole treatment of Gloucester is structured by the grotesque disproportion between the dignified picture Gloucester wishes to have of his own suffering,

[30] *The Wheel of Fire* (London, 1939), pp. 175–93.    [31] II. iv. 219–23.

and what then happens. When Gloucester prepares for suicide he
prays on what he believes is the edge of Dover Cliff:

> O you mighty Gods!
> This world I do renounce, and in your sights
> Shake patiently this great affliction off;
> If I could bear it longer, and not fall
> To quarrel with your great opposeless wills,
> My snuff and loathed part of nature should
> Burn itself out.[32]

Wilson Knight makes this penetrating comment: 'Gloucester has
planned a spectacular end for himself. We are given these noble
descriptive and philosophical speeches to tune our minds to a
noble, tragic sacrifice. And what happens? The old man falls from
his kneeling posture a few inches, flat, face foremost . . . The
grotesque merged into the ridiculous reaches a consummation in
this bathos of tragedy.' One can add to Wilson Knight's examples.
After the failed suicide, Gloucester says to Edgar:

> . . . henceforth I'll bear
> Affliction till it do cry out itself
> 'Enough, enough', and die.[33]

And Edgar responds: 'Bear free and patient thoughts.'[34] Even now
something remains of a sort of stoic dignity. But all dignity is
immediately dispersed with: '*Enter Lear, fantastically dressed with
wild flowers.*' Lear is completely mad. In his madness he seems to
recognize Gloucester, before he acknowledges him, for all his
remarks seem slyly and sadistically directed at him:

> I pardon that man's life. What was thy cause?
> Adultery?
> Thou shalt not die: die for adultery! No.
>
> .    .    .    .    .    .    .
>
> Let copulation thrive; for Gloucester's bastard son
> Was kinder to his father than my daughters
> Got 'tween the lawful sheets.[35]

Lear then makes a series of jokes about Gloucester's blindness,
perhaps at the same time alluding to his adultery:

[32] IV. vi. 34–40.          [33] IV. vi. 75–7.
[34] IV. vi. 79.             [35] IV. vi. 112–19.

LEAR. I remember thine eyes well enough. Dost squiny at me?
No, do thy worst blind Cupid; I'll not love.
Read thou this challenge; mark but the penning of it.
GLOUCESTER. Were all the letters suns, I could not see it.[36]

Later Lear begins to make a dignified speech—he says that he will
'preach'—which begins with a traditional trope and turns suddenly
into murderous rage:

When we are born, we cry that we are come
To this great stage of fools. This a good block!
It were a delicate stratagem to shoe
A troop of horse with felt; I'll put it in proof,
And when I have stol'n upon these sons-in-laws,
Then, kill, kill, kill, kill, kill.[37]

Shakespeare regularly disappoints our expectations in this play,
and he regularly removes consolation just when it seems about to
materialize. How then can we be sure that the play enacts the
greatest consolation—that Lear has come to know that all is vanity
in the world except love? And that this is true knowledge? May not
this also be a false consolation?

Christians would not be wrong in finding the play resonant with
Christian ideas. Humility is an important theme. But does Lear
discover humility as Christians understand the word? After his
madness he describes himself as 'old and foolish', and 'a very
foolish fond old man'.[38] There is certainly a humbled quality in his
words to Cordelia:

Thou art a soul in bliss; but I am bound
Upon a wheel of fire, that mine own tears
Do scald like molten lead.[39]

There is little more than that. Bradley thinks that Lear finds
knowledge in his madness. Is it then that he discovers humility?
Before he actually goes mad, in the storm scenes, he is filled with
rage and grief at the ingratitude of his daughters. He realizes that he
had been flattered during his time of power: 'When the rain came to
wet me once and the wind to make me chatter, when the thunder
would not peace at my bidding, there I found 'em, there I smelt 'em

[36] IV. vi. 134–8.         [37] IV. vi. 180–5.
[38] IV. vii. 84, 60.        [39] IV. vii. 46–8.

out. Go to, they are not men of their words: they told me I was everything; 'tis a lie, I am not ague-proof.'[40] And he sees human society as pervaded with hypocrisy:

> Robes and furr'd gowns hide all. Plate sin with gold,
> And the strong lance of justice hurtless breaks;
> Arm it in rags, a pigmy's straw does pierce it.[41]

There is something in all this that could be called humility, and more that could be described as being humbled. It is possible, however, that a Christian-inspired readiness to discover a redemptive humility in Lear leads us to exaggerate the former. It is surprising that critics can be so sure that we should see Lear as having discovered humility, rather than as having been broken and *therefore* humbled by his sufferings. In the Christian tradition humility is a virtue, because it shows an awareness of man's sinfulness, ignorance, and impotence, as compared with the goodness, omniscience, and power of God. But to be broken and humbled as Lear is is not of itself good, even in the Christian tradition. And outside that tradition, what happens to Lear may not make sense at all. It is possible that many people are not troubled by a possible confusion in the play, because they allow themselves inertly to be influenced by a secularized version of Christian belief.

It is in fact difficult to argue that the play sets forth, in any coherent way, a vision of renunciation of the world and its glory, power, and resentments. The Fool is generally allowed to be a very important character. Yet we might remember that everything the Fool says to Lear is about his *folly*—his folly in trusting Goneril and Regan, in giving up his power, in believing that without power he will be respected, or even safe. The Fool talks all the time in proverbial, worldly wisdom. He never once urges Lear to remember humility, or to think of renouncing the world and its pomps. Quite the contrary. He never once suggests that Lear should feel guilt about Cordelia. Indeed, when Lear seems to be thinking of her ('I did her wrong')[42] the Fool immediately diverts his attention from her. (It is possible, of course, that, on this occasion at least, the Fool wishes to spare his master's feelings. In general he is quite cruel to Lear, constantly drawing his attention to his folly in an unsparing way.) It may be argued that the Fool's view of things is hardly

[40] IV. vi. 102–8.     [41] IV. vi. 163–5.     [42] I. v. 24.

decisive; and, as Bradley says, it is probably right to think of the Fool as half-mad.[43] Nevertheless, the Fool provides by far the main body of comment on Lear's behaviour, and none of it has to do with the desirability of renunciation, or humility, or love.

If we do not simply assume—as Bradley apparently does—that everything in the world is vanity, except love; if we think (for instance) that for 'the gods' to have touched Lear with 'noble rage', and for him to have found the means of translating this noble rage into revenge upon his ghastly daughters, would have been the greatest good for him (although not the best material for a tragedy), then the play becomes much more painful and unconsoling than Bradley, and many other critics, would allow. Indeed, it becomes the play that eighteenth-century theatre-goers could not bear. The defeat of Lear's manhood; his being left only with the pathos of his love for Cordelia; his delusion that this love could be all, even in prison—all this is intensely painful. Lear's final words, perhaps suggesting that he thinks Cordelia is alive, do not suggest redemption in any sense that matters. The experience of the play does not firmly, or consistently, encourage us to find values decisively higher than worldly ones.

Yet at the same time, critics who have found in Cordelia an intimation of something saving are right. Not only does she stand for love; she stands, shiningly and explicitly, for an unselfish love— a love which 'seeketh not her own'[44]—which is very like Christian charity. Furthermore, Cordelia's love for Lear does point to the way in which the play entertains other-worldly values. Lear has throughout believed that he *merits* the love of his daughters, because he is a father, a loving father, a kind father who 'gave you all'.[45] Justice requires their gratitude and a return of love. Even Cordelia initially speaks the same language:

> I love your Majesty
> According to my bond; no more nor less.
>      .      .      .      .      .
> You have begot me, bred me, lov'd me: I
> Return those duties back as are right fit,
> Obey you, love you, and most honour you. . . .[46]

[43] *Shakespearian Tragedy*, pp. 311–12.          [44] 1 Cor. 13: 5.
[45] II. iv. 252.                                 [46] I. i. 91–7.

But the love which Cordelia finally offers Lear has nothing to do with her 'bond', or with justice or desert—she simply loves him. When Lear says that she has 'some cause' either not to love him, or to do wrong to him (it is not clear which in the passage) she replies, 'no cause, no cause.'[47] This does not mean that Cordelia thinks that Lear still merits her love despite the wrong he has done her, or that he has done her no wrong, but that the question of merit, desert, the 'bond' is rejected altogether. This all resonates with a Christian understanding of a love which seeks no return.

But Cordelia is hanged by a common soldier—an especially degrading death. Can we really say that the consolation offered to our moral sense by the love she exemplifies is any less undermined by the events of the play than is the dignified stoicism affected by Edgar and Gloucester? Surely there is a similarity between the two? If that is so, then we are left with a play in which stoic values of noble patience, feudal loyalty (Kent), Christian values of humility and selfless love, keep emerging into prominence, but are never fully endorsed by what happens in the play. At the same time there is the pain of Lear's horrible humiliation, the defeat of his manhood, his childlike 'sweetness' (the word is Bradley's)[48] after his awakening in Cordelia's tent, and his helplessness to prevent her murder. Some may feel that for an old man to know his helplessness, to lapse into a childlike dependence, suggests 'salvation'. Others may find it inconsolably painful, and may think that it makes Lear, in the end, an object of overwhelming and fearful pity.

It is possible that *King Lear* embodies an unresolved conflict between 'pagan' and Christian values, and between the 'irascible' and 'concupiscential'. It is possible also to see the play as entertaining, but then destroying, a series of visions of human possibility that console the moral sense. It is easy, on that reading, to understand why Samuel Johnson found the play intolerable.

In the *Iliad* we do not feel *this* sort of painful pity for Priam, for he is not, even when he humbles himself, humiliated. He is not broken by calamity, but retains his pride and his courage. Our pity for him includes a sense of the common fate of man. That Achilles and Priam can join in recognizing this common fate, so that Achilles weeps for Priam, and for his own father, and for Patroclus, and for the shortness of his own life, preserves a severe, unpathetic, tragic dignity.

[47] IV. vii. 74–5.          [48] *Shakespearian Tragedy*, p. 285.

Part of the greatness of *King Lear* lies in what, ethically speaking, could be regarded as confusion. It makes use, opportunistically, of some of the most potent images and emotions in our culture—the humbling of pride, the survival of love, finding oneself through losing oneself, redemption. At the same time, and even as a condition of the power to move us of such things, there is in the background a recognition of the good of 'noble rage', of outrage at ingratitude, of horror at the comprehensive defeat of manhood.

> I am ashamed
> That thou hast power to shake my manhood thus,
> That these hot tears, which break from me perforce,
> Should make thee worth them.[49]

It may be that *King Lear* deliberately offers no consolation, that stoic ideas of human dignity surviving amid suffering, the belief in the triumph of justice, a faith in providence, Christian ideas of redemption through love, are all subverted. If that is so, then the play is coherent, but disturbingly nihilistic, even sensationalist. It is more cruel than tragic. However, it may be that *Lear* uncomfortably combines, without reconciling, 'pagan' and Christian elements. This could be taken as evidence for T. S. Eliot's suggestion that 'the thought behind Shakespeare is of men far inferior to Shakespeare himself'[50]—i.e. Seneca, Machiavelli, and Montaigne. My own opinion is that there is confusion in the play, that the discordant elements are not reconciled, and that it is impossible that they should be reconciled. We fully respond to, and understand, what is outrageous in Lear's humiliation; we subscribe to a 'pagan' wish that he be revenged upon his daughters. We find the impotence of his anger distressing. At the same time, we are willing half to believe that there is a transcendent value in Cordelia's unselfish love. And many critics, drawing on Christian presuppositions, translate this vague belief in Cordelia into a clear redemptive pattern which (I suggest) is not warranted by the text of the play. Such critics agree in dissenting from the unhappiness of the eighteenth century with *King Lear*, but they also discover a consolation in the play which is as false as Tate's happy ending.

It has been a theme implicit in this book that we inherit a

---

[49] I. iv. 294–7.
[50] 'Shakespeare and the Stoicism of Seneca', *Selected Essays*, ed. T. S. Eliot (London, 1951), pp. 135–6.

confused system of values; that when we think most rigorously and realistically we are 'pagans' in ethics, but that our Christian inheritance only allows a fitful sincerity about this. It would therefore be wrong to assume that any thorough return to 'pagan' ways of thinking about ethics is being suggested. *King Lear* is a central text in our culture, and it suggests—even, perhaps, shows— that the impossible attempt to reconcile discordant elements is what we are committed to whether we will or no.

# BIBLIOGRAPHY

ALTHAM, J. E. J., review of Michael Oakeshott, *On Human Conduct, The Cambridge Review*, 97 (Oct. 1975), 23–5.

ANSCOMBE, G. E. M., *Intention* (Oxford, 1963).

AQUINAS, ST THOMAS, *Summa theologiae*, gen. ed. T. Gilby (London, 1972).

AUGUSTINE, ST, *De libero arbitrio*, trans. Benjamin and Hackerstaff (Indianapolis, 1964).

ARISTOTLE, *Nicomachean Ethics*, trans. W. D. Ross (Oxford, 1915).

—— *Nicomachean Ethics*, trans. Rackham (London, 1934).

—— *Politics*, trans. Ernest Barker (Oxford, 1948).

—— *Rhetoric*, trans. Ross (Oxford, 1924).

ARNOLD, MATTHEW, 'John Keats', *Essays in Criticism*, 2nd ser., ed. S. R. Littlewood, (London, 1938), pp. 60–72.

AUSTEN, JANE, *The Novels of Jane Austen*, ed. R. W. Chapman (Oxford, 1965).

BENNETT, JONATHAN, *Rationality* (London, 1964).

BIBLE, Authorized Version.

BRADLEY, A. C., *Shakespearian Tragedy* (London, 1926).

BROWN, PETER, *Augustine of Hippo* (London, 1969).

BURNABY, JOHN, *Amor Dei* (London, 1938).

BUTLER, JOSEPH, Sermons II and III 'Upon the Natural Supremacy of Conscience', *The Analogy of Religion and Sermons*, ed. M.A. (London, 1886).

BUTLER, MARILYN, *Jane Austen and the War of Ideas* (Oxford, 1975).

BYRON, GEORGE GORDON, *Don Juan, Poetical Works*, ed. F. Page (Oxford, 1969).

CARLYLE, THOMAS, *On Heroes, Hero Worship, and the Heroic in History* (London, 1891).

CASEY, JOHN, 'Practical Wisdom', *Essays in Criticism*, 27 (Oct. 1977), 348–54.

—— 'The Autonomy of Art', *Royal Institute of Philosophy Lectures*, 6 (1971–2) 65–87.

CLARENDON, EDWARD HYDE, EARL OF, *History of the Rebellion*, ed. W. Dunn Macray (Oxford, 1888).

CONRAD, JOSEPH, *Nostromo* (London, 1957).

—— *Lord Jim* (Harmondsworth, 1957).

DALEY, HARRY, *This Small Cloud* (London, 1986).

228            *Bibliography*

DANTE ALIGHIERI, *La Divina Commedia*, de. *R.H.W.* (London, 1900).
DAVIDSON, DONALD, 'How is Weakness of Will Possible?' in Joel Feinberg (ed.), *Moral Concepts* (Oxford, 1969), pp. 93–113.
DENNETT, DANIEL, 'Conditions of Personhood', in Amelia Rorty (ed.), *The Identities of Persons* (Berkeley, 1976), pp. 175–96.
DESCARTES, RENÉ, *The Passions of the Soul*, trans. Haldane and Ross (Cambridge, 1931).
DICKENS, CHARLES, *Great Expectations* (London, 1890).
—— *Hard Times* (London, 1890).
DONALDSON, IAN, 'Jonson and Anger', *Yearbook of English Studies*, 14 (1984), 56–71.
DONNE, JOHN, *Songs and Sonets, Poems*, ed. H. Grierson (Oxford, 1933).
DOSTOEVSKY, FYODOR, *The Brothers Karamazov*, trans. Magarshack (Harmondsworth, 1958).
ELIOT, GEORGE, *Middlemarch* (London, 1901).
ELIOT, T. S., Introduction to Samuel Johnson, 'London: A Poem' and 'The Vanity of Human Wishes' (London, 1930).
—— 'Little Gidding', *The Complete Poems and Plays* (London, 1969), pp. 191–8.
—— 'Shakespeare and the Stoicism of Seneca', *Selected Essays*, ed. T. S. Eliot (London, 1951), pp. 126–46.
—— 'The Metaphysical Poets', *Selected Essays*, ed. T. S. Eliot (London, 1951), pp. 281–91.
—— 'Virgil and the Christian World', *On Poetry and Poets* (London, 1957), pp. 121–31.
FREUD, SIEGMUND, 'Three Essays on the Theory of Sexuality', *Works*, vol. vii, ed. Richards, pp. 45–169.
GOLDBERG, S. L., *An Essay on King Lear* (Cambridge, 1974).
GRACIÀN, BALTASAR, *The Oracle*, trans. Walton (London, 1962).
HAMPSHIRE, STUART, *Thought and Action* (London, 1959).
HEGEL, G. W. F., *Aesthetics*, trans. Knox (Oxford, 1975).
—— *The Phenomenology of Spirit*, trans. Miller (Oxford, 1977).
—— *The Philosophy of Mind*, trans. W. Wallace (Oxford, 1971).
—— *The Philosophy of Right*, trans. Knox (Oxford, 1967).
HEIDEGGER, MARTIN, *Being and Time*, trans. Macquarrie and Robinson (Oxford, 1978).
HOBBES, THOMAS, *Leviathan*, ed. M. Oakeshott (Oxford, 1957).
HOMER, *Iliad*, trans. Murray (London, 1924).
—— *Odyssey*, trans. Murray (London, 1919).
HUME, DAVID, *An Enquiry Concerning the Principles of Morals*, ed. L. A. Selby-Bigge (Oxford, 1902).
—— *A Treatise of Human Nature*, ed. L. A. Selby-Bigge (Oxford, 1888).
JAMES, HENRY, *The Wings of the Dove*, ed. L. Edel, *Works*, vol. vii (London, 1969).

JOHNSON, SAMUEL, *Johnson on Shakespeare*, in *Works*, ed. A. Sherbo, vol. viii (Yale, 1968).
—— *The Rambler*, in *Works*, ed. Bate and Strauss, vols. iii–v (Yale, 1969).
JOYCE, JAMES, *A Portrait of the Artist as a Young Man* (London, 1956).
—— *Ulysses* (London, 1960).
JUVENAL, *Satires*, *Works*, ed. G. G. Ramsay (London and Cambridge, Mass., 1918).
KANT, IMMANUEL, *Critique of Practical Reason*, trans. Beck (Indianapolis and New York, 1956).
—— *Fundamental Principles of the Metaphysic of Ethics*, trans. Abbott, 10th edn. (London, 1965).
—— *Lectures on Ethics*, trans. Infield (New York, 1963).
KEATS, JOHN, *Letters*, ed. Rollins (Cambridge, 1958).
—— *Poetical Works*, ed. H. W. Garrod (Oxford, 1956).
KEMPIS, THOMAS À, *Imitation of Christ*, trans. Bishop Challoner (London, 1948).
KNIGHT, G. WILSON, *The Wheel of Fire* (London, 1939).
LA ROCHEFOUCAULD, FRANÇOIS, DUC DE, *Maxims*, trans. K. Pratt (London, 1931).
LEAVIS, F. R., *Revaluation* (London, 1964).
—— *The Common Pursuit* (Harmondsworth, 1962).
—— *The Living Principle* (London, 1975).
LIVY, bk. viii, trans. B. O. Foster (London, 1926).
LOCKE, JOHN, *An Essay Concerning Human Understanding*, ed. and abridged Pringle-Pattison (Oxford, 1924).
LUCRETIUS, *De rerum natura*, trans. Dryden, in Dryden, *Poems*, ed. J. Kinsley (Oxford, 1958), vol. i, p. 403.
MACHIAVELLI, NICCOLÒ, *Discourses*, trans. Walker (London, 1970).
—— *The Prince*, trans. Bull (Harmondsworth, 1961).
MACINTYRE, ALASDAIR, *After Virtue* (London, 1981).
MARX, KARL, *Economic and Philosophic Manuscripts of 1844*, trans. Milligan (Moscow, 1959).
MERLEAU-PONTY, M., *The Phenomenology of Perception*, trans. Smith (London, 1962).
MILL, J. S., *A System of Logic* (New York, 1950).
MILTON, JOHN, *Poems*, ed. H. Darbishire (Oxford, 1952).
MURDOCH, IRIS, *The Sovereignty of Good* (London, 1970).
NAGEL, THOMAS, *Mortal Questions* (Cambridge, 1979).
NEWMAN, JOHN HENRY, *A Grammar of Assent*, ed. Ker (Oxford, 1985).
—— *An Essay on the Development of Christian Doctrine* (New York, 1968).
NIETZSCHE, FRIEDRICH, *Beyond Good and Evil*, trans. Hollingdale (Harmondsworth, 1973).

NUSSBAUM, MARTHA, 'Shame, Separateness, and Political Unity: Aristotle's Criticism of Plato', in Amelie Rorty (ed.), *Essays on Aristotle's Ethics* (Berkeley, 1980), pp. 395–427.
—— *The Fragility of Goodness* (Cambridge, 1986).
OAKESHOTT, MICHAEL, *On Human Conduct* (Oxford, 1975).
—— *Rationalism in Politics* (London, 1962).
OVID, *Metamorphoses*, trans. Miller (London, 1916).
PLATO, *Gorgias*, trans. Lamb (London, 1925).
—— *Laches*, trans. Lamb (London, 1967).
—— *Republic*, trans. Shorey (London, 1935).
—— *Symposium*, trans. Lamb (London, 1925).
PLUTARCH, *Lives of the Noble Grecians and Romans*, trans. North (London, 1899).
POPE, ALEXANDER, 'Epistle to Dr Arbuthnot', *Poems*, ed. J. Butt (London, 1963), pp. 597–612.
POUND, EZRA, 'Hugh Selwyn Mauberley (Life and Contacts)', *Selected Poems*, ed. T. S. Eliot (London, 1959), pp. 173–87.
POWELL, J. ENOCH, 'A Conservative Estimate', *The Cambridge Review*, 100 (Nov. 1978), 52–4.
PROUST, MARCEL, *Remembrance of Things Past*, trans. Scott Moncrieff, Kilmartin, and Mayor (Harmondsworth, 1983).
RICKS, CHRISTOPHER, *Keats and Embarrassment* (Oxford, 1974).
RORTY, AMELIE (ed.), *Essays on Aristotle's Ethics* (Berkeley, 1980).
—— (ed.), *The Identities of Persons* (Berkeley, 1976).
RORTY, RICHARD, *Philosophy and the Mirror of Nature* (Oxford, 1980).
RYLE, GILBERT, *The Concept of Mind* (London, 1949).
SARTRE, J.-P., *Being and Nothingness*, trans. Barnes (London, 1957).
—— *Critique of Dialectical Reason*, trans. A. Sheridan-Smith (London, 1976).
—— *Sketch for a Theory of the Emotions*, trans. Mairet (London, 1962).
—— *The Psychology of Imagination*, trans. Frechtman (London, 1972).
SCHILDER, PAUL FERDINAND, *The Image and Appearance of the Human Body: Studies in the Constructive Energies of the Psyche* (London, 1935).
SCHILLER, FRIEDRICH, 'On Naïve and Sentimental Poetry', in H. B. Nisbet (ed.), *German Aesthetic and Literary Criticism* (Cambridge, 1985), pp. 179–232.
SCHOPENHAUER, ARTHUR, *The World as Will and Representation*, trans. Payne (New York, 1958).
SCRUTON, ROGER, *Sexual Desire* (London, 1986).
SHAKESPEARE, WILLIAM, *Antony and Cleopatra*, ed. M. R. Ridley (London, 1965).
—— *A Winter's Tale*, ed. J. H. P. Pafford (London, 1963).
—— *Coriolanus*, ed. P. Brockbank (London, 1976).

—— *Julius Caesar*, ed. T. S. Dorsch (London, 1965).

—— *Henry IV, Part II*, ed. A. R. Humphreys (London, 1966).

—— *King Lear*, ed. K. Muir (London, 1962).

—— *Macbeth*, ed. K. Muir (London, 1962).

—— *Othello*, ed. M. R. Ridley (London, 1962).

SKINNER, QUENTIN, *The Foundations of Modern Political Thought* (Cambridge, 1978).

SPINOZA, BENEDICT DE, *Ethics*, trans. Gutman (New York, 1949).

STRAWSON, P. F., 'Freedom and Resentment', *Freedom and Resentment and Other Essays* (London, 1974), pp. 1–29.

SWIFT, JONATHAN, *Works*, ed. J. Nichols, 19 vols. (London, 1801).

TAYLOR, CHARLES, *Hegel* (Cambridge, 1975).

THACKERAY, W. M., *Vanity Fair, Works*, vol. i (London, 1879).

THESIGER, WILFRID, *Arabian Sands* (Harmondsworth, 1964).

THUCYDIDES, *The Peloponnesian War*, trans. Marchant (London, 1923).

TRILLING, LIONEL, *Sincerity and Authenticity* (Oxford, 1972).

VIRGIL, AENEID, *Opera* (Mannheim, 1779).

WAGNER, RICHARD: *Sämtliche Werke*, ed. C. Dahlhans, E. Voss, *et al.* (Mainz, 1970–).

WARNOCK, MARY, *The Philosophy of Sartre* (London, 1965).

WIGGINS, DAVID, 'Locke, Butler and the Stream of Consciousness: And Men as Natural Kind', in Amelie Rorty (ed.), *The Identities of Persons* (Berkeley, 1976), pp. 139–74.

WILLIAMS, BERNARD, 'Moral Luck', *Moral Luck* (Cambridge, 1981), pp. 20–40.

WITTGENSTEIN, LUDWIG, *Culture and Value*, trans. Winch (Oxford, 1980).

—— *Lectures and Conversations on Aesthetics, Psychology and Religious Belief*, ed. C. Barrett (Oxford, 1970).

—— *Philosophical Investigations*, trans. Anscombe (Oxford, 1958).

YEATS, W. B. 'In Memory of Eva Gore-Booth and Con Markeiwicz', *Collected Poems* (London, 1950), pp. 263–4.

XENOPHON, *Oeconomicus*, trans. Marchant (London, 1923).

# INDEX

Acedia 107, 109–10
Adam and Eve 35
  in Milton 36–7, 125
Addison, Joseph 93
Admiration
  objects of admiration 26
  and respect 27
*akrasia* 158–9
Altham, J. E. J. 192
Ambrose, St 59
*amour propre* 128–35, 210
  and carnality 131–2
  La Rochefoucauld's *Maxims* really
    about *amour propre* 128
  and paranoia 132
  as pervasive, infinitely various 129
  and vanity and envy 129–30, 132–4
Amyot 203
Anger 10–15, 19, 27, 44–5, 117, 180,
  186
  and acknowledgement of wrongdoing
    12, 122
  appeased by apology 21, 22
  appropriate anger 14
  and bodily gestures 16
  and courage 56, 58
  and equality 21, 56
  and forgiveness 12
  and freedom 15
  good temper 14, 21
  having same object as justice 10, 12,
    22, 173
  ira and excandescentia 13
  and jealousy 13
  and justice 12, 19, 22, 173
  as melancholy (towards a more
    powerful person) 12
  as moral achievement 56
  objective attitudes to 19
  pain of 12
  proper 14
  and rebuke 12
  and respect 13–15
  seeks to harm its object *sub specie
    boni* 12

and slight 10
rancorous (*kotos*) 13
Anglo-Argentinian War 171
Anscombe, G. E. M. 124
Aquinas, St Thomas *Summa Theologiae*
  ix, 1, 3, 51, 83, 112, 113, 114, 134,
  136, 157, 166, 170, 181, 182, 186,
  188, 195, 196, 197, 198, 206, 211,
  212
  on *acedia* and *tristitia* 107, 110
  on *akrasia* 159
  on *amor amicitiae* 185
  on anger 10, 12, 22, 173
  on charity 177–8
  on courage 56, 58–9, 63, 100
  on cruelty 135–6
  on *dulia* 198
  on duties towards rulers 197
  on grace 112
  just revenge 22
  on physical and spiritual beauty 111
  on *pietas* 194
  on pleasures arising from the sense of
    touch 104
  on the saved rejoicing in the sufferings
    of the damned 135
Aristotle 8, 11, 13, 22, 28, 49, 52, 54,
  56, 57, 58, 61, 64, 67, 70, 72, 73,
  76, 82, 83, 101, 114, 117, 128,
  129, 130, 138, 142, 152, 153, 166,
  192, 211
  on actions done from ignorance or in
    ignorance 62, 156–60
  on *akrasia* 158, 159, 160
  on anger 10, 12, 14
  on benefactors 182
  on courage 51, 69, 92, 100
  on *eutrapelia* (playfulness, ready-wit)
    110
  on friendship 177, 183, 184, 185,
    188, 189, 190, 191
  on justice 172, 173, 190, 191, 193,
    194, 197
  on the magnanimous man 63,
    199–202, 206

Aristotle *(cont.)*:
 on the magnificent man 201, 202,
  207–8
 on man as political animal 5
 on practical wisdom 146, 148, 157,
  159, 160, 167, 170, 171
 on slavery 5
 on temperance 104, 107, 108, 159,
  160
 on virtues v, vii, 208, 209, 210
Arnold, Matthew 140, 214
arts
 hierarchy of 153–4
 higher than skills 152–4
 household arts 152–3
 and politics 152–4
 and rules 151
 and tradition 151–2
assent 169–70
attitudes 7, 8
 'inter-personal attitudes' 8
 objective attitudes to anger 19
Augustine, St vi, 49, 104, 116, 117,
  128, 129, 134, 135, 180, 181, 199
Austen, Jane 53, 178, 197
 as conservative writer 160–1
 *Emma* 162–5
 ethic implied in Jane Austen's
  writings 160
 *Mansfield Park* 161–2, 164–5
 relation of intelligence to moral
  goodness 160–6
 and self-knowledge 162–5
 and Sentimentalism 160–2, 164–5

Barker, Ernest 190
Barrett, C 71
Battle of Britain 101
benevolence, *see* love
Bennett, Jonathan 17, 60
Bible, Holy
 1 Corinthians 177, 208
 Ecclesiastes 217
 Ecclesiasticus 85, 86
 Galatians 3
 Genesis 35, 179, 180
 Jeremiah 138
 Luke 172
 Magnificat 130
 Mark 207
 Matthew 208
 Proverbs 153–4
 Psalms 135

Romans 208
body, the 8, 33–49, 106–10
 and anger 16
 and courage 39–42
 as emblem 95
 and expression 41
 fitness of 108–10
 as 'an idea in intelligent perception'
  (Schopenhauer) 33
 as instrument 94–5
 as noble 36
 and self-consciousness 35
 sexual expressiveness of 16, 38–9, 43
 and shame 35
 and signs 41–3
 and sloth 106–10
 and will 33, 34, 38, 41–9
 and the world as 'to be acted upon'
  34
Bradley, A. C. 215, 216, 217, 218, 221,
  223, 224
Brown, Peter 128
Burrow, Colin 212
Butler, Joseph 130
Butler, Marilyn 160, 161, 162, 163,
  164
Byron, Lord 175, 176

cardinal virtues v
 temperance as cardinal virtue 104,
  106
Carlyle, Thomas 53
carnality 131, 132
Casey, John 74
Cervantes, Miguel de 69, 170
Charity
 as friendship 177–8
 and *King Lear* 223, 224, 225
 as seeking no return 177
 sloth as sin against 107, 110
 as surviving into next life 3
chastening, of the will 114–18
Chevalier, Maurice 15, 16
choice
 distinctively human capacity 59–62
 necessary to courage 58–62
Christ 146, 181, 192, 207, 208, 211
Christianity 131, 134
 Augustinian tradition 104, 128, 180
 and carnality 217, 219, 226
 and the magnanimous man 200
 and moral goodness vi
 and pagan virtues v